D0842039

Attic Alone

An Ex–Jehovah's Witness Finds the Church

A. McGinley

iUniverse, Inc.
New York   Bloomington

Attic Alone
An Ex–Jehovah's Witness Finds the Church

iUniverse books may be ordered through booksellers or by contacting:

iUniverse
1663 Liberty Drive
Bloomington, IN 47403
www.iuniverse.com
1-800-Authors (1-800-288-4677)

Because of the dynamic nature of the Internet, any Web addresses or links contained in this book may have changed since publication and may no longer be valid. The views expressed in this work are solely those of the author and do not necessarily reflect the views of the publisher, and the publisher hereby disclaims any responsibility for them.

ISBN: 978-1-4502-4908-9 (pbk)
ISBN: 978-1-4502-4909-6 (cloth)
ISBN: 978-1-4502-4910-2 (ebk)

Library of Congress Control Number: 2010911486

Printed in the United States of America

iUniverse rev. date: 9/9/10

For my family and friends

A crowd is not company and faces are but a gallery of pictures, and talk but a tinkling cymbal, where there is no love.

—Francis Bacon, writer, philosopher, and statesman

Introduction

This book was written to reveal the life of a child from a large family, who was raised as a Jehovah's Witness and spent many years preferring to be in an attic alone where she could hide. Since many years have passed, some of the events may have melded together, and some of the Watchtower teachings may have changed. Anyone associated with the Witnesses can verify that the teachings do change as their leaders receive what is called "new light," and what was the truth yesterday or years ago is no longer considered to be the truth today.

The attic became a mental refuge where this person would retreat for many years through her life, even after she broke free from the religion at the age of twenty-six. As a young woman, she spent ten years in a spiritual void, and then someone asked her a life-changing question that she did not know how to answer. She spent the next thirty years thinking, searching, learning, and believing the answers to question after question. One day she found a new door to open—and the journey continues.

A. McGinley
atticalone.amcginley@gmail.com

Chapter 1

In 1905 a new federal law required all children about to enter American elementary schools to receive a smallpox inoculation. The Supreme Court of the United States ruled that all states require these vaccinations for the "common good." This was an important decision to wipe out the dreaded and devastating disease that killed many people worldwide.

Of the people vaccinated, less than two percent developed smallpox and less than one percent of them died. In the unvaccinated, almost fifty percent of the people became infected with the disease and of those infected, about ten percent died. In general, the danger of death from smallpox was much greater in people who were unvaccinated than it was in those who were vaccinated.

In the late summer of 1943, before my first day of school, Dad said, "I'm going to give you a smallpox vaccination mark on your arm. It will grow a brown scab in a few days." My father was a big man of German and Turkish parentage, six feet two inches tall and very muscular. He was somewhat olive-skinned with dark wavy hair that rose high on his head and seemed to add another three inches to his handsome face. His deep, dark brown eyes reflected his Turkish heritage. Dad looked like a giant to me; he was steely and scary when he became angry. He always wore shorts, but no shirt in the summer. I was a very frightened, thin little girl at the time with dark brown eyes and straight, shoulder-length hair that was light blonde. Six of us children inherited our father's dark Turkish eyes and the others have blue eyes like our mother.

Dad took me into the kitchen where the late-afternoon sun didn't shine, and the darkness of the approaching evening added to my gloomy apprehension. This was a traumatic event that I never forgot; it was my first vivid childhood memory. I knew it would hurt because my older brothers and sisters had marks and I had heard them talk about getting theirs. My father proceeded to stretch out my small tanned arm on the worn, wooden kitchen table that was used for good times and bad times. Here was where our family of eight children enjoyed Mom's flavorful cooking by the plateful, and here was where the children served long quiet-time punishment for making too much noise when our father was home.

Mom was there, about ten feet away, watching from the other side of the spacious kitchen. We watched as Dad opened a small amber-colored bottle with a long glass dropper that held the heavy liquid used for fraudulent smallpox vaccinations. Letting a small amount of the liquid drip onto my upper arm, he spread it around in a small circle. He was holding my arm so tightly against the table that I wasn't sure which hurt more, the flesh-eating drops or my father's large, strong fingers that clamped my arm to the table while I cried and screamed, "Stop! Stop!" Mom was watching with a look of consternation on her usually smiling face. She shouted, "Blow on it! Blow on it!" and my dad began blowing on the wound in a futile attempt to stop the terrible burning of the acid that was eating a hole into my arm.

Dad released my arm and I ran to Mom to be held and comforted. Mom was a stout, five-foot-two-inch woman with dark, curly hair framing her pretty face that showed all her emotions. Her blue eyes shed tears easily, but inside she had the fierce determination of all her Scotch-Irish ancestors. She was no match for my father when he intended to do something she didn't like.

The kitchen seemed to be her domain, where she always wore a homemade apron over her sleeveless, flower-print cotton dress. Her aprons were styled from washed chicken feed sacks purchased from a local farmer, Mr. Renner, who traveled down our street with his horse and wagon almost every week in the summertime. The sacks were very pretty printed material, and everyone on our street bought some of them.

Farmer Renner was short and wore thin blue overalls over a plaid shirt. A straw hat sat on his head of gray hair and shaded his face from the sun. His slow old horse was brown with white markings. The wooden wagon held baskets of fresh produce, a wooden crate full of live chickens, and an assorted pile of washed chicken feed sacks. He stopped in front of our house because Dad always wanted my mother to buy two chickens from him. Farmer Renner took the chickens into the backyard with a chopping block and an axe. He chopped off their heads, and the headless chickens flapped their wings and ran around in circles before falling over dead. My mother put them in a large tub full of very hot water from the stove, and as the water cooled, she pulled all the feathers off the chickens.

Mom cooked a big dinner every day. After dinner, she had to make sure we were ready to go to the Kingdom Hall with our father on meeting nights. He would get really angry if we made him late for the meeting. The day of my vaccination, I said, "Mom, my arm hurts. I don't want to go." My father told me to stay home.

From the 1930s to the 1950s, good Jehovah's Witnesses who obeyed the rules of the Watchtower Society did not allow their children to be vaccinated against smallpox, and they saw nothing wrong with using a liquid acid on their children's skin to skirt the law. Doctor certificates were forged to avoid hassles with the schools and law enforcement agencies.

The reason for not getting vaccinated goes back to earlier Watchtower days. Their *Golden Age* magazine of May 1, 1929 claimed that people should rather have smallpox than the vaccine because the vaccine plants seeds of syphilis, cancer, eczema, consumption, leprosy and many other diseases. It called vaccinations a crime and an outrage.

About 1950, a reader of the *Watchtower* magazine wrote a letter to the headquarters asking about the vaccination policy. It is the most important magazine to the Witnesses if they want to keep up with the current truth. The magazines, published twice a month, are purchased by all Jehovah's Witnesses. They are required to read and study the magazines before they distribute them.

A young man, Bill, worked at the Watchtower headquarters and was struggling to answer the letter about the smallpox vaccination ban. It was commonly thought that the vaccine contained blood. Bill felt that simply replying, "Because the vaccine contains blood and we do not accept any blood products," was not a very complete answer. In order to give a firsthand account of the blood being added during the manufacturing process, he wanted to visit the company that made the vaccine, Lederle Labs.

He was told by the pharmaceutical company "There is no blood in the vaccine," and they gave him a written statement to confirm that. Bill reported to the Watchtower leaders, "There is a mistake in the smallpox policy. No blood is used in the manufacturing process of the vaccine, and the ban against the vaccine should be lifted. Children should be vaccinated." The leaders did not appreciate that this young man had thought for himself. He was reprimanded and told not to run ahead of Jehovah God or his organization.

In 1952 the Watchtower leaders let it be known that it was now okay to give the smallpox vaccination to children because there was no scriptural evidence against the vaccine. In 1958, Bill left the Bethel Home living quarters of the organization and could not be silenced about the blood transfusion issue. When asked about taking blood, Bill advised a Witness to give a transfusion to a dying child. He was considered a troublemaker for questioning the Watchtower. Now, he was accused of being an apostate and was disfellowshipped. His wife, Joan, was disfellowshipped later for attending a church where Bill was speaking against the Watchtower ban on blood transfusions.

Bill and Joan began searching for true Christian doctrine and tried to persuade their family and friends to do the same thing. Most of them turned away from them because they were disfellowshipped. Joan was disowned and disinherited by her wealthy Pennsylvania family.

For more than half a century, a ministry founded by Bill and Joan has been helping Jehovah's Witnesses leave the false teachings of the Watchtower. Bill passed on, and Joan continued the ministry with the help of her grown children and her Christian friends.

They have inspired many others to do the same. By revealing the experiences I lived as a child and young adult, it is my prayer that many struggling to escape or those who have escaped controlling organizations will find comfort in knowing they are not alone.

Chapter 2

Needless to say, my mother was upset about the acid burn on my arm and gave me lots of hugs. For distraction, Mom said, "Let's go up in the attic and sort through some of the boxes that have school clothing from your sisters Jean and Millie." Clothing that was worn to school was packed away every June and unpacked before Labor Day in September.

Going to the attic was a rare treat for me. It was semi-dark, somewhat peaceful, and yet spooky at the same time. There was one small window that allowed the light from the late afternoon sun to enter. The noises of everyday family living from downstairs were muffled, and every corner had a large pile of what seemed to be lost treasure.

It was like a different, private world up there in the attic as Mom opened bags and boxes of clothing. She pulled out clothing that I didn't remember seeing before. Some of the size 6 school dresses from my two older sisters fit me now. Mom also opened a big box of used clothing that my father recently brought home. Mom was humming as she helped me try on some dresses. We children never knew what she was humming, and Gram hated when she hummed. Gram was my dad's mother and lived near us; she was always at our house and ruled the family with him.

My grandmother was short, stout, and somewhat cranky; she was bothered by her arthritic body joints hurting all the time. I always admired how pretty her pale skin was. Her salt and pepper hair was always curly; she gave a nice appearance in her best blue dress, especially when she went to the Kingdom Hall or out knocking on doors with the *Watchtower* and *Awake* magazines. One day her dress pulled up above her knee and I could hardly believe my eyes. She had a large, colorful butterfly on the side of her thigh. "That butterfly is so beautiful!" I exclaimed. She quickly pulled her dress over her knee and screeched, "No, it isn't. I'm ashamed that I have it!" "Why?" I asked, and she answered, "Before I was a Jehovah's Witness, I did some crazy things. I was a real flapper!" I had no idea what a flapper was, but I stopped asking her questions because she looked angry to me.

She had sewn one special dress for me to wear to the meetings at the Kingdom Hall of Jehovah's Witnesses. The Hall was a converted old theater without any windows where we sat during the meetings. Buildings with no windows were considered to be very desirable. Windowless walls were highly prized by the Witness leaders because it gave a sense of isolation from the outside world. However, in recent years Jehovah's Witnesses have been required to install windows in some of their buildings in order to comply with building codes or to obtain lower fire insurance rates. I always thought it would be dangerous to be at the Hall if there was a fire. I worried about fires because we'd had a small one in our kitchen at home when a candle on a small table ignited the curtains on a window.

Mom was hand sewing some repairs to the school dresses in the kitchen the next day and said, "You can wear your Kingdom Hall dress the first day of school." Gram didn't enjoy sewing very much anymore, but she could put a small dress together in one afternoon. She would sit at the old sewing machine that worked by foot power, put her feet on the treadle, a metal-grated platform three inches from the floor, and then pressed the front of her feet downward. She pushed the treadle down and then up again quickly. Back and forth her feet would go repeatedly as each movement sewed a stitch in the material under the needle.

I liked the dress my grandmother made for me and I wanted to go to school like the older kids did, but some things worried me. Gram and Dad warned me, "Don't salute the flag. The flag is a wicked symbol that Satan devised to mislead people away from Jehovah God and his kingdom. Satan is the ruler of this old world and we are not part of this world." My reply was, "What world are we part of?" Dad just ignored that. I looked forward to my first day of school, but feared being in a room with a wicked Satan symbol.

Jehovah's Witnesses around the world were not allowed to salute or pledge allegiance to the flags of their countries. They may not realize that the use of flags has the approval of God. In Numbers 1:52 (NIV), God said, "The children of Israel are to set up their tents by divisions, each man in his own camp under his own standard." The standards were banners or flags to identify the individual twelve tribes and their purposes. They helped to keep order among the Israelites as they lived, traveled, and fought under their flags. Most people recognize the Lion of Judah flag. Using national flags was not condemned in the Bible, but it was criticized by the leaders and writers of the Watchtower Society. They strongly objected to anyone pledging allegiance to the flag.

During World War II, Americans were very patriotic and supported the war effort. Witness children were expelled for refusing to salute the flag. An early 1943 Supreme Court decision said that it was unconstitutional to force anyone to say the pledge to the flag. When I started school in September of 1943 my father said, "The Watchtower says no one can expel you for not saluting the flag or saying the pledge of allegiance to the flag, so don't do it!"

Jehovah's Witnesses obey whatever the Watchtower says, even though they do not know the anonymous authors of the magazines and books after the first two presidents of the organization passed away. The third president believed, "It is not right to honor men who are the writers because the information they publish comes directly from Jehovah God through his channel, the Watchtower, Bible and Tract Society."

When the teachings change, as they do, the Witnesses do not wonder why Jehovah didn't give them the right information to start with because they are told that Jehovah is giving them new light.

They usually accept the changes with excitement and enthusiasm, like a gift from God.

Most of the time, Mom was very quiet and just hummed to herself as she ignored what Dad and Gram were saying about any new light from the Watchtower Society. On the rare occasions that she questioned what they were saying, she was told to be quiet because she didn't go to enough meetings to know anything. Being quiet was her way of coping in a house where her opinions didn't mean much.

Chapter 3

I was registered for first grade at Cleveland Elementary because our school district did not have kindergarten classes in the early 1940s. My father gave me a piece of paper to give to the teacher the first day. It was a forged doctor certificate saying I'd had a vaccination. That first morning while walking to school with my older brothers, my heart pounded with so much fear that I thought I would fall over and die before we even got to the building. I tried to remember all the instructions my father gave me: "Don't salute the flag, don't tell anyone how you got your vaccination, and be very careful what kind of songs you sing."

I had never been in a classroom before and was happy to see that it had so many desks and chairs. It was actually a nice bright room with yellow-painted walls, large windows, and a big long chalkboard. The desks were shiny clean and faced the teacher's desk, where she had an assortment of books. My teacher was a terrible, cranky woman according to my two older brothers, Rod and Harry. She was standing at the door near the front of the room when I arrived. The words "Mrs. Fisher" were written with bright white chalk on the blackboard.

Mrs. Fisher resembled Mom except Mrs. Fisher was taller, wore glasses, and had lighter brown hair. She looked stern and didn't smile like my mother, though I wished she would, at least once. After taking the forged vaccination certificate from my outstretched hand, she pointed me in the direction of a desk and chair near the middle of the room. There were name cards on all the chairs, and my eyes searched for the familiar letters of my name. When I finally sat down and looked forward, the first thing I saw was the large and dreadful American flag.

As other children filed into the room and were directed to their seats, I wondered if they were afraid of the flag and Mrs. Fisher. They didn't seem to be and some of them were happy and smiling. After everyone was checked in and sitting in the seats, Mrs. Fisher told us to stand up as she read a few verses from the Bible. I was happy to stand for that. We heard Bible verses read from the Watchtower magazine all the time at the Kingdom Hall, but we never stood up to read any of them.

After reading many verses, our teacher said, "Next, we will say the Lord's Prayer." Watching as most of the other children folded their hands in front of them, closed their eyes, bowed their heads, and said, "Our Father, who art in heaven—" I felt like such an idiot! I had no idea what the Lord's Prayer was! My quieted heart started pounding again because I was still frightened in spite of the fact that the other children seemed to be okay.

The real terror came when Mrs. Fisher pointed and said, "Look at the flag, put your right hand across your heart like this, and say the Pledge of Allegiance to the flag. If you don't know how to say it, just listen to me and learn the words, because we will recite the pledge to the flag every day." There was special emphasis on the words "every day."

Mrs. Fisher and a few of the children began saying the pledge at the same time. "I pledge allegiance to the flag of the Unites States of America." Like me, many of the children did not know the words. Mrs. Fisher looked at me, and my small heart started beating double time. I truly feared that my teacher might be part of the wicked plan Satan had, and she knew that I knew it was his plan to turn people away from God. "But why would Mrs. Fisher read the Bible to everyone if she wants to turn the children away from God?" I thought. "That doesn't make any sense."

After school I asked Shirley Holland, the blonde, curly-haired girl who sat next to me, "Where did you learn the Lord's Prayer?" and Shirley said, "At church." That explained it! My family had never been in a church; we went to the Kingdom Hall of Jehovah's Witnesses!

We passed a large, gray stone church with many tall, colorfully stained glass windows and two large red-painted doors on the way to school. I felt kind of scared because Gram had told me, "People worship a three-headed god in the churches. The doors are painted red because it is the color of blood and they are responsible for people killing each other in all the wars." I went as fast as I could past the church, almost running because my mind conjured up images of a terrible false god with three heads reaching out for people. Gram said, "The churches are to blame for people killing each other in the big war against Germany."

Dad blamed the war on all the churches too, but especially the Catholic Church for meddling in government affairs. I was so glad to live in America where there were no bombs or soldiers trying to kill everyone. At the end of that first day of school, I decided I liked school and was happy to go there.

Mrs. Fisher told our class, "Try to memorize the Lord's Prayer and the Pledge of Allegiance as quickly as possible." When I privately and quite proudly told Mom that I had learned to say the Lord's Prayer after my first week of school, she didn't get angry with me. She whispered to me, "Be quiet; don't tell your father or grandmother. They don't want you to say that." This was just another of the many warnings we all got from Mom that we should not do this or say that when our father or grandmother was within hearing distance.

In school, it made me feel good to be with other children who prayed to God. There were few children at the Kingdom Hall, and we never sat with each other or prayed together. At the Kingdom Hall with no windows or decorations, all members, including the children, were expected to look at and listen to the speaker during the meetings. I recited the prayer every day because I liked it, and Mom said, "The Lord's Prayer is in the Bible." (Matthew 6:9–13; KJV)

When I asked Gram about the prayer, she explained, "Jesus doesn't want us to say the same prayer he said. It was to be used as a model to make our own prayers. Saying that prayer all the time is like being a heathen person. They have a prayer wheel where people write down their prayers on paper and put them in the little wheel. Then they turn the wheel thinking that every time it was turned, the prayer was being said. People who say the Lord's Prayer think the prayer will save them, but it won't." I knew in my mind and in my heart that we were not being like the heathen. Thinking to myself, "Jesus wouldn't tell us that prayer if it wasn't good for us to say," I continued saying it every day. School was helping me to think for myself.

Eventually, I was not afraid of the red, white, and blue flag or the Pledge of Allegiance. After all, my dad would never know if I saluted the flag or not, and I didn't think there was anything wicked about the flag. I didn't believe that Satan had anything to do with the flag, because Mrs. Fisher told us, "A nice woman in Philadelphia named Betsy Ross sewed the first American flag for George Washington when the early Americans wanted to be free from the king of England." I also learned that the pledge was started in Boston by schoolchildren and their teacher. It was for a school celebration of four hundred years since Columbus came to America. The pledge spread to other schools and then all across the country.

I said the pledge, but nevertheless I was feeling very guilty and fearful about disobeying my father and grandmother. In my mind, I would often doubt what they told me. Even Mom didn't seem to agree with everything they believed, but she was usually afraid to express her own opinion. Jehovah's Witnesses are often told that independent thinking and independent Bible study will cause them to fall away from the truth and into false teachings.

They can be disfellowshipped from the organization for these offenses. Other offenses that are punished by shunning include smoking, voting, saluting the flag, celebrating holidays, serving in the military service, and taking blood transfusions. As a matter of fact, if anyone takes a blood transfusion, they are automatically disfellowshipping themselves. They will be shunned when they need help the most from family and friends. They will be left all alone.

We were never alone at home. I had four brothers and three sisters when I was in first grade. Our family was the largest one at the Kingdom Hall, where many times we heard it said, "Woe to those with children in the last days." This warning was taken from Matthew 24:19 (KJV) where it says, *"And woe unto them that are with child, and to them that give suck in those days!"*

We were living in the last days according to everything that was taught at the meetings. It made me feel as though I should not have been born. I began to worry about the end of the world. Dad said the war was proof that we were living in the last days.

Chapter 4

At home, we looked at the daily newspaper every day, which was full of pictures about the air and sea battles in Europe and the Pacific. In school, the first-grade class talked about the newspaper pictures with Mrs. Fisher because a few of the other children had fathers, uncles, cousins, or older brothers who were soldiers, and they wanted their loved ones to come home from the war. I felt sorry for them, but at the same time everyone in my class was so proud of those soldiers who were fighting for freedom and America. Mrs. Fisher was the only adult that told me the real reasons why the soldiers were fighting.

Her explanation of the value of fighting for freedom made more sense to me than blaming it on the churches. Jehovah's Witnesses didn't believe in going to war or fighting in the war, and I could certainly understand the reasoning that war is a bad thing, but we had also been taught by Dad and Gram that, "When there is a job to be done, someone must do it!" My family pretty much lived by that rule in our house because our father and grandmother gave all of us children many chores to do.

A few weeks after school had begun in September, one of the boys had a birthday. Mrs. Fisher told the class it was his birthday and we should all sing the happy birthday song to him. When the whole class began smiling and singing the song, a red embarrassment crept over my face because I had never heard the song before. I felt so stupid!

After school I told my mother what we did. She shushed me and said, "Don't let your dad or grandmother hear you sing that song." We could always talk to Mom without being afraid of what she would do to us. With each passing day and week, the difference between my family and other families became more and more uncomfortable. Sometimes it seemed as though we were not a normal family. We were different. I wanted to go to the houses of the other girls from school when they invited me, but Dad and Gram did not approve of many people.

The weeks passed quickly in first grade, and Halloween was just around the corner, as the saying goes. It was the only holiday that our father allowed us children to celebrate in spite of the fact that Jehovah's Witnesses were told not to participate in any of the activities. My father told us, "Make sure your face and hair are covered so no one knows who you are." We enjoyed the excitement of going out that night. My older brothers and sisters helped us younger ones to dress like ghosts and farmers and hobos.

Dad sent all of us children out to the neighborhood for hours with an old hat and some old pillowcases. We sang, "Halloween is coming and the geese are getting fat. Please put a penny in the old man's hat. If you haven't got a penny, then half a cent will do. If you haven't got a half a cent, then God bless you." Our nearby neighbors always guessed who we were, but our father didn't seem to care about that because we didn't have any neighbors who were Jehovah's Witnesses. Everyone was very nice and enjoyed seeing us. We went home with a full hat and heavy pillowcases.

While we sat on the floor and divided up the candy, apples, and popcorn balls, our father would take the money that had collected at the bottom of the hat and pillowcases. All of those nickels, dimes, and quarters added up to a hefty reward for him. I suppose that was why he allowed us to break the Watchtower rule.

We all enjoyed eating the treats, and it certainly made me feel happy. We did not have many happy times in our house. Halloween made me feel more normal because all the other kids from school were out doing the same thing. I realized that even my dad broke some of the Watchtower rules, so I didn't feel as bad about breaking them in school. However, when children came to our house and knocked on the door, no one opened the door or gave any treats. Dad did not allow that.

Chapter 5

When Thanksgiving was near, we learned about the pilgrims and their desire for freedom to worship God. I admired the pilgrims for leaving their homelands to search for religious freedom across the ocean in another land. Mrs. Fisher read many Psalms of Thanksgiving from the Bible.

Our first-grade class learned so many songs about America and freedom that my heart was overflowing for the first time with love for my God and for my country. We never sang any children's songs at the Kingdom Hall, and the meetings were very boring for children to sit through quietly. Mrs. Fisher's class was always fun and exciting. Contrary to what my brothers said, Mrs. Fisher was not terrible; she was only cranky if someone wasn't paying attention. Secretly, I wanted to be just like the other children; I didn't want to be afraid of singing and celebrating. I wanted the American soldiers to win that war and come back to their families. I wanted to be normal.

At home, we had a turkey for Thanksgiving Day, and I asked Mom if we were actually celebrating the holiday because my mother knew Dad and Gram didn't approve of celebrating anything. Smiling, Mom said, "Not really, but your father gets a free fresh turkey from his dairy company, and he lets me make it because it is a sin to waste good food." She always made the best turkey, the best pumpkin pies, and the best cakes.

My birthday was exactly one week after Thanksgiving, but my mother didn't tell me it was my birthday. Mrs. Fisher said, "Today is Arlene's birthday, so everyone gather around and sing the birthday song to her." It felt so good to have the other children sing to me. I had tears in my eyes and said, "Thank you." After school, I found my mother in the kitchen.

She was cooking some great-smelling tomato sauce for spaghetti. I excitedly told her, "Mom, they sang the birthday song to me in school. Is it really my birthday today?" Mom hugged me and said, "Yes, today is your birthday, Honey, but don't say anything about it to anyone because Daddy will get mad. How about if I bake a cake especially for you? Everyone can have some later tonight, but please don't tell anyone it is your birthday cake. This is our secret."

I thought my dad probably didn't even know it was my birthday because nothing was ever said about them. While Mom began putting all the ingredients on the table, I sat on the steps at the end of the first-floor hallway that opened into the big kitchen. I began looking at a first-grade book. From the stairs, I could sneak a peek around the corner into the kitchen and watch Mom while she made the secret birthday cake.

My brothers and sisters were shouting and playing noisily out in the backyard when our father came home wearing his white milkman's uniform. As usual, he entered the house through the back door of the kitchen. Our dad was angry! "The dairy company took my horse and wagon away from me and gave me a g—d— truck! Now when I get to the end of the block, I must run back down the street to get the truck. My legs are so tired, I can hardly walk. I want my horse and wagon back! My horse always followed me up the street and was waiting for me at the corner!"

Dad began shouting and cursing at my mother because the table was full of cooking and baking stuff. "I can't find a blank-blank place on the table to lay down my customer book and money bag! What are you doing? How can I sit down at the table when you have it all cluttered?" Mom, using her scared voice, said, "I'm baking a cake for the children. Here, I'll make room for you."

We could always tell when Mom was scared because her voice kind of shook when she spoke. I thought Dad was going to figure out that it was a cake for my birthday, and we would both get in serious trouble. I crouched on the stairs, out of sight, not knowing if I should stay or quietly crawl up the steps. I was so afraid he would see me.

"Why aren't you baking pies? You know I like pies, not cake!" he said, raising his voice even louder. Then suddenly I heard a noise that sounded like a train being dragged across the kitchen table. I peeked around the corner from the stairs just in time to see my dad's large arm sending two of the bowls on the table crashing to the floor! Flour and sugar scattered everywhere!

He hit my mother across her face with the backside of his hand, and she fell down on the floor with the flour and sugar. Then he seized her by the back of her hair and shouted, "Clean up this g—d— mess right now!" He pushed her head down into the floor as my mother sobbed. His face was red and twisted with anger. Fearing that he might see me, I quickly began sneaking up the stairs, hoping with all my heart that he would not come up the steps until I was safely under a bed. Even though I was the only one that actually saw what happened, I knew my brothers and sisters could hear everything out there in the yard.

I could hear my dad in the kitchen, screaming obscenities at Mom as she wept openly and heavily. Shaking and crying, I crawled under my bed while muffling my mouth on my arm. My dad went into the living room and turned the radio on. In my heart, I knew that Mom was still weeping as she labored to clean up the mess on the kitchen floor. I wanted to help her, but I was too afraid to move.

I stayed under the bed a long time, hugging my book, until my brothers and sisters came in from the yard. Mom called all of us to dinner. She served us a dinner of spaghetti and butter bread, which we all ate solemnly while our dad snored and slept on his chair in the living room. I was afraid to look at my mother because I didn't want to see her with red swollen eyes and the red mark from my father's large hand still showing on her face. There would not be a secret birthday cake for me, and I was so ashamed of myself for wanting one. "This is my fault for wanting a birthday cake. I will never, ever mention my birthday to Mom again."

I was too young to realize it at the time, but many years later while recalling that frightening scene, I realized that my father had been intoxicated that day in the kitchen. He always had the same smell on him when he came home in the afternoon, but we didn't know it was alcohol until many years later. He didn't usually drink in front of us children when we were young; he drank at Tinkle's Bar & Grille most of the time until all of his children grew older.

Chapter 6

As my first-grade Christmas neared, a different world opened up to me. I had never sung Christmas carols before and never heard the Bible verses that were about the birth of Jesus. My family and our Jehovah's Witnesses friends never celebrated holidays.

The birth of Jesus was not even being discussed at the Kingdom Hall, but in school we sang songs, made decorations, trimmed a small tree, and talked about Saint Nicholas. Mrs. Fisher said, "Print your name on a paper, fold it up, and put it in this box. We will shake up the box and then everyone can pick one of the papers. You will make a Christmas card for the person on the paper. Write that person's name on the front of the card." After we all took a paper out of the box, she led us to a table full of colored papers, lace doilies, pictures, cotton, crayons, gold stars, scissors, and paste that we all could share.

She helped many of the children, including me, who were kind of lost and were not sure what to do or make. When we were finished, she told everyone, "Print your name inside the card so the person you give it to will remember you." After we printed our names on the cards, she helped us to exchange the cards. Then we had a party with cookies, pretzels, and punch before we went home for Christmas vacation.

Some of my school friends were saying, "Merry Christmas!" to me, and I said the same thing to them. It felt so good to say those words, I almost cried. The card I received from another classmate was as beautiful as the one I had made.

My mother had friends in our neighborhood called the Herb family. They sent a card inviting her to a small party one afternoon to see their decorated tree. They decorated their whole house for Christmas. Other neighbors were invited too and it was like a party. Mom told us younger children, "I am taking you to visit the Herb family. They want us to see their Christmas tree and have snacks, but don't say anything when your father gets home or we will all get in trouble."

The Herbs had two daughters, Catherine and Mary, who were older than me. They were young teenagers, but were always kind to me. They both had blue eyes and Catherine had pale skin topped with curly red hair. She told me she liked school every day. Mary had pale skin too, but darker auburn hair. Mary was a little cross-eyed and was often teased. The boys would make faces at her and hurt her feelings, so she hated school. I liked talking to them when I saw them outside the house.

I could not talk very much at home about what I liked at school. I wondered if my older brothers and sisters had the same feelings when they were in first grade. They warned me about cranky teachers, taking tests, and getting homework, but they never said anything about birthdays or holidays. Surely, they must have been just as confused as I was about the differences between home and school.

We all wondered why it was okay for our dad to get a huge holiday-wrapped gift box full of cheeses, crackers, nuts, candies, and jellies from his dairy, but it was not okay for him to give his own children a gift. Many of Dad's dairy customers gave him Christmas cards with money inside. He didn't let us see the cards. He just removed the money and never looked at the cards before dropping them in the trash can.

I was usually the first one to wake up and be with Mom. As we looked through the cloudy window on Christmas morning, the people in the houses across the street and down the block were turning on their Christmas lights. We saw wreaths on the doors and decorations in the windows. Christmas trees filled some of the windows. I could not help but wonder, "What would it be like to have a decorated tree and wrapped presents? How nice it must be! What fun it would be!" My mother was obviously pleased to see all the lights, so I questioned her, "Mom, why is it so wrong to have a tree and presents? Why is it so bad?" She hugged me and said, "I'm sorry, but I don't know how to answer that question. Your father will not allow us to celebrate anything. It is against his religion."

According to my dad, celebrating Christmas was a terrible thing to do. In fact, according to him and the Jehovah's Witnesses, it was a pagan holiday that a real Christian would never think of celebrating. The Bible says not to make graven images or worship other men. "It is idolatry!" he said, "It is ridiculous to worship a tree or a baby! We only worship Jehovah God!"

I knew from school that people were not worshipping a tree. I could not say anything to my father to make him angry, but I thought, "No one is worshipping a picture of the baby Jesus either. They are celebrating his birthday, so I guess no one can have a party, not even Jesus." This Watchtower rule was made because they said, "Birthdays are idolizing people," and because, "It was a birthday party that caused John the Baptist to lose his head," so birthday parties were not allowed.

We could not talk to Dad. We could never say anything about what we thought because to disagree with our father meant having our mouths punished. He would sprinkle hot pepper on our tongues for arguing or talking back to him, and sometimes give a spanking on top of that if we dared to kick or try to get away from him. After being punished, we were sent to our beds for the rest of the day.

The radio would be kept off today because there would be church messages and holiday music on most stations. The family was not allowed to listen to ministers or church music or any other program that our father did not like. He controlled the radio, and no one was allowed to turn it on when he wasn't home, not even Mom.

I was helping one of my little brothers stay out of our father's way and wondered what games I could play to keep him occupied. One of his favorites was wooden clothespins. He took the clothespins, made airplanes by connecting them in a crisscross manner, lined them all up in a row, and then flew them off the floor one at a time to crash into another airplane field three or four feet away. The boys liked the pictures of the airplanes that showed up on the front page of the newspaper almost every day. My little brothers and I could also sit behind the large stuffed chair in the living room and look at books or draw pictures on paper. Mom liked when we drew pictures of our family and colored them.

When the whole family was up, my older sisters helped in the kitchen. My older brothers were out in the yard working on the clubhouse they were building with wood scraps they brought home from God knows where. I was watching them through the kitchen window when the lady from next door came to the fence carrying a large round tray of cookies and gave it to my brothers.

Mrs. Landrock was giving them a gift! There was even a big green bow on top of the cookies. My brothers were all smiling and happy. I could see them saying, "Thank you," to our nice neighbor. Even though I couldn't hear them, I watched their mouths and thought they said, "Merry Christmas!" They were all smiles as they brought the tray through the kitchen door. Mrs. Landrock was a very nice lady and a friend to our mother. They often had tea together in the early afternoon, and Mom enjoyed talking with her.

My brothers brought the cookies through the kitchen door with big smiles on their faces. We watched our mother's expression turn into one of happiness. Hearing Dad walking toward the happy squeals in the kitchen, I was afraid that he would throw the decorated cookies away, but he didn't. He just complained about the stupid shapes of the angels, stars, and trees, before walking out of the kitchen with a big handful of them.

After giving each of us children two cookies, Mom put the rest on the table for later. We all wanted milk and kind of got in her way, but she was so happy to have Christmas cookies that she didn't mind at all. Our father wouldn't allow Mom to bake them. My brothers and sisters and I were so thankful that he didn't believe in wasting food. We will never forget Mrs. Landrock and the kindness she showed to us.

Chapter 7

Catherine and Mary came to our house late on Christmas morning to ask if I could have lunch with their family. I was so happy and excited to be invited somewhere on Christmas Day because I had two older sisters that didn't want to be bothered with me and one little sister that didn't know how to play anything. Fortunately and surprisingly, Dad said I was allowed to go to their house.

I had a wonderful afternoon with them. The multilighted pine Christmas tree was full of ornaments that I could touch and play with. After a wonderful meal, there were plates of Christmas cookies, candies, and nuts to nibble. They had Christmas music playing on the radio, and Catherine gave me a beautifully wrapped present.

I was so embarrassed because I had learned in school that Christmas was about giving, and I had nothing to give her in return. At first I told Catherine that I could not accept the gift. The truth is that I didn't know how to accept a gift because I had never received one before. Crying, I told Catherine that my father did not allow us to celebrate Christmas or get gifts.

Catherine said, "Then this is not a Christmas present, it is just something we want to give you because you are a nice little girl." I thanked her and carefully opened the box that was wrapped with bright gift paper and had a large red bow. Inside was the most beautiful doll I had ever seen. Catherine said, "We bought it because it has blonde hair and brown eyes just like you." I thanked her with tears running down my cheeks while Catherine gave me a big hug and kissed my forehead. I wished I could stay there forever.

Everyone in the Herb family gave me a hug and said Merry Christmas—even the very tall and skinny father who kind of scared me because he never said anything. Mrs. Herb was a very thin woman who tired easily, so she often took naps. After hugging me, she said, "I will take a nap now. Thank you for having dinner with us and Merry Christmas!" Catherine said, "You can stay longer until it is almost dark. We can work on a puzzle, and then I will walk you home."

This Christmas Day was the happiest day of my childhood. It was the only new doll I ever had. I named her Sally after the girl in my first-grade reading book. Knowing that the doll might look like a little idol to my dad, I hid the doll under my coat when I entered the house and quietly snuck through the hallway outside the living room. Dad was sleeping in his chair, so I went from the hall into the kitchen where I showed the doll to my mother. Mom whispered, "Take it upstairs where your father won't see it. Hide it and don't play with it when anyone is around." Still hiding it under my coat, I went upstairs.

I tried to reach the hook latch on the attic door, but it was a little too high. Since the attic was out of reach, I hid Sally under my bed. Our beds were high off the floor, and my mother would store boxes under the beds. Pushing the boxes together to make a hiding place for Sally was easy to do. I was so happy with the doll that I was almost bursting from not being allowed to tell anyone about her. I played with Sally whenever an opportunity opened, which wasn't very often because there were so many children in my family.

I wanted desperately to be alone to play, so I kept stretching to reach the hook on the attic door until one day it finally unhooked and we could go to the attic. The attic became an excellent hiding place from the rest of the family. Mom gave me permission to play up there, but warned me there was lots of dust and dirt. She said, "Clean a little bit of it every week in exchange for being in the attic alone."

Chapter 8

What an escape the attic became! It was loaded with boxes of old clothing, shoes, records, books, and army cots. One box held an old beat-up and stained feather quilt that was made by my grandmother when she was much younger. Putting it on the floor, I spent many happy hours quietly playing with a box nearby so I could hide Sally in it if someone came up the steps.

Eventually, Mom helped me pry open one of the folded old army cots. Someone gave them to Dad when he went on a camping trip with my older sisters and brothers. They went to a Jehovah's Witness convention campground in Ohio where they spent about five days learning how to be good Jehovah's Witnesses.

I filled an old pillowcase with clothing from one of the boxes. A pile of old books kept me company, and I found a small lamp with an extension cord that reached to the one outlet that was near the steps. I loved being in the attic alone. I was hardly ever alone in the bedroom because it had no door and my parents walked through the room to get to their room.

My bedroom was large and had two double beds. One bed was for my two older brothers, Rod and Harry. I shared a bed with my three year-old brother, Paul, and little eighteen-month-old sister, Judy. There was also a new baby brother, Lenny, who slept in the crib. Jean and Millie, my older sisters, had a small room at the back of the house. Gram was at our house almost every day and took her afternoon naps in Jean and Millie's bedroom.

At school, the other girls began talking about Easter. I didn't know anything about that, but had learned to listen for all the little pieces of information in order that I could know everything they knew. About the same month as Easter, Dad decided it was time for me to start going door-to-door with Gram on Saturday and Sunday mornings. He said, "If you are old enough to go to school, you are old enough to go door-to-door." I wasn't sure what that was all about, but I knew my older brothers and sisters had been doing it, so off we went.

While it was nice being with the older ones, it wasn't much fun at all. Some people were very nasty and slammed their doors in our faces. Other people argued that the Witnesses should not be bothering them. They seemed not to like the Witnesses, but I didn't know why. Some people would say, "I'm Catholic," or "I'm a Baptist," or some other religion and then shut their doors while Gram was still talking and trying to sell them a *Watchtower* or *Awake* magazine.

One bright and sunny day, a woman who opened her door was extra nice to us. She wore a gold cross on a chain around her neck and she had a big, warm smile for my grandmother and me. She politely listened to Gram's two-minute sales pitch for the *Watchtower* magazine and then said, "I don't believe the way you do, but I'm going to pray for you." Looking right at me, she quickly added, "and I'm going to pray for you too."

My heart instantly felt warm; I smiled at the woman and was about to say, "Thank you," when Gram angrily said, "Keep your prayers to yourself, we don't want them!" She put her hand across my shoulder and began pushing me off the porch. In shock, I said nothing, but looking back at the woman, she was still there smiling at me. I knew in my heart that the woman would say a prayer for me, and it made me happy because no one had ever said that they would pray for me before. I felt in my heart that it was a good thing.

Gram told me, "We don't want any prayers from people who go to churches. Their prayers never reach God's ears because they don't use his name Jehovah when they pray. If they don't pray for the truth, the work, and Jehovah's organization, their prayers are wrong, and God will punish them at Armageddon. We don't want any of those church people to mention our names in their prayers. Satan hears their prayers." The way Gram always warned me about Satan, I began to think, "Satan is always doing this and that, but what is Jehovah God doing other than secretly channeling information to the men of the Watchtower organization? Does Satan have more power and more followers than Jehovah?"

The prayers at the Kingdom Hall were all about thanking Jehovah for the so-called truth, the weekly magazines, the books, and the organization. They asked Jehovah to help everyone to understand them, give everyone the time to study them, and go door-to-door with them to reach all the people of the world before his great day of wrath and destruction would come. All personal prayers for people were for them to continue to be able to serve Jehovah God, the work, and the Watchtower Society. Selfish prayers were not allowed.

The Lord's Prayer was never said because the leaders said that Jesus gave it to his followers as a guide to prayer, nothing more. Witnesses were not allowed to use it like the churches do. The Witnesses were always admonished to be careful not to be like the churches, and that was one of the reasons they didn't have Sunday school classes for the children.

They didn't want to be anything like the churches because when Armageddon arrived all churches would be destroyed along with the people who went to the churches. Gram said, "I wouldn't want to be in a church when Armageddon comes! I would die with all those church people!" That is why she always told me to never go into a church. The thought of all those people dying always made me very sad.

While churches are celebrating Easter, Jehovah's Witnesses have a celebration called "The Memorial." It usually falls on or near the Jewish Passover. They all are expected to be in attendance at the Kingdom Hall and bring visitors to observe this once-a-year passing of the unleavened matzoh crackers and wine.

No one was allowed to take the crackers and wine except those who were born before or during 1935 and are part of the heavenly class of one hundred forty-four thousand who have been chosen by Jehovah to go to heaven. In many Kingdom Halls, no one takes the once-a-year crackers and wine because there are so few people old enough to take it or who believe they have the calling to go to heaven. Most Jehovah's Witnesses believe they are part of the earthly class who will live on earth forever. It is a two-class religion, the earthly class and the heavenly class.

The *Watchtower* says that Armageddon will come while a few of the heavenly class are still on earth leading the organization. The numbers of those born before 1935 were decreasing every year when they counted how many took crackers and wine. The Witnesses were encouraged that Armageddon would soon arrive. That teaching has been changed a little bit in the not-too-distant past. Some of the original heavenly class members had fallen into sin and were disfellowshipped. They never returned to the Watchtower before they died, so they were lost in everlasting sleep.

Jehovah needed to call a few more people that were born after 1935 to make up for the lost ones. The new ones that were called, of course, were often junior leaders at the Watchtower headquarters. This new light was not received with joy by many of the Witnesses who were tired of knocking on doors. They still believe that all peoples of the earth will die except those closely identified with the Watchtower publishing company.

In recent years, the partakers of the memorial have actually increased in numbers. This has caused some confusion among the Witnesses; they are having a problem understanding how this could happen. The decrease always made them feel good. Now, with the yearly increase in partakers, it seems as though Armageddon might be delayed for a long time. Leaders have been trying to allay those fears by coming up with new guidelines for who may be chosen as part of the one hundred forty-four thousand and who may not.

With new rules from the organization, fewer will be allowed to be in the heavenly class. My Dad and Gram never believed they had the heavenly calling. My grandmother said, "Who wants to go to heaven and fly around all day? I want to live right here on earth after Jehovah God destroys the wicked."

Back then, when I was a child, Gram was busy making sure we had nice dresses to wear to the Memorial meeting. She wanted my brothers to have white shirts and ties because this was such a special day. The Kingdom Hall would be full because no one would think of missing this once-a-year meeting. To me it was boring, but to Gram, it was exciting. She carefully watched to see who would take part of a matzoh cracker and drink a little wine.

Chapter 9

My grandmother was meticulous about some things, like recording the number of every house on every street where we knocked on doors. I thought, "Maybe she will be scolded if she doesn't keep the records properly." The Kingdom Hall had a territory file where all the records were stored. One of the men would assign the territories and records to the members before they went out knocking on doors. They tried to systematically visit every door in the whole town at least two times a year.

At age seven, I was able to keep the house-to-house record for Gram by marking every house number with a code letter. The letter I was for *interested*, NI was for *not interested*, O was for *opposed*, and NH for *not home*. These record cards were dated and turned into the Kingdom Hall along with the territory envelope. When that territory was scheduled to be pulled out of the file for another door-to-door visit, the Witnesses knew the attitude of the householder before they knocked on the door. They hoped that the NI and O people were not home or that someone new would open the door.

There was never a choice about knocking on doors or in what I was allowed to do, and felt as though I lived in two very different worlds that opposed each other. My home world was home and the Kingdom Hall of Jehovah's Witnesses where it was like walking on a dangerous tightrope. My school world was school and normal people, like our neighbors who made me happy. Dad and Gram didn't want me to enjoy school and they warned, "Don't believe everything the teacher says."

Shirley Holland was my best school world friend, and I managed to stop at her house a few times. Her family was very different from mine. They had a picture of Jesus on the wall, and Shirley's mother decorated their house for every holiday. She had time to sit with us at the table and talk while having a snack. Her mother was always smiling and happy. Shirley had an uncle who was serving in the army in Europe, but she had no brothers or sisters.

Catherine, Mary, and their parents were my friends too. When their family moved several blocks away, they kept in touch with Mom. I was allowed to visit them on weekends several times a year. Sometimes I stayed overnight. They gave me little gifts whenever I visited them, and they took me many places over the next few years. They took me on some bus trips with their parents to New York City. One time we went to the beautiful Christmas show at Radio City Music Hall. It had a big impact on me, and the joyful celebration of Christ's birth thrilled me to the core of my being.

They also took me to the circus, the state fair, and the ice show. My father always gave me a *Watchtower* magazine to take to the Herb house each time I stayed overnight on Friday or Saturday. He said, "Give this to Catherine and invite her to the Kingdom Hall lecture Sunday." I always told her, "This is from my father," and gave her the magazine, but never invited her to the meetings. Instinctively, I knew she would never go to them because she did not like my father. Dad's magazine always went on the pile of old newspapers to be thrown out.

My father knew I enjoyed doing large puzzles at their house. Mary was the best puzzle-doer I ever knew, but Catherine would get bored and sit on the comfy sofa to read jungle comic books. They taught me many of the little tricks of putting puzzles together systematically, and it became a thoroughly enjoyable challenge. It became my favorite way to pass time, but the trips they took me on were utterly fantastic. Dad and Gram never knew all the places I went because I never told anyone except Mom, and she warned me not to tell anyone else.

When I was almost eight, Gram said, "We are going uptown to do placard service." We met other Witnesses at the Kingdom Hall to get our white cardboard signs. There were two sizes: the small ones for children and the large ones for adults. The signs had slogans on them like, "The World's End is Almost Here!" and "Religion is a Racket and a Snare!" Gram began taking me every Friday night when all the stores in the shopping district were open until nine, and the sidewalks were full of people. Sometimes we also had to do this on Saturday afternoons.

Some of the men wore heavier sandwich boards, but most of us had white cardboard signs. They were tied together with pieces of heavy string around our waists and over our shoulders. The fronts and backs had advertisements for the Kingdom Hall. Paper leaflets were handed to all the people we walked near. These leaflets were inviting them to come to the Kingdom Hall to hear the one-hour public speech that would be given Sunday afternoon. I didn't like doing this, and it might have shown on my face because people would look at me so strangely and pitifully. Some of the people took the leaflets I was holding out, but most of the people just stared at me and refused the leaflet. Very few people smiled. I told my grandmother, "People don't like that we are doing this. They stop smiling when they look at us."

Gram barked at me, "Then you smile! What is wrong with you? You should be happy to be doing God's will. Maybe if you smile, people will smile back at you." It didn't work for me. When other children walked down the street with their parents, I would turn around and try not to be seen by them. I wasn't sure why, but I felt ashamed. I wanted to be home in the attic alone. My father and grandmother were always scolding me and telling me not to be ashamed of serving Jehovah. That made me ashamed of being ashamed.

My brother Harry was not forced to wear the sandwich boards. Harry was excused from doing door-to-door and placard service for the most part because he had a lame leg. It upset me that I had to do this service for God and he didn't. He was seventeen months older than me and was treated special because he was born with what my mother called "water on the knee." His one leg did not develop properly. When he needed new shoes, my mother took him to a shoemaker. The shoemaker did all kinds of shoe repairs and he knew how to put a cork lift on the bottom of the new shoes. Harry didn't especially like me either when we were children. Sometimes we played mean tricks on each other. I could run and jump better than he could. Some people thought we might be twins because we looked like each other. I had gotten as tall as him, and he resented me for that. I resented him for being treated nicer than me.

Dad told me, "God knows what we each can do. You are healthy and strong. When you go out doing service, you are pleasing Jehovah God." I never understood why everything the Witnesses did was pleasing God. I never heard it from the Bible that we should walk around wearing big cardboard signs or that we should bother people by knocking on their doors in the morning. The instructions only came from the men at the Kingdom Hall. The men at the Hall, including my dad, took turns giving the Sunday speeches.

The Watchtower organization provided a speech outline and the scriptures they must use during the lecture to support the doctrines that were being presented to the public attendees. My father gave me his outline and the job of looking in the Bible to find the scriptures. He said, "Put a piece of paper at each of the scriptures for bookmarks where I can find all of the verses. Then I don't need to look for them myself. It will save me a lot of time." It saved him time and it also helped me to find the books of the Bible much faster.

Hunting for scriptures became like a game for me. At the Watchtower study every Sunday afternoon, I often sat with the magazine and the Bible looking for every verse that was quoted in the magazine. The Watchtower study followed the one-hour public speech after a brief intermission, and all the visitors were invited to remain for one more hour of studying the Bible.

Whenever Dad gave a speech, people would come up to him afterward to praise him for his speaking ability and ask him questions about the Bible. Although Dad's school education stopped in the sixth grade, he always seemed to know everything about everything.

He liked to read and had an excellent memory, like an elephant that never forgets, and had memorized many Bible verses.

Each time someone asked him a question about the Bible, he would open his Bible to a verse, or else he would quote a verse word for word to support everything he said. He enjoyed the attention very much and would usually be in a good mood the rest of the day.

When he was in a good mood, everyone else in the family was happy, including my mother. When he was in a bad mood, Mom and all of us children trembled with fear because his violent temper would explode into physical violence. His love of attention and alcohol kept him going to Tinkle's Bar between his dairy route and home. It was the ideal location for someone who didn't want his customers or his neighbors to know how much he enjoyed drinking. He also enjoyed talking.

One day at our house, someone asked him a question about the Bible verse in 1 John 4:20 (KJV) that says, "If a man say, I love God, and hateth his brother, he is a liar: for he that loveth not his brother whom he hath seen, how can he love God whom he hath not seen?" The person told my father, "If we do not love our neighbors, then we cannot love God either."

Dad knew that verse by heart and said, "Love for our neighbor is the motivation for everything Jehovah's Witnesses do. Love is why we go door-to-door with the Watchtower literature to warn people about the impending battle of Armageddon that is right around the corner." Deep inside, I knew very well how capable my father was of hating people that were not only neighbors, but also relatives. My grandmother hated people too.

Gram had a brother and sister-in-law who lived on the same block where we lived. She never spoke to them and warned all of us to never go near that house, "because they don't want to hear about the truth, Jehovah and his organization." They were good friends until she had tried to convert her brother to the Witnesses, and he argued the Bible with her that they were wrong. She would have nothing to do with her brother after that.

Dad spoke about them as though they were "devil dirt," and that is exactly what he called them. He hated many people and would often curse them and judge them as being Satan's children or devil dirt because they were not Jehovah's Witnesses. All religious clergy and politicians fell into the same category.

There were times when I was convinced that my grandmother and my father were so full of hate that they didn't know how to love their own family. My father would often get angry when talking about his childhood; how, at the age of twelve he had to quit school and help his mother and family by going to work at the coal company where his father had been fatally crushed during a cave-in.

My grandmother and my dad had had a hard life, and maybe that accounted for their desire to see the old world destroyed and a new world ushered in with cheers. All Witnesses are expected to try to convert people to their beliefs about the end of the world. No other beliefs are tolerated.

Witnesses are not allowed to read the publications of other religions in spite of the fact that the Watchtower will sometimes quote things out of context from other religious literature. When I questioned this, my grandmother said, "It is okay to read the quotations in the Watchtower literature. The Society will provide us with any information we need to know. The Watchtower saves everyone from wasting time, like reading magazines and books with false teachings. Wasting time is not allowed because the end of the world is so near."

In spite of having restrictions on what the Witnesses are allowed to read and what organizations they are allowed to join or support, the Watchtower goes to great lengths to get access to information and publications from around the world. They join large organizations to further their own interests.

For example, in 1991 the Watchtower Society secretly sought and received membership into the United Nations as an NGO, a Non-Governmental Organization. Historically, the Watchtower Society has strongly attacked and denounced the League of Nations and then the United Nations as being part of Satan's last world empire predicted in the Bible. I was taught as a child that the UN was part of the beast of Revelation that was doomed for destruction. We, the Witnesses, were not allowed to join worldly organizations, yet the

Watchtower became an NGO member of the United Nations. They willingly joined the evil beast of Revelation.

When this information was posted on the Internet nine years later in 2000, many Jehovah's Witnesses were so upset they left the organization. To avoid further damage to their authority and leadership, the Watchtower organization announced in 2001 that they had withdrawn their United Nations membership after ten years as an NGO participant. It was claimed that they just wanted to use the UN library. Most of the Witnesses happily accepted this excuse.

Chapter 10

Gram always supported the Watchtower. She made excuses for them when they were wrong and needed to replace the truth with new truth. She clung to the organization like a child clings to a parent. My grandmother was not treated very well as a child, but I suppose many poor children of her era were treated badly. I am not sure if she ever had any real love.

It was easy for her to get caught up into an organization that was harsh and controlling; that was the way she was raised. My grandmother was only fifteen years old when her father, a coal miner, arranged for her to be the wife of another miner she had never met. She was a pretty teenage girl with long, light brown hair and brown eyes. Her mother taught her how to cook, clean, and take care of her younger brothers and sisters. Gram's ancestors came from England on both sides of her family; her father's family name was Adams.

There were many European immigrants working in the coal mines. One man, John Ossman, was part of an immigrant family from Germany. He was considered an outcast in Germany because he had Turkish blood flowing through his veins. The Turks were not very popular in Germany in the 1800s or near the turn of the 1900s as memories of the Ottoman Empire rulers had not been forgotten. Handsome John had a German mother, but looked like his Turkish father, with very dark eyes and dark, wavy hair. He had light coffee-colored skin. His ancestral family name was Oman, but it was Germanized by adding two letters to the name to make it Ossman. However, they were still discriminated against, so the family emigrated to America and became coal miners.

They settled in a Pennsylvania coal mine town where the men worked all day and often drank all night at the company bar. At the end of the month, many of them were in debt to the coal company. While drinking in the bar room with his fellow workers after a long day of working in the mines, the thirty-year-old John Ossman confessed, "I am very lonely and wish I had a wife. I want to be married and have children."

My great-grandfather offered to sell his daughter, my grandmother, to John. Gram's father saw her as a liability because she could not work in the mines the way her brother did, and there were no factories close enough to where they lived. My grandmother never told anyone what the price of a bride was at that time, but it could not have been very much because they all lived in the same coal town in small, crowded housing provided by the mine owners. She married John when she was fifteen and became pregnant after her first month of marriage.

My grandmother began raising her children under difficult circumstances. They were poor. She told me, "I felt very fortunate that all of my children survived the 1918 Spanish flu epidemic. We had a Catholic doctor who was accused of wanting the Protestants to die. When he was called to the homes in the middle of winter, he told them to open the windows a little and let some fresh air into the stale, smelly houses. Many people didn't have enough sense to close the windows after the doctor left. Some people died of pneumonia, and their families accused the doctor of wanting to kill them because they were not Catholic."

It is estimated that half a million Americans and about fifty million people worldwide died of the Spanish flu. Some people, like my grandmother, would rather have died from their illness than have the doctor come to the house. Hatred for all Catholics was born in my father's heart as a child of eight and never left.

There were two churches near Dad's coal town; one was Catholic and one was Lutheran. Organizers of the Ku Klux Klan were working in the coal regions of Pennsylvania at this time when my father was a boy. The KKK members were against the Catholics, especially the Irish, and blamed them for many of the economic ills that befell the people. Irish immigrants were usually targeted because they were Catholic. Most Germans were Lutheran. They tolerated the fewer Anglican and Methodist families who were English and Scotch-Irish. My grandmother's family was Anglican in England, but in America, they were separated from the church.

My grandmother was thirty years old and seven months pregnant with her ninth child when her husband, my grandfather, was crushed in a cave-in and carried home dead from the mine. Twelve men died that day, and many others were injured. Her husband was laid to rest as part of the Lutheran community service. Gram had never gone to church before, and when she was heavy with her ninth child, decided to go again. She told me, "I decided one Sunday to take my children to the Lutheran church. The usher gave me and my eight young ones a pew near the back and escorted the better-dressed families to the front pews. I was offended and never went inside a church again."

She became very angry with me when I asked her, "Gram, did you tell the usher you wanted to sit in the front of the church?" She said, "The churches only want people with money. They cater to the well-dressed rich and don't care about the poor and the orphaned." I was shocked to hear that and wasn't sure I should believe what Gram said. I knew nice, kind people like my schoolteachers and friends who went to churches. I also knew that small children might make a lot of noise in the front of a church and my grandmother had eight young children to control, with another one on the way. Gram told me, "Some people think that they are buying their way into heaven by going to church, but we know that they aren't going to heaven because only one hundred forty-four thousand Jehovah's Witnesses are going to heaven. Hah!" she remarked, "Too bad there isn't any real hellfire for the church-goers to burn in."

I was shocked that she would wish that fate on anyone. The Witnesses do not believe in the immortality of the soul or in hellfire. They believe the soul dies because it is nothing more than the flesh and blood. To them, hell is nothing more than sleeping in the grave.

It appears she became very bitter when she lost her husband and was left alone with nine children to support.

She had virtually no support system outside of her older sons. John Jr. and William quit school immediately and took full-time jobs helping the miners. Two years later when my father turned twelve, he quit school after sixth grade and went to work at the mine. Dad worked above ground as a slate picker. He told us, "My hands would bleed every day because the slate even cut through my bandages. I picked sharp pieces of slate out of the coal. After a while, I worked on the coal chutes of the breakers where the coal was crushed and rolled down the chute. When I was fourteen, they put me underground in the mine as a trapper. A trapper opens and closes the doors between the sections of the mine when the coal carts go through. I liked that job. It helped develop my muscles. My brothers and I made enough money to buy food for the whole family at the company store. When I was sixteen, I became a miner like my older brothers and made more money. My mother lived frugally and began saving money. She wanted to get us out of the mines before we were killed."

My father quickly became involved in the Ku Klux Klan while a young teen. Although he had little education, by the time he was fifteen he was recognized as being a youth leader because of his outstanding memory and public speaking ability. In 1925, he helped organize a KKK group from his county near central Pennsylvania to march with thousands of other members in Washington DC during a national gathering of the KKK. They wore their white sheets and white hoods.

The only thing religious about my father at that time was his hatred for Catholics. Burning crosses on the lawns of Irish Catholics in the coal region was his expression of the contempt in which he held all of them. How ironic that his father escaped being discriminated against for being part Turkish and then his son, my dad, discriminated against others because of their religion. It was a hatred he carried with him throughout his life. By contrast, my mother never said anything mean about anyone.

My mother had a hard life too. She was a petite and pretty girl of twelve when she was orphaned. Her mother was taken with a stroke at the age of forty. Her father had been killed two years earlier at the same time and the same mine where my dad lost his father along with the other miners, so both of my grandfathers were killed on the same day and at the same place. Mom was very close to her mother, and it broke her heart when she died.

Mom was in the kitchen where her mother was sitting on a rocking chair near the black coal stove that heated the house and where they cooked their food. They lived in the same house as her older brother, Joe, who worked in the coal mine and supported them. My mother was sitting on the homemade rag rug on the floor. She watched as her mother pulled all the long hairpins out of her dark brown hair that was piled high on top of her head. Mom told me she thought she looked so beautiful, with her long, wavy hair cascading down to frame her face. Then her mother closed her eyes and let her head fall to the side. My mother thought she was napping. When her brother came home, they tried to wake her up, but she was gone. They buried her next to their father.

Mom's mother was part of the Maguire family, and she told me many stories about the Molly Maguires. According to her, "My family was just antagonizing the mine owners and being troublemakers to protest the working conditions, but then some violent troublemakers began to call themselves the Molly Maguires. They were a group of men who stole horses, then tried to rob, beat, and murder the mine owners and mine bosses. They were protesting the poor working and living conditions of the miners while the owners reaped huge profits. The mine owners fought back with hired ruffians who beat and murdered the members of the Molly Maguires. No one felt very safe." Mom claimed, "The Molly Maguires were the reason the Mine Workers Union was eventually legally established. They gave their lives for a good cause."

After they buried her mother, Mom went to live with her recently married sister, Mattie, short for Matilda. Mom was an orphan, but she was loved very much by her sister. My mother needed to drop out of school because of anxiety and other health problems. The Catholic doctor said, "She has St. Vitus's Dance, a twitching of the muscles that causes her legs to shake when she walks. Children between the ages of five and fifteen get this disorder more than adults, but adult outbreaks of the disorder were also reported in Europe. Saint Vitus is the Catholic patron saint of dancers and children, so the ailment carries his name."

My mother told me, "When I had St. Vitus's Dance, Mattie would walk me to the train tracks every day and help me to walk on the rails to help me get control of my legs back. If I had not done that, my legs would have gotten weaker. Mattie was good to me."

Mom's sister provided her with good, nourishing food and daily exercise to strengthen her legs and her body. She eventually made a complete recovery. Other children were afflicted with the disorder in the coal regions where they lived. My mother and my father had been born seven days apart in January of 1910 and shared the same background of growing up in the same coal mine town. They knew each other all of their lives.

My grandmother wanted to get her sons out of the mines. She had saved enough money to move her nine children out of the coal region by the time my father was eighteen. They took a train south as far as they could afford to go and still have enough money to rent a house with an apple tree in the yard. In Allentown, they began a new life away from the dust and death of the mines. Gram's oldest daughter, Gertrude, found work in a sewing factory, and my dad found work driving a delivery truck. My father was still eighteen when he brought his orphaned girlfriend, my mother, to Allentown as soon as he was working steadily. Mom had lived with her sister for six years, but Mattie had her own children now and needed room for them. Mom said, "I could never repay Mattie and her husband for supporting me and taking care of me all of those years." Mom looked for work, but could not find a job.

They all looked for work in Allentown, but jobs were few and then the stock market collapsed in 1929. The Wall Street crash, bank failures, and lowering of real estate values led to several years of economic decline in most industrialized nations. My mother told me, "Neighbors would share food and plan meals according to what they could each provide. They all had vegetable gardens in the yards. One neighbor made lots of good pasta and would exchange it for other foods she wanted." My mother enjoyed cooking and baking. She collected the apples from their tree to bake very good apple pies that she often exchanged for fresh pasta. My father wanted to marry her.

Gram was opposed to them getting married during such hard economic times and refused to sign the consent form. Early one morning they secretly eloped in the old delivery truck. The age of marriage consent in Maryland was eighteen, as opposed to Pennsylvania where the age of consent was twenty-one. They did not need a blood test or a parent's signature in Maryland. There was no waiting period either, so they were married in a wedding chapel by a justice of the peace in Elkton, Maryland. At that time in the 1920s and 1930s, Elkton was known as "the elopement capital of the East Coast." People from the surrounding states could marry and drive back home the same day. Gram was not happy about the elopement, but she took them back into her house when they returned.

Dad shared Gram's resentment against all the churches, especially the Catholic Church because of his KKK connections. Gram was easy prey when Jehovah's Witnesses came knocking on their door. The Watchtower man and woman asked if they could visit her and the family every week to study the Bible with them because the churches didn't tell the people the real truth about the Bible. Gram liked hearing them assail the churches, and she wanted to hear more.

When the Witnesses conduct Bible studies with people in their homes, they are actually using Watchtower literature in their studies and not the Bible. Scriptures are quoted and twisted out of context to support their teachings. If the Witnesses would read the entire chapter in context, they usually would get a different meaning out of the verses than the one that the Watchtower teaches.

I have experienced that the Witnesses are subject to mind control by repetition of the same verses for the same teachings used over and over again. The Witnesses are kept so busy going to many meetings a week, reading the monthly publications, and going door-to-door, that most of them have no time to actually read the Bible chapter by chapter. Sometimes I saw my grandmother sleeping in her rocking chair with an open *Watchtower* magazine. Reading helped her to sleep.

Gram and Dad had a hard life, but lots of people have a hard life and yet don't want to see all the people in the whole world destroyed. Other Witnesses I knew shared the same desire as my father and grandmother for Armageddon to come quickly. They did not consider themselves to be part of this worldly system. Witnesses thought they were part of a new world system and showed no sympathy for all of the outsiders who would die.

Chapter 11

Every time natural disasters occurred, my grandmother was hoping it was the beginning of the end. Her biggest fear was dying before she saw the old world destroyed. Going door-to-door and placard service was not much fun for me, but I sure didn't want to see Armageddon start and kill me for not going.

I was more interested in what I learned at school than in what was taught at the Kingdom Hall. By spending many hours in the attic alone with magazines, newspapers, and schoolbooks that had lots of pictures, I learned to escape from my family and surroundings by mentally traveling through the pages of history books into other times and other places where Jehovah was never mentioned.

My older brothers showed me where the public library was and then would not take me there again. Begging them did not help. Desperately wanting more books, I tried to go by myself one Saturday. It meant crossing two busy streets that I was warned by my father not to cross.

Stepping off the curb while looking to the right to see if any cars were coming, a car hit me on my left side. I went flying through the air, landing hard on my side in the street. A car had been coming from my left, about to make a right turn, just as I reached the curb and was looking in the other direction. Luckily, the car was not moving very fast when I stepped out in front of it. My first thoughts were of the beating my father would give me if he found out I was disobeying him by crossing that street.

The fear of getting a beating from Dad far outweighed the pain I felt. As the man and woman jumped out of their car, I got up and ran like a frightened animal. The man and woman shouted after me, "Stop! Come back!" but I ran as fast as I could. The pain was throbbing through my left side as I made it home and quietly crawled up the steps to hide in my attic alone.

Crying softly and stifling the noise with my hands, I lay there on the old cot and quilt, fearing that someone would find out what I had done. Sleeping intermittently in spite of the pain, hours passed and my mother came up the attic steps looking for me. Dinner was over and she had not seen me since that morning. I told Mom that I had a bad headache and didn't feel well enough to eat anything.

Mom believed me and left me to sleep in the attic alone. Luckily, I had a small snack box stashed in one of the larger boxes where I had squirreled away some treats. It was an accumulation of candy, pretzels, and crackers. I kept an extra glass bottle or two of soda and a bottle opener in my snack box.

As I lay there, I thought about my three other close encounters with death. First, Mom told me, "You fell out of the baby carriage onto the top of your head when you were a baby. Blood began running out of your mouth, and you were dazed. I was afraid you would die, but then you began screaming." Our family doctor lived one block away from us, so Mom ran with me to his office. I had several teeth by then and had bit through my tongue. My mother said, "It took me, the nurse, and the doctor's wife to hold you still while the doctor treated your mouth."

The second time, I was almost three when my brother Harry held a big balloon in my mouth and then stuck it with a sharp pin. The balloon burst, shot down my throat, and I almost choked to death. I fell backward, hitting my head against the wall. Harry started screaming for Mom. My mother came running into the room and dug the balloon out of my throat as I passed out. I had nightmares for years about a large, unknown dark object suffocating and killing me.

The third incident was a few months before being hit by the car. While swimming with my older brothers at the first cement pool in Fountain Park, a brain-damaged boy, about twelve, jumped off the side of the pool. He landed on my back and sat on me, pinning me under the cold, clear water. He thought he was just playing. I struggled to get free and scraped my abdomen on the rough cement bottom of the pool before losing consciousness. The lifeguard rescued me and as I began to open my eyes, I saw a bright light. A handsome face was smiling at me. I thought I had died and gone to heaven. For some reason, I thought he must be Jesus. He looked like the picture of Jesus that my friend Shirley had on the wall at her house. Comforted by that thought, I closed my eyes and when I opened them again, he was gone. My older brothers were making me stand up and they took me home.

How I wished this night in the attic that someone was there to help me. I wanted to close my eyes and wake up without pain. Thoughts of lying there until I died, maybe bleeding inside, went through my mind. At first it was frightening to think that I might die, because according to what Gram had recently told me, "Little girls and boys don't go to heaven when they die. They simply cease to exist unless they are very good Jehovah's Witnesses and then they will be in God's memory. Jehovah God will resurrect them someday in the future to live on a paradise earth after Armageddon."

Now I thought, "I am a very bad Jehovah's Witness because of praying the Lord's Prayer and saying the Pledge of Allegiance to the American flag in school. Maybe I don't deserve to live in the new world because of disobeying my father and grandmother all the time. Jehovah will probably kill me at Armageddon and maybe he is going to let me die now from my injury."

While thinking about this, I realized that dying wouldn't be so bad. "Dying means there won't be any pain if I am sleeping forever in a grave. I don't really mind sleeping, and maybe it might be better than living as a Jehovah's Witness without birthdays and holidays. Maybe it would be better to die." I hugged my doll for some comfort.

Very early the next morning, Sunday, I crept down the steps quietly and slowly because the pain made it difficult to move. After eating some cereal and changing clothing, I slowly went back upstairs to the attic alone. My left hip and buttock were severely bruised and discolored. Thank goodness it was still the weekend. When my mother came up, I said, "I'm not feeling very good and didn't sleep." When Mom went downstairs, she told Gram, "Arlene is staying home from service today. She doesn't feel well."

Every time someone came up the steps, they found me looking at an old Witness book called *Children* and sometimes pretending to be asleep so they wouldn't disturb me. The *Children* book was not for children. It predicted dire problems for people who had children in "the last days." At some point when I was napping, my mother left some food on a plate so I wouldn't need to go down the steps. She was very thoughtful.

Monday, the second day after the accident, my pain was worse. I was afraid to tell Mom the pain was in my backside and legs, so I pretended to have a really bad headache. "My head hurts. Can I stay home from school and have something to take the pain away?" If my mother knew the truth, she would want to examine me and then get very upset. My father might find out. Mom said I could stay home from school. She hardly ever gave us children any pills, but she gave me some aspirin with warm milk and toast. It helped for a while, and then she gave me more pills that night. She gave me a little castor oil too; she thought that cured everything.

The next day, Tuesday, my side felt a little better, but it was still difficult to sit on anything hard. I told Mom that my leg was hurting, but didn't know why. She told me to stay home from school again and gave me some more aspirin. Mom told me she was very worried that I might be getting polio; polio was a big item in the newspapers, and researchers were trying to develop a vaccine to prevent the disease. She said, "You can stay home from school again today, but if you are not better by tomorrow, you are going to the doctor."

I was afraid to go to the doctor because he might see the huge black and orangey-blue mark on my upper left leg into my backside and then Mom would need to know the truth. I was still afraid of what punishment my dad would give me. Maybe he would beat my left side just for spite to teach me a lesson.

With my clothing hiding the black and blue marks from my mother's eyes, I began walking around and feeling better, so I went downstairs with a book and lay on my bed while the older ones were in school. It was nice to be all alone in that big bed. My little sister and my youngest brothers were enough to keep Mom busy all day. I went back to school the next day.

There were many old Witness books up in the attic, like seven volumes of *Studies from the Scriptures*. They were very difficult to read, but they gave me a great deal of practice for sounding out words. Little did I know that my love of reading was actually promoting my Watchtower indoctrination and doing me harm. The logic used by the Watchtower to explain everything is very misleading. People allow themselves to be influenced by the writings of men instead of the Word of God. Many completely close their minds to true Christian doctrine when they study the books written by the leaders of Jehovah's Witnesses.

Chapter 12

Gram started a so-called Bible study with a woman she met going door-to-door. The woman was almost as old as my grandmother and had invited her into the kitchen for tea while they talked about the Bible. Mrs. Malone was a very lonely person because her husband had recently died.

Lonely people often answer the doors when the Witnesses knock. A Bible study meant going to the private home for one hour every week at a set time in order to study one of the Watchtower books, which, of course, quoted Bible verses. The verses were taken completely out of context to prove the doctrine that was being presented. Gram wanted me to learn how to do this. She said, "If you go to the study with me, you can count an hour on your service report. You need to get more hours to report to the Kingdom Hall."

Mrs. Malone was very nice and always made me a cup of tea with lots of milk; she usually had some fresh-baked cookies to go with the tea. I liked her. She was somewhat like Mom because she was the same size and always wore a flowered cotton housedress. She smiled often—and her kitchen always smelled good.

My grandmother would say, "The study books and magazines are so important because no one can really understand the Bible by just reading the Bible. There is so much confusion and so many churches that believe in the Bible differently. The churches are like the tower of Babel that men built, and God confused their languages. They are not doing what God wants them to do. God does not approve of all these different religions that pretend to understand the Bible. They don't understand it at all. If they did, they would all be Jehovah's Witnesses."

I didn't like when Gram began assailing the churches. It was not a very nice thing to do, because lots of nice people went to churches, like our neighbors and my schoolteachers. My grandmother thought people who went to the churches belonged to Satan, especially the Catholics. She always made fun of the Catholic priests who wore long robes. She made fun of the nuns, too, and said terrible things about them. Gram said most of them were prisoners of the church and were not allowed to leave. If they did, they would be hunted down and killed.

She hated the Catholic Church, not only because of the doctor in the coal regions, but because they claimed to be the church founded by Christ. They claim Jesus wanted Peter to rule the church and be the first pope. She said, "Jehovah's Witnesses go all the way back to Cain and Abel. Abel loved Jehovah and was the first martyr for Jehovah."

After the Bible study, we walked home in the dark. On the way home from Mrs. Malone's house, we passed a building that had a red neon sign reading, "JESUS SAVES." I said, "Look at that sign, Grammy! What does Jesus save?" In my mind, I was thinking in terms of the tin cans that everyone saved during World War II, or soda bottles or string, but Gram gave me a slap on my mouth. The slap told me that I had just spoken about something Jehovah's Witnesses should not talk about.

"Jesus doesn't save anything! Those people are all crazy!" Gram shouted at me. Whenever we passed near that sign, I wondered why the city allowed those crazy people to put that big sign on the building. We walked across Allentown's longest bridge at the time, which was at least two blocks long. It gave us a view of the east and west sides of the city. In the evening, we could see all the lights, so that was my favorite part of walking home. After more than two years of going and coming back home from the Bible study with Mrs. Malone, Gram gave up on converting her.

The home Bible studies started when Charles Taze Russell, a co-owner of a haberdashery, founded the Watchtower organization. It was 1879 in Pittsburgh, Pennsylvania. He asserted that he had rediscovered the true religion that started with Abel, the son of Adam and Eve. Mr. Russell was an average-looking man of his time, with hair that stopped at his shirt collar. He had a full beard that was kept at a stylish length. Greatly influenced by magazine articles written by Nelson H. Barbour, Russell collaborated with him to do some writing. Mr. Barbour was a spiritualist and eventually a leader of a splinter Adventist group in Rochester, New York. They were sometimes called the Second Day Adventists. He wrote articles for the *Herald of the Morning* magazine.

Mr. Russell also wrote *Studies in the Scriptures,* a seven-volume set of books that sold almost ten million copies. The volumes were printed in thirty-four languages at a time when there was great social unrest in America and the rest of the world. He used the unrest to persuade some people that God had a plan to take care of everything and give the world another chance.

His followers thought he was inspired by God and believed him when he claimed, "Jehovah God resides on a star in the Pleiades constellation." I was taught that as a child and believed it until 1953 when the teaching was changed. At that time in 1953, the Watchtower Society said they do not know where God has his throne. Many Witnesses were disappointed with that announcement because they had spent many nights looking at and adoring the stars in the Pleiades. No doubt, in the 1950s the Watchtower became aware that with new and bigger telescopes, the study of outer space and the universe was expanding, and they might disprove what their founder had said.

Mr. Russell wrote many books, and his salesmanship technique of making converts was widely used by his followers. Many of them would put a foot in the doorway when the householders tried to shut the door, then forcibly complete their sales pitch for the books and magazines. Mr. Russell gave himself the title of "Pastor."

In 1912, Russell's Watchtower publication advertised expensive "Miracle Wheat Seed" for sale at $1.00 a pound. That was much higher than the price of a normal pound of wheat seed, but Russell claimed that his seed would grow five times more wheat than any other brand. The proceeds went to Russell's Watchtower Society.

Russell owned nine hundred ninety-nine of the one thousand shares of Watchtower Society stock. By this figure, ninety-nine cents of every one-dollar profit went in Pastor Russell's pocket. After a January 1913 mail fraud court trial about the wheat, the *Brooklyn Eagle* newspaper implied that Russell's religious cult was nothing more than a money-making scheme.

Government agents testified that the wheat was no better than common wheat sold everywhere for much less money. If stricter laws regulating postal fraud had been in existence at the time, there might have been more serious charges brought against Russell. He could no longer get away with advertising his miracle wheat seed, and the offer was withdrawn from the magazines.

For almost twenty years Russell and his wife Maria fought, in and out of courts, much to the consternation of their followers. There were many reports of the court cases in the newspapers. Mr. and Mrs. Russell had many marital problems and she accused him of immoral conduct. Mrs. Russell claimed that dogs had more rights than she had, and Mr. Russell retorted that she had no rights at all because she was a woman. He accused her of being a suffragette.

When a court ordered him to pay alimony to his estranged wife, Russell transferred all his property and money to the Watchtower, Bible and Tract Society. He left himself personally penniless, but in complete control of the Watchtower Society and the money. (A history of this has been written and can be found on the Internet for all those who desire to know more. The newspaper accounts about the Russell divorce are there for all to read.)

Mr. Russell is often referred to as Pastor Russell by the Witnesses and the International Bible Students, a splinter group of Jehovah's Witnesses. Or as the IBS believers say, the Witnesses splintered from them. Either way, there was a big power struggle after Russell died in 1916 and Joseph Rutherford took control of the printing company. He and his followers eventually took the name of Jehovah's Witnesses.

Mr. Russell was buried at the Rosemont United Cemetery in Pittsburgh, Pennsylvania, where a headstone with a cross marks his grave. His site has an eight-foot-high pyramid, because Russell had visited Egypt and measured pyramid bases to ascertain some of the dates of his prophecies. He reinforced his teaching of the 1914 return of Christ from his measurement of the great pyramid of Giza. He called it "the very center of the earth." When Jesus did not appear, he explained that the return of Jesus was actually an invisible return. His Armageddon dates fell by the wayside when it did not start on time, and then the holy cross fell out of favor when his successor, Mr. Rutherford, became the second president of the Watchtower. He had been raised as a Baptist in Missouri.

Mr. Rutherford was a cigar-smoking, boisterous man who dominated those around him. In his younger years he was a court reporter and was given a license to practice law in 1892. Back then, if a judge was ill, he could appoint an attorney to sit on the bench for him and judge the case. Rutherford was asked four times to sit on the bench for one day each time. After that, he preferred to be called Judge Rutherford.

In 1920, President Rutherford had proclaimed, "Millions now living will never die," and everyone believed him. He published a book by that name that predicted 1925 would see "Abraham, Isaac, Jacob, and the faithful prophets of old" restored to human life.

Under Rutherford, the Watchtower purchased property in San Diego and built a small mansion called Beth Sarim for the patriarchs (Abraham, Isaac, Jacob, Moses, David, Daniel, Jeremiah, and more)—who would come back before Armageddon. They would have a warm and comfortable climate to live in during the cold months. It was a climate similar to the Middle East where they lived in the past. The mansion was even deeded to the Watchtower Society and Abraham, Isaac, and Jacob, among others. Rutherford lived a life of luxury as their leader.

It was said that as president of the Watchtower, he could afford to own two new Cadillac automobiles, and Al Capone, Mafia leader, could only afford one of them. Rutherford kept one Cadillac in New York and one in San Diego, at the Beth Sarim mansion where he spent his winters. Other leaders enjoyed wintering there until it was quietly sold in 1954.

While he was the president, Rutherford denied that Christ died on a cross. He taught that Jesus died on an upright stake or tree, without a crossbeam. All Witnesses were told to get rid of their crosses. He saw the cross as a symbol of the Catholic Church. He was anti-Catholic—and my grandmother adored him.

"If people really love Jesus, they should hate the cross," said Gram. I had many doubts about the things my grandmother told me. Many things did not jive with a loving God. She made him sound like a judgmental, revengeful, and destructive God. Until this day, most Jehovah's Witnesses privately will sneer at the cross. They shake their heads in disgust that anyone would wear one around their neck or hang one on their wall. They regard it as being repugnant. The only thing religious we were allowed to wear was the mustard seed necklace. The mustard seed was entombed in a small glass or plastic ball and hung on a neck chain. My grandmother said, "That is okay to wear as long as you don't worship it or idolize it like people do with the cross."

After Rutherford did away with the cross, he initiated more aggressive ways of preaching. Phonograph players were used at the doors and they would blast the volume on the records if the householder shut the door. He was the one who initiated the placard work. When President Rutherford died in 1942, square-shouldered, square-faced Nathan Knorr became the third president of the Watchtower Society.

This caused a great stir in my Kingdom Hall because Nathan Knorr was from our congregation. His mother and sister still attended our Kingdom Hall. As an interesting side note, his sister Isabelle and another young woman named Davita loved the same young man. They became rivals for his attention. Isabelle was also slightly square-faced, but very tall and attractive. Davita was more petite with a softer, rounder face.

The young man they both loved was killed in an automobile accident, and, according to Witness teaching, he would be resurrected in the new world as the same young man. I was told that Isabelle and Davita both swore not to marry until the new world and then he could choose one of them. They never thought they would grow old before the new world arrived, but they did. As they aged, the two women became friends instead of rivals because they realized that the young man would not choose either of them. They had grown too old for him and were past their childbearing years. Both women were very loyal to Jehovah's Witnesses and the organization in spite of their dashed dreams.

Mr. Knorr praised the deceased president for his loyal and dynamic leadership, but he insisted on a dynamic membership. Great pressure was put on the Witnesses to distribute more of the literature and spend more time going door-to-door. More printing plants were built in foreign countries, and Watchtower printing presses around the world were pushing out literature twenty-four hours a day.

The Witnesses were encouraged to "become pioneers of the new world" by working only part-time and spending one hundred hours every month going door-to-door with the literature. He promoted the importance of starting and conducting home book studies. Knorr zealously persuaded the Witnesses that their making it into the new world after Armageddon depended upon whether they would be faithful to the organization by preaching the good news of God's kingdom as they understood it from door-to-door and distributing the literature. The pressure didn't stop as long as he was the leader; one of the five weekly meetings became like a big sales demonstration meeting. It was called "The Theocratic Ministry School." My father and grandmother thought he was a living saint.

In 1945, Mr. Knorr decided that Jehovah's Witnesses may not have blood transfusions, even if their life depended upon having one. He claimed that a transfusion might temporarily save this life, but they would lose their everlasting life in the new world after Armageddon. Therefore, all Witnesses believed it was better to die now without a transfusion in order to live forever in the new world.

This policy has caused thousands of children and adults to die prematurely. They leave behind heartbroken families.

About ten years later, when his sister Isabelle was in the hospital for surgery, the family barred all visitors from her private room. Everyone at the Kingdom Hall was wondering if she might have secretly accepted a blood transfusion, and they didn't want anyone to know. No one dared to question the Knorr family.

Chapter 13

When I was nine, a tragedy occurred that planted a big seed of doubt in my mind and heart about Jehovah's Witnesses. A little boy that played with my younger brothers when the parents came to visit our family was in the hospital. The doctors wanted to give him blood transfusions. They said he needed surgery immediately and would die without blood.

His parents had this one and only child late in their life. As good Witnesses, they didn't want to have children because of Rutherford's advice that people should not have children in this old world. These people wanted to wait until after Armageddon to have children because Armageddon was so very close.

Rutherford and Knorr had promised their faithful followers that they could have their children in the new world after Armageddon, but this couple had their wonderful little boy. They loved him very much and were very proud of him, but because the Watchtower leaders said no one was allowed to have blood transfusions, they sat by his bed and watched their only son die. This mother was past her childbearing years and knew she had no hope of having another child. She never recovered from her loss.

I asked Dad, "Why did he die? Why didn't they give him blood?" My father opened his Bible and read from Leviticus 17:11–14 (KJV). Those verses say:

For the life of the flesh is in the blood: and I have given it to you upon the altar to make atonement for your souls: for it is the blood that maketh atonement for the soul.

¹²*Therefore I said unto the children of Israel, No soul of you shall eat blood, neither shall any stranger that sojourneth among you eat blood.*

¹³*And whatsoever man there be of the children of Israel, or of the strangers that sojourn among you, which hunteth and catcheth any beast or fowl that may be eaten; he shall even pour out the blood thereof, and cover it with dust.*

¹⁴*For it is the life of all flesh; the blood of it is for the life thereof: therefore I said unto the children of Israel, Ye shall eat the blood of no manner of flesh: for the life of all flesh is the blood thereof: whosoever eateth it shall be cut off.*

If Jehovah's Witnesses take a blood transfusion, they are disfellowshipped, cut off from living among all the other Witnesses and treated as though they are dead. If Armageddon would come, that person would have no hope of living in the new world.

The Leviticus chapter was not talking about taking a life-saving blood transfusion. If my dad had continued reading for one more verse, it would have explained how the person would be "cut off." Verse 15 says:

And every soul that eateth that which died of itself, or that which was torn with beasts, whether it be one of your own country, or a stranger, he shall both wash his clothes, and bathe himself in water, and be unclean until the evening: then shall he be clean.

In Leviticus, punishment was a temporary thing until the offender performed a ritual of washing his clothes and bathing in water. That evening he was clean again. Being cut off was being separated for a short time until the offender cleaned himself. It was a sanitary law, as most of the hundreds of laws were. There was not a period of time, like a whole year or more, of shunning—and no everlasting damnation judgment against them.

If a Jewish person is asked about this passage, he or she will tell you that it does not apply to blood transfusions. There are hundreds of laws in Leviticus, and most of them were for sanitary reasons. They have little bearing on today. For example, the entire chapter of Leviticus 15 speaks of the rules governing men and women who are bleeding. They were considered unclean. A woman was unclean when she had her monthly blood flow and needed to live apart from her family. I cannot image anyone today following these rules. Verses 15 to 25 are very specific:

And if a woman has an issue, and her issue in her flesh be blood, she shall be put apart seven days: and whosoever toucheth her shall be unclean until the evening.

And everything that she lieth upon in her separation shall be unclean: every thing also that she sitteth upon shall be unclean.

And whosoever toucheth her bed shall wash his clothes, and bathe himself in water, and be unclean until the evening.

And whosoever toucheth any thing that she sat upon shall wash his clothes, and bathe himself in water, and be unclean until the evening.

And if it be on her bed, or on anything whereon she sitteth, when he toucheth it, he shall be unclean until the evening.

And if any man lie with her at all, and her flowers be upon him, he shall be unclean seven days; and all the bed whereon he lieth shall be unclean.

And if a woman have an issue of her blood many days out of the time of her separation, or if it run beyond the time of her separation; all the days of the issue of her uncleanness shall be as the days of her separation: she shall be unclean.

Clearly, these rules no longer apply today. Back then, women stayed in a separate tent at that time of the month. What if modern-day Witness women were asked to live in a separate tent or house once a month because she was considered unclean? I don't think the women would obey that rule. It would be the downfall of the publishing company. Yet, loyal men and women watch their children die or give their own lives to be in obedience to the organization.

I had been falsely taught that it was okay for people to die instead of taking a lifesaving blood transfusion. I truly believed that if I ever took a blood transfusion, Jehovah would destroy me at Armageddon. We carried cards on our person that directed that no blood transfusions were permitted to be given to us in the event of an accident or medical emergency.

The Watchtower also uses Acts 15:28–29 to support their "no blood" policy. It says to "abstain from blood," so they think that applies to blood transfusions. They take three words out of context and drum them into the minds of the Witnesses. Scriptures should always be read in context. It was common for non-Jews, like Romans, to drink the blood of animals sacrificed to idols.

Many of these Romans were becoming Christians. They were to no longer be part of a ritual of drinking the blood of animal sacrifices. They were not to eat the meat or drink the blood of sacrificed animals. These verses have no connection to lifesaving blood transfusions or to everlasting condemnation. Acts 15:28, 29 (KJV):

It seemed good to the Holy Ghost, and to us, to lay upon you no greater burden than these necessary things; That ye abstain from meats offered to idols, and from blood, and from things strangled, and from fornication: from which if ye keep yourselves, ye shall do well. Fare ye well.

Taking verses out of context and twisting them to mean something else is dangerous. It says, "*Ye shall do well.*" It does not say that they must follow the old law, or Jehovah would destroy them. That entire statement was made because there was a controversy in the early church about circumcision and other Jewish laws. Some thought that the Gentiles needed to become Jewish before accepting Jesus, which meant they would need to be circumcised. Circumcision was not necessary to become a Christian, but they would do well if they abstained from the meat and blood offered to idols and from strangled animals and from fornication.

Why would they do well to abstain? The Jews and the Gentiles ate meals together. The Jews were horrified that the Gentiles ate meat that was not kosher (1 Cor. 11:17–34). This was a practical concern to keep the unity of the early church. The apostle James disassociated with the Jewish Christians who said following the Jewish law was needed for salvation in Jesus. It seemed good to James and the Holy Spirit that no greater burden should be put on the Gentiles, except for the ones mentioned.

Those same rules apply today, but they have nothing to do with blood transfusions. We do not live in a society that has animal sacrifices that would have us eating the flesh or drinking the blood of the sacrifices. What Christian would want to do that today?

The Watchtower rules caused me to live under an umbrella of fear. No matter what I did without their approval, Jehovah would destroy me. "Why was I born? Why even bother trying to be good enough to please Jehovah?" I said to myself. "It seems impossible."

By the age of ten, I was trained to talk at the doors about the *Watchtower* and *Awake* magazines while Gram or someone else was with me. New information about Bible chains was being presented in one of the weekly meetings at the Kingdom Hall. Everyone could use the chains by writing the first verse of the chain in the front of our Bibles. If people at the doors asked a question about our denial of any doctrines like the Trinity, the soul, or hellfire, we could answer the questions by looking at the first verse of the chain on any given topic.

Specific chains of Bible passages all related to one subject to support their doctrines. Other relevant Bible passages are left out if they seem to be contradictory. Other than these Bible chains, which are easily marked in the Bible, the average Witness at your door is not very knowledgeable about the Bible. The Seventh Day Adventists, Christian Science believers, and Mormons have been known to use this same system.

All the Witnesses do is look at the first verse. After reading that verse, the second connecting verse followed, written in the margin of our Bible at the top or the bottom of the page. Then we could turn to the next verse and continue with our chain for five or six more verses without letting the person at the house get a word in edgewise.

Witnesses would practice on each other at our meetings and would be critiqued by the leader. We were coached to keep the householder's eyes on the verse we were reading by turning the Bible toward them and pointing our finger to what we were reading to them. That way, they would not notice that the next verse was written somewhere on the same page. The householders at the doors would often say, "Wow, you really know your Bible," but we were only following our chain, jumping around the Bible from one verse to another.

Many of the chains are used for two- to three-minute sermons that Witnesses present at the door. The most popular one leads people through the terrible conditions of the world and into the "new heavens and new earth" presentation from the Bible book of Revelation. People who do not attend church regularly or have little knowledge of the Bible are often amazed to see and hear the message the Witnesses present. It appears to be different from what is considered basic Christian doctrine. Witnesses claim, "The churches do not teach the Bible."

If the householder did interrupt the chain, we were taught how to get them back to the Bible chain by passing over their comments and completely controlling the conversation. We were using the verses completely out of context, but I didn't realize that it was the wrong way to study doctrines. The surprised householder most often did not realize that either.

The Witnesses give Bible literature that they claim, when studied, will help people understand the Scriptures. Because I loved books and loved to read and search for things in books, this was very interesting to me as a child. In the attic alone, I began to study the Watchtower material more intently. My grandmother did very well with the chains and memorized some of them.

My grandmother planted a big seed of doubt in my mind when she showed me the large palatial house she wanted to live in after Armageddon. We were going door-to-door with the magazines in the west end of town where wealthy people were building new homes. Gram pointed to a huge and beautiful new house sitting on a large knoll. It had been landscaped to perfection and looked like a picture from a magazine. She said, "That is the house I am going to live in after Armageddon."

I replied, "But Grammy, how can you afford that house?" I knew Gram didn't have any money. She said, "The people living there are not Jehovah's Witnesses. They will all die at Armageddon and then we can move into their house."

A cold chill went through me, right down to my bones. "How many children live in that big house? Why is God going to kill all the children because their parents aren't Jehovah's Witnesses? Why should all my friends in school die? Where does the Bible say that we can just move into their nice houses?" I asked myself these questions, but I knew I was not allowed to ask Gram because she would slap my mouth or might tell my dad that I was questioning the teachings of the Witnesses.

Instead of asking what was really on my mind, I asked, "Gram, how do you know that Jehovah will not destroy the house when he destroys the people?" Gram always had a Bible answer for everything. She said, "Because the Bible says that Jehovah knows the desires of our hearts and he will give us those desires. Psalm 37:4 says, *Delight thyself also in the LORD: and he shall give thee the desires of thine heart.* He knows that in my heart, I really want that house and he will give it to me as a reward for being a faithful Witness to him."

I had a suspicion that the Bible wasn't talking about giving us new homes. Many people who open their door to the Witnesses are impressed and think the Witnesses know their Bibles. The truth is, the Witnesses don't know the Bible very well, but they can find all the books and verses that they use regularly. Most people don't know the danger of taking a scripture out of context or the danger of twisting the scripture, bending it to support a false doctrine. As a preteen child, I actually enjoyed this challenge tremendously because it required studying and searching for the right verses to say about any topic. It was a game I played.

Recently, in the twenty-first century, Jehovah's Witnesses are adopting a new game. They have a new method of reaching people at the doors. They only talk for one minute or less to offer a free Bible study course and they push some literature toward the householder. The surprised householder will often just take what is placed right in their hands and say, "Thank you." The Witnesses take that as an acceptance of the free Bible study course and they call back on the person the next day or in a few days to discuss the first lesson, thus trying to gain a foothold into the house on a weekly basis.

The more I studied the books, the more confused I became about the Bible. If I questioned anything, I was told that I should just read the books and use only the scriptures that were quoted for that particular topic. Dad said, "Don't bother looking for verses that say something different or don't agree with the Watchtower. And don't try reading the entire Bible. It is a waste of time. No one can understand the Bible just by reading the Bible." He believed the Watchtower organization was inspired by God and that they would explain everything to us in the magazines.

I began to think that maybe the Witnesses were told they couldn't understand the Bible by reading it chapter after chapter because that might put a different slant on the Watchtower teachings. I doubted what the Watchtower magazines and books were saying about many things, like the blood issue, but I lived in fear of ever saying anything that might contradict the Watchtower organization. After all, I was taught that this was God's organization on earth, and if I questioned the teachings, Jehovah would kill me at Armageddon. It could begin very soon—maybe even that day I questioned them.

The goal of the Watchtower is to get people baptized so they can become one more official statistic on their roll book of members, one more unpaid laborer for the Watchtower. Unsuspecting householders have no idea how dangerous false teachings can be to their family. Most Jehovah Witness families have no idea that their everlasting lives are in peril. They are good people who are being misled.

Chapter 14

In 1950, when I was a few months shy of turning twelve, my grandmother began putting pressure on me to be baptized. "Jesus was twelve when Mary and Joseph found him in the temple teaching. It is an age of accountability, and Jesus was showing us what we should be doing for God," said Gram. She insisted that I was old enough to make a lifelong decision of whether or not I was going to follow Jehovah and his organization through baptism. At this time, all of Jehovah's Witnesses called themselves "Kingdom publishers." Actually, we were only unpaid distribution workers, a free labor force for a large, wealthy publishing company.

We were all taught that there was no life or hope outside of the Watchtower. We were told, "The organization is like a modern-day Noah's Ark. If you are not on the ark when Armageddon comes, you will die!" By this point in my life, I was afraid to live and afraid to die! Living was being a Jehovah's Witness; dying was missing out on school, friends, and becoming an adult. I could not figure out why Jehovah's Witnesses were so obsessed with wanting Armageddon to start. They were living for Armageddon, a day of death and destruction.

The Witnesses believe that the life is in the blood, and when you die, your blood stops, so your soul is dead because the soul is in the blood and there is no life after death. However, if you were a good Jehovah's Witness, then someday after Armageddon, you would be brought back to life and be given a new perfect body. If you are not a good Jehovah's Witness, suicide is an easy way out. Some have committed suicide, and some have killed their families. They would rather sleep forever than live as a Witness. Some realize that no matter how hard they try to be good, it is not good enough to please God. Unwavering obedience is not always possible.

I talked about going to college. Gram and Dad laughed at me. They both shouted, "Jehovah's Witnesses don't go to college!" I protested, "There are two school teachers at the Kingdom Hall. They went to college!" Gram said, "They went to college before they became Jehovah's Witnesses." My heart felt like it was sinking.

I loved school, and it was a staggering, crushing blow to know that I could not plan on going to college or even think about being a schoolteacher. Gram shouted, "You will never finish high school because Armageddon is almost here! Armageddon could come tomorrow! Don't worry about going to school!" I began thinking that sleeping forever would be okay with me. I was already tired of living under the Watchtower rules.

One day my grandmother asked me to walk with her to visit someone in the hospital, so I did. The woman was very ill; Gram said I should wait in the lobby for her. As I sat down, I noticed among the magazines there was a *Watchtower*. It was the first time I realized that some Witnesses carry extra magazines with them everywhere because as long as they leave a magazine, they can count time on their service record.

My father always took the magazines with him went he went places, like the barbershop and the shoemaker. When Gram returned, I pretended I was reading it. That pleased her, so she offered to buy me some ice cream. We walked across the street to the fairgrounds. The Ritz restaurant made wonderful flavors; my favorite was raspberry. Gram said, "I heard some good news from one of the brothers at the Hall."

She went on. "A few leaders of the Watchtower Society are translating the Bible." The first installment was released the next year. It was the Greek scriptures from Matthew to Revelation. It was the beginning of the New World Translation. By 1961 they finished and published the completed New World Translation (NWT) of the Bible—an amazing feat, considering that none of the translators had college degrees or any qualifications to translate the biblical languages.

The names of the translation committee members were withheld from the Witnesses, but were later revealed by former workers at the Watchtower offices. The translators reportedly said, "We don't want to be put on a pedestal for what Jehovah has accomplished through us." Personally, I never thought anyone would put them on a pedestal. As another ex-JW remarked to me, she thought, "Now they can make the Bible say anything they want it to say."

Jehovah's Witnesses are not allowed to question the leadership, so we gladly accepted the so-called new translation with great enthusiasm because we were told that Jehovah and the translation committee made it easier to understand the Bible. Every Witness was expected to purchase one and use only their translation when knocking on doors. Needless to say, the NWT changed the Bible to support the doctrines taught by the Watchtower Society. The NWT has had at least two revisions made to further strengthen their teachings and to purposely remove all traces of the deity or worship of Jesus.

Witnesses do not question where all the changes come from. They think it comes from Jehovah, but former workers at the New York headquarters revealed that the Watchtower translation committee was not at all qualified to translate the Bible. The chief translator of the NWT had some higher education. Frederick Franz had twenty-one semester hours of classical Greek and some Latin. He claimed to be self-taught in Spanish, Biblical Hebrew, and Aramaic. However, in a 1954 court case in Scotland, Mr. Franz was asked to translate a verse from the original Hebrew language in Genesis to test his knowledge. He could not translate the verse. In Genesis 2:4 of the English Standard Version, it says:

This is the account of the heavens and the earth when they were created; when the Lord God made the earth and the heavens.

Franz refused to even try to translate it saying, "No. I won't attempt to do that." Under oath, in a courtroom, he could not translate the verse. Another reported member of the translation committee, George Gangas, had no higher education in languages. He was from Turkey and knew how to speak and write modern-day Greek and English.

Four more of the reported NWT translators had little to no education in biblical languages. Their names were Milton Henschel, Karl Klein, Nathan Knorr, and Albert Schroeder. Mr. Schroeder studied mechanical engineering for three years before dropping out of school.

When Nathan Knorr was sixteen, he tried to drop out of high school. He left his home in Pennsylvania and ran away to Brooklyn, New York. He wanted to see the president of the Watchtower. Knorr was forced back to Pennsylvania by Mr. Rutherford to finish high school. Rutherford promised him a position when he graduated high school. Knorr has no higher education that we know about.

If they want to prove that the NWT is really a scholarly translation, the Watchtower must produce positive evidence that the translators possessed the skills and qualifications necessary to translate the Bible from the original languages into English. No evidence has been provided by the organization.

The evidence shows that the New World Translation is misnamed. It is more of a sectarian paraphrase of the Bible, written to support the Watchtower doctrines. Jehovah's Witnesses are not allowed to question the NWT because they believe Jehovah provided it for them.

In later years, I discovered that the name Jehovah has incorrectly been inserted into the Watchtower's New Testament two hundred thirty-seven times where the Hebrew name YHWH does not appear in the original Greek. The NWT actually replaced the words *Kyrios* (Lord) and *Theos* (God) with the name Jehovah. The name Jehovah itself is a common mistranslation of the Hebrew name for God. Yahweh is a better translation of the Tetragrammaton YHWH, which is unpronounceable.

The Watchtower purposely tried to lower Jesus to the level of Adam, a perfect man. In an attempt to support the Watchtower claim that Jesus had no divine nature, where Jesus referred to himself as *I am* in John 8:56–59, the NWT says, "I have been." They deny that Jesus claimed to be the same *I am* as in the Old Testament in Exodus 3:14 where God told Moses, "I am," when questioned about His name. The question to ask Jehovah's Witnesses is this: When Jesus claimed to be *I am*, the crowd stoned him. Why would they stone Him unless they thought He was committing blasphemy by claiming to be God? Anyone can read about that in the tenth chapter of the gospel of John. They accused Jesus of blasphemy. Bible scholars agree that the NWT Bible is not a real translation.

You don't need to be a Bible scholar to prove that the Watchtower translation committee has changed and twisted the meaning of many verses in their Bible. Like an old house that sways back and forth in the wind, the Watchtower can change things whenever it is good for their own purposes.

Chapter 15

A storm that struck the East Coast of the United States in November of 1950 is listed as one of the top ten storms of the twentieth century. It has been called by several names including a hurricane, the Thanksgiving Storm, and the Appalachian Storm. It developed over the Carolinas and pushed northward. One hundred and sixty people perished.

It spawned snow as far as West Virginia and Cleveland, Ohio. The New Jersey shore suffered extremely high tides, flooding, winds, and as a result many homes were destroyed. Part of the storm seemed to veer off from the coastline when it reached southern New Jersey and roared up the Delaware Bay into the Delaware River. Philadelphia and eastern Pennsylvania were windswept and flooded as the storm came at us from the south and the east at the same time. We suffered a great deal of wind and water damage.

Trees and electric wires were lying across many streets, and other streets were closed due to flooding. I was a few days away from my twelfth birthday, and my family was still living in the three-bedroom house where most of us children were born. Our house was severely water damaged by the storm as part of the roof blew away that evening. We heard a loud, ripping noise up in the attic that sent chills through all of us.

Mom, who was eight months pregnant with her ninth child, went upstairs to my beloved attic with my dad and brothers. They were trying to prop pieces of wood and sheet metal against the beams where the storm had torn the roof loose and open. As Mom and my oldest brother were lifting a wooden beam up against a section of the metal, the beam slipped on the wet floor. The side of the beam came up and hit my mother's lower abdomen. It knocked her off balance and onto the wet, slippery attic floor where she cried in pain. She could barely make it down the steps because of the pain.

My father called the police. He said, "My wife is going to have a premature baby, and we need you to take her to the hospital." Before the electricity went out, the radio operator said no one was allowed to drive cars because of the many electric wires that fell down. When the police took Mom away, I wasn't sure I would ever see her again. The storm seemed to rage without end, and I was afraid that this might be Armageddon.

Hour after hour, the rain and wind pummeled the old house. Rain was pouring into the attic and making the bedroom ceilings dripping wet. Our beds filled with water. We huddled together on blankets in the middle of the floor in the living room, with only the light of a candle. The windows were rattling so hard, we were afraid they would burst in on us. We talked among ourselves that if this really was Armageddon starting, there was no way that we would even know about it. "Maybe the whole world is storming and shaking," we said. The electricity was out, the radio was not working, and we thought we might never see our mother again. We were absolutely terrified and cried for her.

As it turned out, the police got Mom to the hospital just in time. She gave birth that night to her ninth child, our youngest brother, Albert John. No one in the family was talking about Jehovah and his protection that night of the storm; we were shaking with fright. I compared our night in the storm with the stories in the newspaper the next few days about other people who had prayed and asked God to protect them. Some of their stories sounded miraculous.

Jehovah's Witnesses scoff at these people because they don't pray to Jehovah, and they claim God doesn't hear selfish prayers or the prayers of people who are not Witnesses. All I knew was that other people talked to God in their time of need and we didn't. In my heart, I had wanted to ask God to protect us, but I was afraid it was a selfish prayer. We were thankful that the scary night did not turn out to be the end of the world and that Mom, with the rest of the family, survived.

People in the Middle Atlantic area of the United States survived the storm in spite of suffering injuries and serious property damage. Some homes were totally destroyed. Volunteers from many Pennsylvania churches helped their local communities, and others journeyed to the Atlantic coast to help feed and clothe any person who was homeless or in need. The Witnesses only took care of their own members.

I wondered why we never gave to anything like the March of Dimes or the Red Cross or any other charity. I asked Gram and she said, "It is wrong to give to any charity that aids people who are not Jehovah's Witnesses." When I asked why, my grandmother replied, "People who do not obey Jehovah God and his organization will all die at Armageddon, so it is wrong for us to give money or assistance to people who God is going to kill anyway. Even if people are starving, it is wrong to feed them if they do not want to follow Jehovah God. They will die at Armageddon anyway, so we can't go against Jehovah's plan for them." I felt sorry for the people who lost their homes in the storm.

Our house needed a new roof. Unfortunately, our family had to stay in the hurricane-damaged house for the entire winter. Minimal repairs were made, and the cold winter air seemed to seep through the old house like never before. Before my baby brother was six months old, we moved.

The minimal repairs and cold winter were probably the biggest reasons that made my father decide he needed to find another house. With so many children, no one wanted to rent another house to him, so he arranged with the owner of the dairy he worked for to buy a bigger house and get a mortgage that he could afford. The company would hold the deed until the mortgage was paid.

It was April, and water still leaked into the poorly repaired roof. I helped to clean out the damaged attic with much regret because I knew the house my father bought did not have an attic where I could be alone. My poor old doll Sally that had given me so many happy hours in my childhood was gone forever. My brother Harry had found Sally and used her for a punching bag, tearing her head off. I had been heartbroken, but I didn't tell anyone except Mom. No one else knew I had the doll. I left the old house sadly, knowing that my beloved attic would never be seen again, just like my Sally.

Our family moved into the new old house and began an endless amount of scrubbing, nailing, scraping, plastering, painting, and wallpapering. It was a larger, better house than the one where we were born. My Uncle Melvin, a short man with a dark complexion, worked in a paint and wallpaper supply store. He contributed many gallons of paint and almost a hundred rolls of wallpaper that he had marked with clearance prices.

The house had a finished third floor with two large bedrooms. Four brothers were allowed to share the largest one. Their room was painted with donated "battleship gray" paint. It was like a dormitory. Jean and Millie could share the other smaller bedroom. They each were planning on getting married to Jehovah Witness young men and then I could have that bedroom. They selected pretty, flowered wallpaper for the room.

There were five bedrooms and a nice bathroom with a built-in bathtub. My father built bedroom closets and laid plywood over the old floors in an attempt to stop the old, worn boards from creaking when everyone walked on them. Gram officially came to live with us and had the largest bedroom on the second floor. Dad built a storage closet for her few possessions.

Working on the house was a new experience and time went by quickly. This was a group activity every weekend after service and meetings for about a year. My mother was happy to have more room for her children. She spent most of her time taking care of our little baby brother while cooking and baking for the Witness friends that were helping with the house. Mom was always humming, but no one paid any attention to that. Her humming really bothered me sometimes, and I wished Mom would stop because some people might think she was crazy. I missed having an attic to retreat to when things bothered me and I wanted to be alone.

After a while, I learned to *feel* attic alone while sitting in the yard with a book or even in a room with noisy siblings. At the Kingdom Hall I would often retreat to my mental attic until the meeting was over. In spite of that, I was afraid that if I didn't get baptized, I would die at Armageddon. Gram told me it was coming soon. Now that she lived with us, there was more pressure on me to dedicate my life to Jehovah and the Watchtower Society by getting baptized. Little did I know that getting baptized into the Watchtower organization meant that they assumed the right to control and judge me all of my life.

I cannot say much about the baptism except that when the candidates all stood before the other Witnesses and were guided through a list of do's and don'ts, I had second thoughts about what I was doing. No one told me we had to take any kind of an oath. We were at a three-day weekend meeting called an assembly where about a thousand Witnesses attended six hours of indoctrination each day. We were seated in the grandstand at the fairgrounds in the morning, and I felt like running away from this assembly—but where would I go?

The Watchtower and the Witnesses always said, "Where would you go if you left the truth?" I didn't know if it really was the truth, and I felt trapped! This was my life. When the baptism candidates changed into their swimsuits and walked to the municipal pool where the baptism was done, I stood in a line with about thirty other people as they filed into the pool.

Several so-called brothers, who had been selected to do the baptizing, were already in the pool waiting for us. I was totally unprepared for being dunked so fast! It was like an assembly line production. Gasping for air as I came up from the water, the brother laughed at me and sent me on my way to the exit steps of the pool while I was still choking. Only the dunkers seemed to be enjoying the baptism.

No one was there for me. My family knew I was getting baptized, but no one really cared because they never celebrated anything. Dad and Gram rigidly expected me to get baptized, and now it was a done deed. It seemed to be a very somber and short occasion for everyone; it was something that was expected of all who studied with the

Witnesses, especially the children. Like robots, we dried off, dressed, and went about the business of living for Jehovah, the Watchtower, and Armageddon. There was no choice in joining the Watchtower Society. We automatically became one of them.

Even the weather was not happy. Appropriately, I thought, it was a very cloudy and gloomy day both outside and inside. I had just become another statistic in the growing roll book of the Watchtower Society publishers, and no one cared that I was totally unprepared for life within the Witnesses or without the Witnesses. Not even my older sisters were there, nor did my mother attend the assemblies.

Chapter 16

My mother missed her oldest sister, Emily, who moved to Oregon that year. Emily was older than their other sister, Matilda, who still lived in the coal region. Emily had moved to Allentown before Mom. My father got her involved with Jehovah's Witnesses, and she married one of them, named Cliff Mayberry. They did not have any children.

Cliff was the congregation elder when all the information about disfellowshipping was revealed in 1952. Uncle Cliff was a very touchy-feely kind of person. He was very affectionate and put his hands on everyone. He was short, half bald, and pudgy. I liked him because he had a happy smile for everyone. I was surprised to learn that my uncle had a long-time affair with Janet, an unmarried woman from the Kingdom Hall.

Janet was almost thirty and quite attractive; she had strawberry blonde hair and blue eyes. She was a pioneer, and I often wondered why she wasn't married. A pioneer was a Witness who spent about a hundred hours a month doing service by knocking on doors with the Watchtower literature and conducting book studies with people in their homes. Even though Aunt Emily suspected the affair, no one would think of questioning an elder about his conduct. After all, Jehovah and the Watchtower Bible and Tract Society had placed him in that position of authority to be an example to everyone else at the Kingdom Hall.

In my family, we didn't think he was a very good example. My Aunt Emily was not a happy woman. We knew the real reason why my aunt and uncle had suddenly decided to move to the West Coast. Poor Aunt Emily was no match for Janet. She was very short, stout, and freckled. She had tried for years to keep Uncle Cliff away from Janet, but he remained her secret lover until the disfellowshipping information came out from the Watchtower. My uncle dropped Janet like a hot potato, and the poor woman tried to take her own life. She had a complete mental breakdown and was hospitalized in a state mental institution.

She was never the same after that; she was unstable. Everything was hushed up to protect the organization, and my uncle quickly moved with my aunt to Oregon. My oldest sister Jean would miss Aunt Emily too because she spent more time with her than the rest of us.

Jean was a very loving and nice sister to me. She looked like a younger version of my mother. A little stout and always smiling, she was married in 1952 to a good Witness man named Al, and they made a good match. They invited me to go with them to a convention at Yankee Stadium in New York City the next summer. We stayed two nights in a medium-sized hotel and traveled the city by subway. It was really exciting to be with them. Other than attending the Watchtower convention every day, we did some fun things too, like taking a train to Coney Island. We wanted to munch on their world-famous hot dogs and ride the world's largest roller coaster, the Cyclone. The Cyclone was built in 1927 and set the world standard for future roller coasters.

Jean was newly pregnant and decided she should not go on the rides, but my brother-in-law was a good sport and went on the Cyclone with me. When we got off, my legs felt like rubber. They were so shaky and wobbly that I had to hold onto Al's arm to walk the wooden platform leading off the ride. I was absolutely speechless for a few minutes, and when Jean asked if I enjoyed it, I wasn't sure how to answer. I told them, "It was the most daring and exciting thing I ever did, and at the same time, it was the most frightening thing I ever did." Jean and Al were very nice to me. I felt safe around Al. They made being with them at Yankee Stadium exciting.

We were at Yankee Stadium when one of the Watchtower speakers said Ezekiel chapters 38 and 39 told us about the end times. He said, "Russia is Ezekiel's biblical Magog, the 'King of the North.' Satan is 'Gog of Magog,' and Israel is modern-day Jehovah's Witnesses. They are being persecuted by Russia and Satan. Like a giant fish hook, Jehovah is baiting Russia and Satan with the Witnesses, and soon he will yank back on his fishing pole to deliver the Witnesses from Satan when the great day of God's wrath begins." The speaker continued, "According to Bible prophecy, Russia and Satan will soon be destroyed by Jehovah God!" This was bold new light, new truth!

All of the Witnesses in the grandstand gasped at the thought that Armageddon was so close. Applause rang out with a standing ovation as all the Witnesses cheered with anticipation of being in the new world very soon. People rose to their feet with great expectation that it could start at any moment. Some people began looking around for the old patriarchs that were going to appear before the end of this old world. Now I was sure—"Gram was right when she told me that I would never graduate from high school because we will all be in the new paradise by the time I am eighteen."

Even though many of the promises of Rutherford proved to be without merit, all the Witnesses, including my father and grandmother, still clung to the hope that someday they would see Abraham, Isaac, Jacob, and the rest of the patriarchs return to earth when the Battle of Armageddon would begin.

Many years after that convention, an investigation into the Gog of Magog topic turned up some very interesting information. The Watchtower taught that the Biblical King of the North spoken of by Ezekiel was:

(1) Germany in 1871
(2) Powers of Germany, Austria-Hungary, Italy, and Japan in 1942
(3) Russia in the 1950s, and
(4) We cannot say, in 1993.

As a child who knocked on doors for the Witnesses, I was taught that we were, in fact, helping Jehovah to separate the sheep from the goats before Armageddon comes. Whenever someone slammed a door in our faces, we could smile and say, "There's a goat!" Today, that teaching is on the scrap pile with all the other false statements from years past. For sixty years, the Witnesses thought they were separating the sheep from the goats.

That was always confusing to me. I thought Jesus separated the sheep and the goats. Watchtower leaders were given new light by Jehovah in 1995 and changed it to teach that the "angels are separating the sheep from the goats. The sheep will inherit the earth and the goats will go to everlasting sleep." The Bible says destruction, but to a Witness, that means sleeping forever.

The Watchtower constantly promotes the doctrine that Armageddon is just a short time away. It has promised this since its very beginning over one hundred twenty-five years ago. Hundreds of thousands refused to have any children in this old world before realizing that they might be too old to have children in the new world. Many people were raised and died in the teachings of Jehovah's Witnesses without ever being allowed to read or investigate any literature other than the Watchtower publications. The Witnesses are afraid to read anything that contradicts the teachings of their leaders. In fact, they can be shunned, disfellowshipped, for questioning the changeable truth as put forth by the leaders of their organization.

The Watchtower purges members and leaders who dare to question them. It doesn't matter that many were thrown out for believing what later became new truth. They will stick to their interpretations until they are forced to come up with a new explanation. In the meantime, millions of Jehovah's Witness souls are hanging in the balance because they refuse to accept Jesus as their personal Savior.

They are not allowed to believe the simple gospel that Christ loves them individually and died for each one. The Witnesses have been assimilated into a mind-controlled group led by a handful of old men in New York. Many ex-Witnesses around the world call them the Watchtower Borganization, a fictional society that believed they needed to assimilate all others into their collective thinking group of robot-like creatures. They needed to plug into the main brain to get their instructions for the work to be done.

One thing I will say about my dad and the organization—they helped people develop a good work ethic. You either worked hard or you perished. We were quoted this verse from Colossians 3:23 (ASV): *Whatsoever ye do, work heartily, as unto the Lord, and not unto men.*

Chapter 17

When we were children, we were taught to bear many tasks and responsibilities. Our father and grandmother were the only authorities that we had to follow besides Jehovah God and the Watchtower Bible and Tract Society that told everyone what Jehovah wanted. As a child, I thought my dad might be next to Jehovah himself the way he pretended to know everything.

He really enjoyed it when we asked him questions about the Witness teachings, as long as we didn't mention what we thought or what other people believed. It gave him a chance to show off his knowledge of the Watchtower. Aside from that, he didn't bother speaking to us very much unless he was screaming threats or work orders. He would find jobs for us as soon as he thought we could handle them, and sometimes even sooner. After being assigned a task, we knew we had better do a good job or else we would suffer the consequences at his hands.

I was thirteen when a nearby assembly was planned and Dad said, "I signed you up for the refreshment stand. I don't know what you will be doing, but I'm sure you will enjoy it." When we got there, my assignment was to chop onions for the hoagie line. It was not something I would have chosen to do, and I smelled like onions for three days. The tomatoes were thinly sliced on a machine. Others were helping to lay out the fixings for the hoagies. They lined up the rolls, cheese, meats, lettuce, tomatoes, onions, Italian dressing, and wrapping papers. We all helped to make the hoagies, about six hundred each day of the three-day assembly.

The week after the assembly, Dad said, "We have an ailing neighbor that needs help with her housework, so you can work for her." I met Mrs. Diehl and began cleaning her apartment every Saturday morning while her husband was at work. She was an attractive, heavyset woman who went to the hairdresser every week to keep her dark, curly, shoulder-length hair under control. She wore a little makeup every day. The Diehls lived in the three-bedroom first-floor apartment of the home they owned. It was a lovely large three-story house that was converted into three apartments.

Mrs. Diehl made lunch for the both of us at noontime. It was usually a ground sirloin burger on a fresh, seeded roll with lettuce, tomato, and a slice of sweet onion. Mr. Diehl always made sure we had a dessert, which was often strawberry shortcake from a local bakery. Mrs. Diehl enjoyed talking with me while we ate.

She began to ask me questions about this strange religion that my family was involved with. I explained the teachings of Jehovah's Witnesses to her, and recorded the one-hour lunchtime on my service report for the Kingdom Hall. Mrs. Diehl, in return, explained many things to me about her Jewish faith. As her health deteriorated over a few months, her only daughter, who was married, began spending weekends at the house, and I was out of a job.

It had been a very nice experience for me to know this kind Jewish woman, and I mourned for her when she died, even though I knew the woman should not mean anything to me according to the teachings of the Watchtower. I took comfort in the Watchtower doctrine that hell is nothing but the grave, and Mrs. Diehl could sleep forever and not be sick anymore. My father was busy trying to find me another job.

At age fourteen, I was still too young to get a real job, so my dad would find housework or babysitting jobs for me on his dairy route. That summer a woman who was going to the hospital for surgery needed someone to stay at her house with her two young children. She needed someone for about four days and nights until she came home. Dad told her that he had a daughter who was experienced with young children and would be allowed to stay with them.

They were very good children, and their father treated them with much love and patience when he came home from the hospital in the evening. I wondered why they were considered to be wicked and worthy of death at Armageddon. When their mother came home from the hospital, she asked me to stay for a few more days until she felt stronger. They paid me well and treated me kindly. That job led to other jobs, like babysitting for Elaine and Sal.

Dad introduced me to a young married couple named Elaine and Sal. They also lived on his milk route and had a small baby girl, Fern, who would be in bed whenever they went somewhere. They would only be gone for an hour or two and then drive me home. They were very much in love and seemed like good parents. Elaine always wanted to come home before the baby woke up for another bottle of milk. She asked me to help her a few Saturdays, so I spent time watching Fern while Elaine was busy doing other things, like baking or sewing. She enjoyed designing and sewing her own dresses.

I had just turned fifteen when New Year's Eve plans were being made, and they were the first ones to ask me to babysit. I was happy to sit for Fern and enjoyed being at their house. They were one of the few families I knew with a television set and the kindness to provide lots of snacks and soda.

Elaine made sure she had things that I liked. She was a smiling, beautiful young mother with reddish highlights in her hair and large brown eyes with long lashes. She told me they would be out late and the baby, who was six months old now, might wake up before they came home, so the instructions were all written out for me. They wanted me to stay overnight in their lovely guest room next to Fern's room.

It seemed like the middle of the night when I heard the baby cry. While trying to comfort her, I turned on the lights and carried her to the kitchen to heat up a bottle of baby formula. Freezing rain was loudly pelting the kitchen window above the sink, and the sound of it made me shiver. Even the kitchen floor made me shiver because it was ice-cold beneath my feet. I heard an unusual noise.

Suddenly, just six feet away from me, someone began making a commotion outside the kitchen door while turning and rattling the knob. I gasped, and fear ran through me. Then it came to me, "They must be home." The door burst wide open, and there stood Elaine's older sister Fran, from across the street. She was dressed in a party dress and a short fur jacket. Her black eye mascara, mixed with tears, was crazily running down her face like a scene from a horror movie. She was sobbing and gasping. Ordinarily she was as attractive as Elaine, but now her wet, streaked face was distorted with pain, and her tangled hair stood up from her head as though she had been trying to pull it out of her skull. She was sobbing hysterically between words that sounded like wailing. "Elaine— car—Seventeenth Street—ice—dead. Oh God—oh God! She's dead!"

I was stunned at what I heard! Fran took the baby girl from my arms and held her tight. I couldn't believe it! Did I hear her right? Fran rocked the startled and now screaming baby girl back and forth in her arms while I finished warming the baby's bottle. Fran kept muttering, "She's dead. She's dead." All the while, the baby was screaming.

Trying to calm down for the sake of the baby, Fran threw her head back and almost strangled from choking back her sobs and tears. She wanted to feed the baby, so she forced herself to calm down and said, "Sit with me. Sit with me." I sat there at the kitchen table, next to her, while she fed the baby the warm bottle. I put my arm around Fran, and we both were quietly sobbing and rocking back and forth. I could feel her overwhelming grief.

Fran's husband, Phil, came in the kitchen door wearing a black tuxedo. He was a very handsome man. Tears were running down his cheeks, and he was carrying a large pile of black cloths. He looked at me and said, "Please help me cover all the mirrors in the house." When I asked him why we were doing this, he answered, "It is our Jewish custom for a few days to cover the mirrors because this is now a house of mourning. It's also to remind us to avoid vanity and focus on our lost loved one." After covering all the mirrors, he told me more details about the accident they had witnessed. They were driving a short distance behind Elaine and Sal when the accident occurred.

"There is a cement monument near the center of the intersection of Seventeenth and Hamilton streets. It is difficult to see in the dark. Elaine and Sal were traveling quite fast, trying to get home before the freezing rainstorm got worse. They didn't know the sleet was already making the street a sheet of ice, so when Sal pressed on the brake to slow down and turn left at the corner, their car never slowed. It slid into the monument. A part of the statue came through the windshield and pierced Elaine's throat." He was crying again. "The passenger side was crushed in and Elaine was dead on arrival at the hospital." He couldn't stop crying.

We all were crying. After Fran finished changing the baby, she put her back to sleep in the crib. Phil gave me several telephone numbers where they could be reached. They had calmed down a little and were on their way to tell Elaine's elderly mother and father about the accident. Elaine was their youngest child. What a terrible heartbreak for those dear old people that I had enjoyed meeting one time. Elaine looked like her mother.

I stayed at Elaine's house for the next two days with a steady stream of relatives, neighbors, and friends coming and going. Everyone wanted to hold the baby girl when she was awake. They helped me comfort her cries for her mother. The poor little thing, six months old, missed her mother terribly. We all cried for Elaine. She was so young, talented, and beautiful. Fran decided it was time to take the baby to her house because Elaine's husband would be in the hospital a long time. Sal had a serious head injury from being propelled into his side of the windshield.

Fran paid me for helping them. She gave me what seemed to be a huge amount of money. I tried to give some of it back, but she insisted I take all the money. When I gave it to my father, he was ecstatic that they paid me so well. In the midst of a crushing tragedy, there was more love and devotion in this Jewish family than I had ever seen before. It seemed that my father only cared about the money in his hand. He showed no sympathy for me or for their family, and it made me feel as though he was happy it all happened just so he could have some extra money.

Money was important to my father, but along with all the jobs he gave to us came the responsibility of keeping regular meeting attendance and going out in the service of the Watchtower. Jehovah's Witnesses are very work-oriented. They believe their faith in Jehovah and his organization must be accompanied by regular door-to-door preaching and distribution of the Watchtower publications they receive weekly.

They need to get the magazines in the hands of other people. They need to convert all the people they come in contact with using love-bomb tactics, among others, that are so typical of cult-like groups. If Jehovah's Witnesses are failing in their works when Armageddon comes, they might not make it into the new world. Those who willfully stop attending the meetings will probably die at Armageddon for not being faithful to Jehovah's program when the end arrives.

Chapter 18

In the spring of my fifteenth year, I went to the Jehovah's Witnesses district assembly in Richmond, Virginia, with a middle-aged husband and wife, the Banks. They were from our local Kingdom Hall and had invited me because they knew I would have no other way of getting to the assembly. They were very obedient to the Watchtower and did not want to have children in this old world. The Banks were short, attractive people; both had dark hair with light complexions. I thought their faces matched each other very well. They were inseparable.

When the three of us arrived at the Richmond stadium and received our room assignments, they discovered that I was not staying at the same location as them. The registrar gave me the directions to my accommodations. "Take this bus number to this street and get off at the second stop. The house is on the corner, and Mr. and Mrs. Richards have a room for you. When you come back to the stadium, you will be getting on the same bus number at 8:30 in the morning." This was somewhat scary to be in a strange city and travel by myself, but in the end, it helped me feel more independent than I had ever felt before.

I don't remember much about the assembly meetings, but I will always remember Mr. and Mrs. Richards, the nice, elderly, white-haired couple who gave me a private room and bath in their home. I was obligated by Watchtower rules to invite them to the assembly.

They declined, telling me they were Methodists. Their home was lovely, and they made breakfast for me each of the two mornings that I was there. As I left them in the morning, they both hugged me and said they would pray for me. They stood at the door until I got on the bus. They found it hard to believe that a girl of fifteen from Pennsylvania was traveling back and forth on buses all alone in the city of Richmond. The second and last morning they hugged me, said they would pray for me, and wished me well in my future. This is a good memory.

I have another good memory of that trip. On the way back to Pennsylvania from the assembly, the Banks decided to take the long way along the Skyline Drive in Shenandoah National Park. It was beautiful, and we stopped at several locations to get out and enjoy the view from the mountaintop. We went to the caverns at Luray and toured the caves. It was incredible to see what could be found deep in the earth. I especially liked the grand ballroom, which was a huge opening underground and was the largest cave I could ever imagine.

The Banks treated me well. Mr. and Mrs. Banks were old enough to be my parents. They told me they expected Armageddon to come very soon and they didn't want any children until the new world. I knew that if Armageddon did not get here very soon, they would be too old to have children. They were considered to be very faithful Witnesses because they had no children to hinder them, and they could spend many hours in the door-to-door work.

Not long after that Virginia trip, the local newspaper was delivered to our door with a story about a slumlord that was fined for not making repairs in his rental properties. There were pictures of the deplorable living conditions of these homes, which were rat-infested and had plumbing that leaked through the ceilings. The story was on the front page for several days. The owners of the properties were ordered to make repairs and bring them up to code.

These homes were owned by the Witness couple, the Banks, who had driven me to Virginia. They claimed that the people living in the properties were responsible for the mess because they allowed their garbage to accumulate and they abused the houses. Everyone at the Kingdom Hall made excuses for them, and they came out of the mess looking like they had been persecuted for being Jehovah's Witnesses.

It seemed to me that all Witnesses have persecution complexes. They are happy when they feel persecuted because it means the great battle of Jehovah was near. The policy of not having children was widely accepted by the Witnesses. They were often reminded that, "woe will come to those with children in the last days." However, my father came from a large family. He had the old-fashioned idea that a large family was necessary in order for him to be provided for by his children when he got old. He wanted children just in case Armageddon didn't come.

My two older sisters were married and tried not to have children, but eventually they had four between them. Pregnant women were considered somewhat of a liability to the Witness work. Those who never had children, like my oldest brother and his wife, were considered to be the best Witnesses. However, they were quite disillusioned when they grew too old to bear children, and the Watchtower's new world was long, long overdue. In spite of that, they remained faithful to the organization and gave many hours going door-to-door.

I was going to turn sixteen that December, and I knew that my dad would expect me to bring him a paycheck every week. My brother Harry could not handle school and a thirty-hour-a-week job, so he insisted on quitting school if he had to work. Dad never cut him a break for having a lame leg. He signed the papers for him to quit school, and Harry took a full-time job in a shoe factory.

Chapter 19

When we each turned sixteen, we had a choice of quitting school and working full-time or continuing in school while working about thirty hours a week, almost full-time, to give Dad our earnings. In other words, we, his children, were expected to give him a paycheck every week to pay for our keep, our expenses. I chose to stay in school, and before my sixteenth birthday, I was hired by Woolworth's five and ten cent store on Hamilton Street. This was our busy, central city shopping district. I thought that working every day after school and all day Saturday was fun.

I made time to get my homework done, even though it meant staying up very late. At first I didn't resent giving all my money home because my family lived rather poorly, and the family really did need to have extra money for food and other necessities. But then I realized, "My family isn't going to be any better treated or fed. Dad just spends more time and money at the bar every week."

Turning sixteen in early December of my junior year of high school was a big deal to me, but no one else seemed to know or care. When the store manager held a Christmas dinner party for the employees, I planned to attend. I socialized with this intergenerational group of co-workers and, being that it was December, I pretended I was celebrating my birthday.

Another part-timer from the store, Hal, was paying an unusual amount of attention to me. When people began dancing to the music, he invited me to dance with him. Hal was a very likable and popular guy. I was quite shocked that he showed me any attention. He was a typical second-generation Italian-American boy with dark chocolate brown eyes and hair. It seemed to be a kind of magical place as he held me in his arms on a dimly lighted dance floor and we slow danced to, "Are the stars out tonight? I don't know if it's cloudy or bright, 'cause I only have eyes for you ..."

After several more dances, he asked me if he could walk me home. It was at least ten blocks out of his way, but he didn't mind at all because we talked and laughed all the way to my house. He told me he was Catholic, went to Catholic school, that he had brothers and sisters, where they lived, and how his father was now gone. Then at my front door, with his arms wrapped around me like we were still dancing, he gave me my first kiss. I thought that was a very nice birthday present and memory.

He said he would like to see me again and asked if he could walk me home when we both worked Friday evenings. Each time he did, we kissed goodnight. After several weeks of being walked home, we considered going to a movie. Knowing my dad would not approve, I told Mom that I was going to the movie with a friend from the store. Hal was waiting for me at the theater.

All along I had been telling Hal things about my family and how my dad was very strict and could be very mean. After a few dates, my father was waiting one evening and heard us talking at the door. He opened the door and his accusing face made me feel as though I had just been caught in a terrible sin.

"What is your name? Where do you live?" Dad angrily fired at Hal. Then a look of recognition crossed his face. "I know your family! You have many brothers and sisters! You live on my dairy route! You're Catholic! You have that statue of Mary in your front yard! You go to Catholic school! What are you doing with my daughter? Just walking her home after the movie?" With every outburst, my father became more enraged and scary. He was shouting.

"My daughter is not allowed to go around with Catholics. Your religion is not teaching you the Bible. Arlene has been taught the truth about Jehovah God, and she has been baptized into Jehovah's

Witnesses. If you want to be her friend, you need to study the Watchtower." Dad shouted at him and chased me into the house. How I wished that I had an attic to hide in until his wrath would pass. He continued his tirade at the door until Hal just turned around and walked away. I was so dumbstruck that I didn't really listen to the words Dad screamed at me that night, and his words meant nothing. I was concerned that Hal would never speak to me again.

The next time I saw Hal at work, I felt so embarrassed because of what had happened, but he was very nice about everything and said, "I understand now what you meant about your dad being a little different." Hal was very kind and sweet and continued to walk me home from work, but movie dates were too risky. We remained friends the whole time I worked at the store. One of the high-school kids that I knew from the store was a Witness boy named Denny, but he didn't last very long on the job. I was extremely happy to see him leave because one day when I went to the stockroom to pull some merchandise for the sales floor, he snuck up on me in the semidark aisle and put his hands on me from behind. I gasped a deep breath in surprise and almost screamed. I tried to push him away, but he caught me by the arms and held them still. Denny had a real mean streak in him.

"What is wrong with you? You are hurting me!" I shouted, and he put a hand over my mouth to quiet me. "It was an accident! I'll let you go if you keep quiet," he said. I nodded my head up and down, and he took his hand away. He told me, "I really like you very much and want you to be my girlfriend." "No thanks!" I replied. There was something too mean and strange about him. Most of the people I worked with were really nice.

I was sad when I needed to quit that job and go work in a factory for the summer. I missed those sweet kisses from Hal, and I wanted to keep in touch with him, but it was next to impossible because of my father. I wasn't allowed any telephone privileges, so I could not speak with him on the phone either.

My dad asked my oldest sister, Jean, to get me a summer job in the factory where she worked. Dad pointed out to me, "You can make more money working full-time in the factory where Jean works." I began working second shift in the sewing machine factory. They taught me to be a folder, then a trimmer, then a trainee on a sewing machine. Jean went home an hour after I started my shift, so I didn't see much of her.

When I left the factory at eleven o'clock to walk home eight blocks in the dark in all kinds of weather, it was scary enough to make me jump out of my skin. About five or six years earlier a neighborhood man by the name of Rufus Keller was accused and convicted of brutally murdering a woman that he befriended in the local bar. He was sentenced to death in "Old Smokey," the infamous Pennsylvania electric chair. Everyone referred to him as Ruthless Killer, and he was executed in 1949. Thoughts of the murder scene raced through my mind many nights because I saw where it happened when I was nine. I never forgot the scene.

Early in the morning we heard an ambulance and police sirens going by our house. Shortly after that, we heard a fire truck going down the street. My brothers said, "Hurry! Let's get dressed and find out what's going on down there." We grabbed something to eat, walked down the block, and turned left through Pine Street toward the cemetery alley. A huge crowd had gathered, and we inched our way around them.

The ambulance was driving away without any sirens. Policemen were talking with some people. Firemen were hosing off the side of the building where parts of intestinal flesh still clung to the wall. Blood was all over the wall and the cement walk. We watched as firemen hosed everything into the street and down the gutter to the drain. We didn't know what they were hosing off the wall until much later in the day when the evening newspaper was delivered to our house. It described the murder scene in every little gruesome detail.

Walking by that cemetery alley where the murder occurred was always frightening, but alone in the dark at eleven-fifteen was body-shaking for a sixteen-year-old girl. I wanted God to help me, but I had been taught that Jehovah God doesn't answer selfish prayers, and he knew everything in my mind. So even if I tried to pretend that I wanted him to protect me just so I could continue to be a Jehovah's Witness and go door-to-door and witness to people, God would know that I only wanted to get home safely. It made me feel ashamed of even wanting to pray.

Chapter 20

In 1955, my father got himself in trouble with the elders from the Kingdom Hall. Dad was making regular visits to the house of a Jehovah's Witness family named Ross. He was very friendly with them. A neighbor of the Ross family told a Jehovah's Witness relative, "Something is going on between these religious people that Mr. Ross doesn't know about. A milkman is spending a lot of time alone in the house with Mrs. Ross." The neighbor was given a telephone number of a JW elder to call if there was anything to report.

The elder was called one day and told, "That Jehovah's Witness milkman is alone with Mrs. Ross again. I think they are having an affair." That elder called another elder, and they both went immediately to the Ross house. After ringing the doorbell, the door opened, and there stood Mrs. Ross in a nightgown and negligee in the middle of the afternoon. She was a tall, attractive woman with a full figure. The elders had a clear view of my dad coming down the stairs from the second floor while pulling up his overalls. "This looks very suspicious," Dad was told.

The elders accused them of immoral conduct. Mrs. Ross protested, "I was not feeling well and didn't get dressed today. He just stopped after work for coffee and went upstairs to use the bathroom." This wasn't a very likely story because by this time, almost everyone knew my father went to a bar after work.

One night after the Ministry School meeting at the Kingdom Hall, they were both called on the carpet before the elders committee. The Ministry School was where Jehovah's Witnesses were critiqued and graded on their door-to-door practice. The elders committee met in a small back room used for a library. They were conducting an investigation into Dad and Mrs. Ross. There was no proof of adultery, and they both denied the charge, but they were put on secret probation. Dad was not allowed to visit the Ross house anymore, and he was not invited to speak publicly anymore. Mr. Ross was not friendly to any of our family after that.

My family probably would not have known about the entire Ross incident except for the fact that while investigating Dad, the elders talked to Mom about their marriage relationship. Needless to say, she was very upset about the entire discussion they had with her and the personal, probing questions they expected her to answer. My mother was angry for one of the few times in her life.

My mother had suspected that my father was having affairs from time to time. He would put on his charming side and flirt with attractive women. One time Mom even mustered up enough courage to ask him about Mrs. Ross, but she was not the only woman that had attracted my father's eyes and attention. Dad protested the secret probation and began attending fewer meetings, but he went to the Kingdom Hall often enough to keep his standing as a Witness.

Time passed quickly, and my senior year of high school was approaching. My younger brothers and sister were allowed to miss many, many meetings because our dad was attending fewer and fewer of them himself, thus saving the younger ones from the pressure of being baptized into the Watchtower Society. I, however, was expected to be at every meeting when I wasn't working because I was a baptized Witness and was old enough to walk to the Kingdom Hall alone if no one else was going.

My grandmother was not a big influence anymore. She was spending less time talking to us and a great deal more time talking on the phone to her oldest daughter, my aunt Gertrude in Florida. Gram's arthritis was getting much worse, and she could hardly go door-to-door anymore. When she talked to Aunt Trudy on the telephone, she counted the time on her service report. When she visited Aunt Trudy, she put the Watchtower magazines in her bedroom and counted them on her literature placement record. Gram preferred the warmer weather in Florida and decided it was time for her to retire.

It was painful for her to walk up the steps to her room at our house. She was beginning to feel useless, and she was depressed that Armageddon had not come yet. She was upset with my father and the whole situation at home, but Dad always drove her to the meetings when she was feeling well enough to attend.

Chapter 21

Around Labor Day, some of the high school students who worked at the factory were going to a square dance to celebrate the end of summer. They invited me to go along. I talked to Mom and told her where we were going Saturday night, and if possible, she wasn't going to say anything to my dad. Some of the other students that were employed in the factory had driving privileges and could use their family's car if they paid for insurance and gas money. Six of us piled into a car and went to the Limeport Dance Barn.

The Dance Barn was really fun, and I was thankful that dancing was not against the rules of the Watchtower. It was mostly square dancing and polka music. I met an older boy, Tim, and danced the polka with him several times. He had blonde hair, blue eyes, and seemed to have an outgoing personality. He joined our table of friends when invited and, as we talked, I warned him about my family and the religion. "I don't have a religion," he said, "Maybe I should look into Jehovah's Witnesses." The following week he began attending the Kingdom Hall.

Everyone was thrilled that another friend of mine was coming to the Hall. The year before, an attractive friend of mine from school, Darlene, began attending the Kingdom Hall with me because she had a crush on my oldest brother, Rod. When Rod lost interest in flirting with her and moved away from home, she gave up trying. He didn't want to write to her, so she began finding fault with all the teachings of the Watchtower. She decided not to attend any more meetings.

I wished that I had that kind of freedom to say what I thought. There was no freedom of speech at our house. I began seeing more and more of Tim because everything at home seemed to be drifting away from the Witnesses. Even Gram was less of an influence. She was getting ready to retire to Florida.

Aunt Gertrude was taking my grandmother to live with her permanently. She was a kinder, softer version of my father. She was a tall, attractive widow of the world who had married well, and she offered my grandmother a nice retirement in her beautiful home in Florida. Gram thought, "I might be able to turn her to the Watchtower if I am there all the time." Aunt Gertrude, however, did not want to be a Jehovah's Witness.

My grandmother quit her job as a part-time housekeeper for a wealthy auto dealer and left for sunny Florida. Before she quit, though, she made sure she cleaned the auto dealer's bar really well. "When I clean the bar, Mrs. Dankle wants me to get rid of all the bottles that have less than two inches of booze," Gram explained. "I don't believe in wasting anything by throwing it away, so I mix all the leftovers into one or two bottles and bring them home." Even though I never saw him drink from the bottles, Dad must have finished them, because Gram brought those bottles home frequently. They just seemed to disappear. My dad was drinking more and talking less.

My father wasn't as interested in the so-called truth when he wasn't being asked to give his one-hour lectures anymore. When he did attend the Kingdom Hall, he would drop us off at the door before the meetings began. Then he would stroll into the Hall fifteen minutes after the meeting started. He always had the smell of fresh alcohol on his breath. The gum he was chewing did not hide the odor. He also had the smell of fresh cigarette smoke on his clothes. The car was always parked down the block near the corner bar room.

"Mom," I said, "I am getting very angry about Dad drinking all the time while he still expects me to give him all my pay. I know

exactly where my paycheck is going! It's being spent at Tinkle's bar!"
I was the oldest one living at home now. My two older sisters were
married to Jehovah's Witnesses, and my oldest brother Rod had
moved away to western Pennsylvania. He tried to pretend to the
Selective Service draft board he was a minister, but it didn't work.

Every Witness man thinks he is a minister, but in the early1950s,
the draft board was usually hostile toward such claims. "Witness men
support themselves by secular employment and not by drawing their
income from preaching the gospel," the board decided. Jehovah's
Witnesses were unpopular because of refusing to salute the flag, or
voting, or serving jury duty. They refused to serve in the military
service of their country. The SS draft board told the young Witness
men, "You will serve in the military, take an alternative job for the
state, or go to prison."

When Rod was drafted, he was classified as I-O, "Conscientious
Objector to all military service." This meant that he claimed to be
"opposed to military training and service in the Armed Forces based
upon moral, ethical, or religious beliefs which play a significant
role in his life and that his objection to participation in war is not
confined to a particular war." Rod accepted alternative service in
a mental institution near Pittsburgh. He was assigned to a job as a
custodian and lived at the institution for two years.

My second older brother, Harry, did not pass the army physical
when he turned eighteen because of his lame leg. The SS board
classified him as 4F, "not acceptable for military service." He married
Geraldine, a girl the same age as me. Gerri had dropped out of high
school when she was sixteen and took care of her mother, who was
dying of brain cancer. Harry was almost nineteen when his girlfriend
Gerri became pregnant. Our father didn't have much choice other
than to sign papers for Harry to get married. Dad immediately
began preaching to his first daughter-in-law.

In my heart, I knew that my father was more interested in being
able to count some time on his weekly service card for the Witnesses
than he was in reaching Gerri for God. Every time someone was
around that wasn't a Witness, he started preaching to them, knowing
he could count the time on his card. He needed to turn his card in

at least once a month to stay on that important Kingdom publisher list. If someone were removed from the active list at the Kingdom Hall, they probably would die at Armageddon.

As my senior year moved on, I was becoming more and more aware of how terribly much I would miss school. My high school friends were talking about the colleges they were going to and what they wanted to study. They all had plans for their future careers and felt sorry for me because I wasn't allowed to go to college. I was feeling very sorry for myself for having been born into a Jehovah's Witness family.

I wished I could stop time and stay in school forever. The few younger teens at the Kingdom Hall were not really my friends. I silently thought, "I hate my whole life! Where is Armageddon? Let's get this over with! I'm tired of living with an axe hanging over my head!" The thought of suicide was there again. Death held no fear for me; I enjoyed sleeping. The future is what frightened me.

There is a long history of suicides with Jehovah Witnesses. Some experts have estimated the rate of suicides associated with the Watchtower is five to ten times the rate of the general population. The exact number of suicides is impossible to obtain because of the secrecy of the organization.

Chapter 22

Jehovah's Witnesses are not to show their dismay or concerns about their future. They are always admonished to smile and be happy no matter what, because they are a special people who will live through Armageddon and inherit the whole earth. Years ago, Gram told me that I would never graduate from high school because Armageddon was going to come any day, any moment.

Well, here I was five years later in my senior year of high school. Armageddon didn't look any closer to me, but expressing doubts about the teachings of the Watchtower was never tolerated in our house. Expressing doubts could put me in danger of being killed by Jehovah, just like he killed Lot's wife when they were fleeing Sodom and Gomorrah. Gram said, "Jehovah turned Lot's wife into a pillar of salt because she was told not to look back at the cities, and she did. She disobeyed God by longing for her old life instead of looking forward to the new home Jehovah would make for her and her family. Keep looking forward to the new world."

Spring of 1956 was getting closer, and I began looking in the stores for a pretty dress to wear on my graduation day in June. I found one that looked dynamite on me and made me feel good about myself. It was purple and white checked gingham with little white pearl buttons down the front. It had three-quarter-length sleeves and a full skirt.

When I told Mom how much it cost, Mom didn't think my dad would let me spend that much money. Mom decided to give me a dollar and told me to ask the saleslady to put it on a layaway plan. Mom gave me a dollar every week until the price was lower and then I asked my dad for the rest of the dress money. You would have thought that it was a fortune the way he carried on, but finally he said, "Okay! But don't look for a graduation gift!"

I knew I wouldn't get a gift anyway. We never got gifts for anything. Dad shouted, "Why don't you just wear your school clothing under your graduation gown? No one sees your dress anyway!" I was really steamed! I needed to feel good about myself and wanted a new dress for my graduation day. I was proud of my accomplishments even if they meant nothing to him. Working thirty hours a week and keeping my grades high had not been easy.

Most of the clothing we had worn through our school years came from the many large bags and boxes that my father brought home regularly from his dairy route. Dad's customers all knew he had a big family, and they put used clothing, shoes, and coats in bags and boxes for him to pick up and take home. His customers lived in a wealthy section of town so we were given famous brands in good condition. Mom dressed in donated clothing too. She was very good at doing repairs and alterations. My dad was the only one that bought new clothing; after all, he was a Jehovah's Witness minister.

Most of the girls I knew from school that could not go to college married young and started families. Some girls at school had gotten engaged at Christmastime before they even graduated from high school. One of the girls that I knew since our elementary years and had always thought was nice became pregnant during our Christmas break from school. Her name was Loretta. She was a very pretty blonde girl with blue eyes and perfectly straight teeth. Loretta and her sailor boyfriend were married when we had days off for Easter vacation.

I couldn't attend the wedding because it was in a church, and I was afraid to set one foot in a church. I went to her wedding reception with some of my fellow classmates from school. Loretta's whole family was there with her, and they all treated her like a princess. She looked like one in her beautiful wedding gown. My father said she was bad company for me when I told him I had been invited to her wedding reception and wanted to buy her a gift. I had to account for every penny he gave me, and since I gave him my entire paycheck every week, he reluctantly doled some back to me.

Loretta had a small rock 'n' roll band playing music at the reception, and we all enjoyed dancing. Some of the most popular songs were "Rock Around the Clock," "Ain't that a Shame," "I Hear You Knockin'," "Great Pretender," and "Tutti Frutti."

We had a pitcher of root beer on our table, and after the first pitcher was empty, someone began mixing the root beer with real beer. I never had an alcoholic drink before and started feeling dizzy and woozy. I was with boys and girls that were friends of Loretta and mine since elementary school. We piled into one car and drove to a nearby water reservoir because all of us were feeling pretty sick. I thought I was going to upchuck, and the driver said, "Everyone that feels sick, get out of the car." I was the first one out, but not the last. It was drizzling outside and we were chilled to the bone from walking around the car trying to get our bearings.

The next morning I stayed in bed. My head felt as though it would explode, and the bedroom was swirling when I opened my eyes. I didn't trust myself to stand upright. I finally had a room to myself. It was my private space, like being in the attic alone, but much nicer and more comfortable than the attic had been. Just as she did in the old attic days, Mom came upstairs to see if anything was wrong with me, and I told her about the night before. Mom went downstairs and made some coffee. She brought it to me in a cup on a saucer, and said, "Don't let your father see you like this."

I started to giggle and then laughed hysterically. I told Mom, "That is very funny because Dad drinks every day and sees nothing wrong with using my paycheck!" I kept giggling, but Mom wasn't laughing as she stirred the coffee with the milk and sugar. She looked grim and did not approve of me at the moment. I took one mouthful of the coffee and spit it back out. "I'm going to be sick!" My mother handed me a wastebasket and took the coffee cup away. She held my head. Later, I promised, "Mom, I will never allow this to happen again. No one will ever trick me into drinking root beer with beer again." I never drank coffee with milk and sugar again either.

Chapter 23

I was five feet two inches of energy in my senior year. My hair was not the light blonde of my childhood. It was dark blonde, almost light brown, and I knew my new graduation dress with purple and white was a good color choice. My beige-tone skin tanned easily and I hoped to get some tan on my skin before I wore the dress.

On my high school graduation day, I had the ninth highest average in the senior class, and I was honored to walk with a small group of ten at the head of the senior body. The other nine honor students would all be going to college. It was a gorgeous, sunny June day, and the ceremony was held in West Park near the school.

Everyone else was excited and happy to be graduating, but I was crying and hurting inside. I loved school and didn't want to leave forever. My friends complimented me on how wonderful my graduation dress looked on me. Wearing that new dress helped me to get through the day.

No one from my family was at the graduation ceremony, not even Mom. It was too far for Mom to walk there with my little brothers. Tim, the boy attending the Kingdom Hall that I had been dating for seven or eight months, was not there either because he was working a new job. As I walked alone through the crowd watching all the other graduates getting hugs, kisses, flowers, and gifts, tears began flowing uncontrollably down my face. I could barely see where I was going as I left the park, wishing I were dead.

I was so upset about leaving school that I could not even force myself to say good-bye to my favorite teachers. I removed the tassel from the cap. After turning in the cap and gown at the school, I walked to a luncheonette two blocks away where my father had said he would meet me to give me a ride home in his dairy truck.

When I entered the luncheonette, he was already inside sitting on a stool at the counter. He was talking to the waitress, Mrs. Ross of the Kingdom Hall scandal. I hesitated right inside the door, and Mrs. Ross looked at me. She said something to my father and nodded her head toward me. He stood up and turned around to face me. Smiling, he shouted, "There she is! My beautiful daughter! All graduated from high school!"

Everyone in the luncheonette turned and looked at him and at me. He might have been drunk when he stood up and came toward me with his arms open as though wanting a hug. I became very angry—angry because he was putting on a show; angry because he didn't care enough to come to my graduation ceremony where I was in the honored top ten students. I was angry because he was sitting two blocks away, having a blast, chatting and laughing with Mrs. Ross, and I was angry because he had never wanted a hug from me before.

Ignoring his open arms, I turned around and stormed out of the luncheonette. He followed me outside, shouting my name. Mrs. Ross followed him. I spun around and shouted back at him, "How dare you? All you care about is drawing attention to yourself! You don't care anything about me! All you care about is making yourself look good in front of other people! You don't care that I am dying inside! I hate you! I hate you!"

I hated him because I couldn't go to college, and because I had been lied to for so many years about Armageddon. I hated him for being with Mrs. Ross, and I angrily glared at both of them. I turned and walked nine blocks to our house in a fog. We never spoke of it after that day, just as though it had not happened. Looking back on that, I realize he might have been afraid that I would tell Mom or someone at the Kingdom Hall that he was still friendly with Mrs. Ross.

Tim came to the house for me late that afternoon when he was finished working, and we drove to a park to walk along the water. I was feeling so down because my life wasn't anything that I wanted it to be, but it was better than nothing. Not wanting to live my life as it was, I didn't really want to die either, even though suicide had become a pleasant thought. Whenever I grew tired and weary of my life, thoughts of sleeping forever comforted me.

Tim and I had been looking at engagement rings in a jewelry store window a few weeks before my graduation, and he surprised me with a lovely engagement ring. Seventeen was a very young age to get engaged. I didn't really want to get engaged and married, but couldn't see anything else in my future. I didn't want to live at home anymore where I would work hard in a factory and then have my father drink it all away. I wanted to escape and change my life.

Dad accepted the engagement, but said, "You and Tim cannot get married until after Tim is a baptized Jehovah's Witness." Fine! My time at home was getting shorter, and I was determined to get Tim baptized. I had hoped that after graduation some of my factory pay would be for me, but nothing changed. I had to give my father my entire paycheck and then had to ask for money and prove the need for everything I wanted to buy. He did not want any of his children to leave home before they were twenty-one years old. Dad always told us, "I will have you arrested and put in a reform school if you run away from home before you are twenty-one." We believed him. Then there was Mom. Life would have been totally unbearable without her constant love.

Chapter 24

After graduation, I suppose I was clinically depressed and didn't know why I felt this way or what to do about it. I didn't even know there was a name for these feelings, but *numb* about sums it up. I could barely function and seemed to be in a persistent fog. Getting out of bed to go to work was difficult. It was like forcing my body to breathe and live.

Many years later, I would discover what clinical depression means. Simply put, it means that you cannot shake off the way you feel to get on with your life. The depression interferes with normal daily routines, and you cannot enjoy activities and pastimes that should be enjoyable. Relationships suffer, self-esteem is very low, and you don't feel well. You lose weight and are no longer fully in control of your daily life.

I forced myself to get dressed and go to work for my eight-hour shift during the day in the sewing machine factory. It was just going through the motions that kept me going. The only bright spot in my day was having a half hour with my sister Jean. I tried to pretend to be happy because that is what Witnesses are taught to do when they are unhappy. When I saw Tim in the evening I was tired and tried to put on a front of being okay, but he knew the tears were right under the surface and could break loose. It was almost impossible to force myself to talk about it with him because that might discourage him from getting baptized.

There was a very popular song recorded by the Platters called "The Great Pretender." It was one of the big hits of the year when I graduated, and it helped me a great deal because I knew I was not alone if millions of other people related to that song, bought it, sang it—and survived.

> *Oh yes I'm the great pretender*
> *Pretending I'm doing well*
> *My need is such I pretend too much*
> *I'm lonely but no one can tell.*

"I'm lonely for school, lonely for teachers, and lonely for my friends that are going to college." Looking back, I think that song is what prevented me from taking my own life, because I was definitely suicidal. Death held no fear for me. It was just sleeping—but I also thought that suicide was too final. It cannot be undone.

Gram came home from Florida for a few weeks in September. I asked her, "Why did you tell me that I would never graduate from high school? Why did you pressure me into getting baptized?" Gram said, "I did it for your own benefit." I replied, "My benefit? How could lying to me that I would never graduate from high school be for my benefit? Armageddon did not come, and maybe the whole Watchtower timetable is a big lie!" Gram got very upset with me and warned, "You can be disfellowshipped for talking like that!" Gram always made excuses for the mistakes of the Watchtower Society. That is what all loyal Witnesses do when confronted with false promises. She said, "Maybe we misunderstood what the Watchtower said." They pretend it never happened. We were all great pretenders.

She said, "The Society cannot be wrong if they get their information directly from Jehovah God, but maybe God doesn't always give them the full information, and they must wait for new light to be shed." New light meant "new truth" or "new meat." The Watchtower says that no one should run ahead of Jehovah. They must be patient because they get "meat in due season," meaning that God gives the leaders a little bit of information over a season of time. They take this teaching from Matthew 2:44–46 (KJV):

Therefore be ye also ready, for in such an hour as you think not, the Son of man cometh. Who then is a faithful and wise servant, whom his lord hath made ruler over his household to give them meat in due season? Blessed is that servant whom his lord when he comes shall find so doing.

The Watchtower Society claims to be the faithful and wise servant that Jehovah uses to feed his people on earth with the meat of the scriptures in due season, or in other words, as required. They claim to be ruler over his household. One need only look at the history of the Watchtower Society to find that many false prophecies and promises were made to, and by, their leaders. There was something wrong with the meat we were being fed.

I thought of my brother Rod working near Pittsburgh. He was free from our house, and that meant he was free to keep his pay, free to do things without getting screamed at, free to think for himself. In the nineteen fifties, young adults had few rights, but they could be drafted into the army. Young Witness men expected to be classified as Conscientious Objectors, like my brother was, and they refused to serve in the military. Some served two years alternate service in a state facility, while others went to jail.

The ones that took alternate service in state institutions were considered to be weak and borderline to make it through Armageddon. The ones who went to jail were thought of as being strong in their faith and were told Jehovah would reward them. My brother said he had a good job in the mental hospital and was happy he chose to do that.

Mrs. Ross's son, Barry, turned eighteen and would soon need to make a decision before the draft board. He was a tall and handsome guy who married a tall, beautiful girl from Tennessee that he met at a national Watchtower convention. They barely knew each other except through letters. A short time after their marriage, Barry was sentenced to jail because he refused alternative service and refused to be drafted into the army.

The Watchtower praised those who went to jail instead of taking alternative service, because they were supposedly being persecuted for their faith in Jehovah. When Barry was released from prison two years later, he was not the same happy, chipper young married man that entered jail; he was suffering from severe mental anxiety and depression.

His wife, who had gone back to her parent's home in Tennessee for those two years, reunited with him. She suffered from emotional stress, and after a few months she returned to Tennessee to file for divorce, against the advice of the elders. The elders warned them they might not survive through Armageddon if they divorced.

They were only twenty-two, and if one of them wanted to move on with their lives and remarry someday, that person would be guilty of adultery and would be disfellowshipped. I was told that their lives were not very happy after that, but hopefully, as the years passed, they did manage to make new lives for themselves.

When young Jehovah's Witnesses divorce, chances are that one or both of the two people involved will want to remarry, and the first one to do so will be disfellowshipped unless they can prove that their divorced mate had committed adultery first. The elders committee requires a confession or two witnesses to prove the adultery. Divorced Witnesses are watched very closely to determine if one of them is having a relationship with another person. It is not unusual for divorced people to change jobs and locations in order to get out from under the Watchtower microscope where they are being scrutinized.

While the Witnesses base the shunning practice on New Testament scriptures, no allowances are made for those people who marry too young and for the wrong reasons or for those who are abused and need to physically depart to protect their sanity or their lives. Women are expected to accept whatever their husbands do to them. The only time divorce is acceptable to the Watchtower is if the spouse opposes the organization or opposes raising the children as Jehovah's Witnesses. In those cases, especially when a Jehovah's Witness is married to a person with another religion, Witnesses are often encouraged to separate. Any opposition from the non-Witness places the married couple under the microscope, especially if the other mate attends a church.

A woman named Josie became a Witness after she was married and had children. She studied with the Witnesses because her husband was working long hours and she was often alone. Her husband, at first, saw no harm in what she was doing.

In a short time after she became a Witness, her husband was alarmed at what she was telling him about their teachings in her attempt to convert him to the Witnesses. Her husband began taking their three children to a Baptist Church every Sunday. He would not allow the children to go to the Kingdom Hall anymore because of their teaching about Jesus Christ being Michael the Archangel and because they deny the bodily resurrection of his body.

Jehovah's Witnesses deny the bodily resurrection of Jesus because they believe that Jehovah dissolved his body into gas and the resurrected one was actually Michael the Archangel going back to heaven, alias Jesus. They cite the scripture that flesh and blood cannot enter heaven without realizing that his resurrected body is a new transformed body.

Josie's husband was also strongly opposed to the Watchtower ban on blood transfusions. The elders told her that she should separate from her husband, take those children, live alone, and take them to the Kingdom Hall meetings. Josie had no higher education and felt she could not survive financially. She also thought her children would suffer great emotional harm if they were to be removed from their father who loved them very much.

The elders put great pressure on this woman and made her feel that she and her children would die at Armageddon if she did not get away from her husband. Her husband was a good loving husband, a good loving father, and a good provider. Her only complaint against him was that he did not want his children to be Jehovah's Witnesses.

Josie lived for twenty years in fear under this cloud of opposition and suffered great mental anguish. Her husband loved her very much. He tried to speak to her about the Bible, but the elders warned her not to speak to her husband about the Bible because he might confuse her and cause her to lose faith in Jehovah. She turned a deaf ear to anything her husband said against the Witnesses. She continued going to the Kingdom Hall and knocking on doors with the Watchtower publications.

Their children grew and married in the Baptist church. Through all those years, they insisted on their mother being included in all holiday celebrations and all birthdays. They showered her with many, many gifts. They helped their father get their mother free from the Watchtower after she lived twenty years in fear that her children would die at Armageddon. Josie began attending a church with her husband that was twenty miles from their home because she was afraid someone would see her going into a church, and she didn't want the Witnesses to know what she was doing.

Her only friend was a Witness, and she wanted to keep her friend. She knew the Witnesses would be spying on her when she stopped attending the Kingdom Hall, and she knew they liked to disfellowship people who stopped coming to the meetings. Josie struggled to be free because she wanted to be happy.

Chapter 25

Back in October of 1956, I was still very unhappy and crying myself to sleep because I couldn't go back to school. For me, it felt really bad to have been such a good student and now face every day in a sewing machine factory. I wanted to be dead, but tried to talk myself out of it by pretending I was really free. The only place I felt even somewhat free was when I was "attic alone" in my own bedroom.

I still had a hard time getting out of bed in the morning and often wished I could be in a perpetual state of being in an attic alone. Those years of hiding in the attic had taught me that I could be free by getting lost within myself and within books. Tim was no help. He talked about getting married all the time because he wanted to have sex, but he didn't want to get baptized. Tim was smart enough to not be baptized the way my father had insisted he must be before we were allowed to get married. He was old enough to know better and would not let anyone push him into the baptism.

Other Witness girls were allowed to marry very young. I knew one who was fifteen when she married a seventeen-year-old boy. Their parents said it was better for them to get married that young than risk having sex before marriage. Dad didn't want any of his children to get married or have sex until we were twenty-one years of age because he really just wanted our paychecks. My younger brothers were not being pressured to get baptized because Gram lived in Florida most of the year. My dad was drinking so heavily he often lived in his own world. I began putting more pressure on Tim to get baptized because I wanted to get married and away from home.

By November Tim had convinced me that no one can wait until they are twenty-one to have sex. I was going to be eighteen in two weeks and, strangely, didn't really care about anything anymore. I thought there was something very wrong with me, but could not figure out exactly what was wrong—except my whole life.

After having sex with Tim, I didn't really feel any different. I had felt so numb for so many months that I couldn't shake the feeling. If anything, I felt ashamed and disgusted and extremely unhappy, but Tim seemed to be the only way of getting free from my father before I was twenty-one. It wasn't college, but at least it was an escape.

When it was my eighteenth birthday in December, no one remembered except me and Tim. He brought me a gift-wrapped present that my dad immediately scowled at then harshly scolded Tim that celebrating birthdays was akin to committing idolatry. I kept the gift of cologne, but as usual, it was not a happy birthday. But then, I had never really known a happy birthday. I wasn't allowed to go out to dinner with Tim. Dad said, "You are not going out to dinner tonight! You are not celebrating your birthday! Go out to dinner some other night!"

My father was getting overbearing. He had been closely watching me in a strange way ever since the day I graduated. He suspected something was very wrong with me, but he didn't know what it was because we couldn't talk to each other. There was a big wall between us, and I never knew how many drinks he might have had. He confronted me one night shortly after my birthday because I had been out past my ten o'clock curfew.

Tim and I had been at his father's apartment while his father was out of town. Tim's mother died when he was twelve years old. That left an empty hole in his life that had never been filled. I had no idea what problems were ahead for me with Tim. Had I known, I might have run away from him and my family.

This particular night, I must have looked like something the cat dragged in, so to speak. My father took one look at me and began screaming and cursing about my being out until 11:00 PM and then coming home looking all disheveled. I didn't really care what I looked like, because I didn't care about anything anymore. There was no fear in me this night either when he was screaming at me, because it didn't really matter what might happen to me if he started to beat me. He could kill me if he wanted to; I almost wished he would. I didn't have the courage to do it myself.

Too numb to care, I began shouting back at him. "You don't care anything about me, about how miserable and unhappy I am about the broken Armageddon promises and about not being able to go to college. It doesn't matter what happens to me anymore, and I might as well be dead because that is how it feels inside. So go ahead and kill me! I am not afraid of dying now or at Armageddon or sleeping forever. I'm only afraid of living!"

Dad grabbed my arm and screamed in my face, "You're having sex with Tim! Aren't you?" I shouted back in his face. "Yes! So what? Who cares?" Even while the words were flying out of my mouth, I knew that he cared, because I could be disfellowshipped by Jehovah's Witnesses for having sex before marriage.

My father wasn't in very good standing himself since the Ross incident, and he was not attending meetings regularly. He was not allowed to give speeches anymore, nor was he going out in the service the way he did in the past. He had his fist raised in the air, and I really expected him to punch me with it, but then he backed away from me and began to blame himself for my attitude. I was so shocked!

My father had never blamed himself for anything before! Everything was always somebody else's fault! Now he said, "This is my fault for not attending the meetings." This totally confused me. Everything seemed to be upside down, inside out and backward.

The next afternoon my dad sacrificed going to Tinkle's Bar and went to see a friend of his from the Kingdom Hall who was the father-in-law of Dad's younger brother, Wayne. Dad confided in this man, Mr. Einhart, and then came home and told me, "I am taking you to see Mr. Einhart." He was from Germany and spoke with an accent. His hair was strawberry blond, and he had blue eyes. He was a nice man, but I didn't want to talk to him about my new sex life.

Dad gave me no choice. He threatened to beat me worse than he had ever beaten me before and drag me there by my hair. I knew he was very capable of doing it. Reluctantly, I went with my father. Mr. Einhart was perfectly quiet while my father sat in his living room and berated me for being a wayward child. It was very embarrassing, and Mr. Einhart gently told me, "You have made a grave mistake that could cost you your life at Armageddon, but I don't want that to happen to you." He said, "By the Watchtower rules, you must meet with the committee of the congregation elders at the Kingdom Hall and they will decide what to do with you."

Surprisingly, he was a gentleman and spoke kindly to me. He offered to speak for me and appeal to the committee on my behalf. I wished that I had a father half as polite, kind, and soft-spoken as Mr. Einhart. He was a widower; he had watched his beloved wife of forty years fight against the cancer that had metastasized in her body. He called for an ambulance one day when he came home from work because she was unresponsive, but still breathing. She died on the way to the hospital.

The police became involved when it was discovered that she had died from an overdose of pain medication. Mr. Einhart confessed to having found an empty pill bottle on the nightstand and he threw it away. The police questioned him and considered charging him with assisting a suicide, but later dropped the investigation for lack of evidence.

A few days after the meeting with Mr. Einhart, I was before the committee at the Kingdom Hall. When they were told by Brother Einhart, "The act happened just recently and she is sorry for what she did," they decided that the only action needed was that I be privately chastised and not be allowed to be alone with Tim until after we were married.

I was hoping that meant that I could get married soon and get away from my father, but Dad and the Kingdom Hall committee didn't see it that way. They said, "Tim must be baptized before you can marry him."

Chapter 26

Just as it was in my father's case, being privately chastised meant that no one else at the Kingdom Hall needed to know what terrible sin I had committed. It was our secret. It was very depressing to think of being tied to my father's house for three more years until I was twenty-one.

A few weeks later I wasn't feeling very well and stayed home from work one day. My periodic cramps and headache were beginning, but nothing else started. As a matter of fact, I felt a little better the next day and went back to work thinking this was going to be one of those difficult months that happened from time to time.

By the first of February I was feeling worse and told Mom. Suspecting I might have gotten pregnant, my mother talked to me about going to a doctor for an examination. Mom offered to go with me, but I wasn't afraid and preferred to go alone. Besides, I wanted to pretend I was already married when I went to the doctor's office, so the people there would not think I was a bad person.

I didn't really feel bad the way my Dad and the Witnesses wanted me to feel about myself, because I was hoping I was pregnant. "This could be my ticket out of the house and away from my dad before I'm twenty-one," I thought. Tim didn't want to get baptized, but he did want to get married. Pregnancy worked for my brother Harry when he wanted to be out from under our dad's rule. He married Gerri and she became my sister-in-law.

I found the entire doctor's visit to be quite embarrassing, but when the doctor said she thought I was pregnant, all I could think about was getting married and away from Dad. The nurse gave me another appointment. Before I went back for the second appointment I really knew what pregnant was from the way my stomach felt every morning and the swelling I was noticing that I never had before. Tim was thrilled to make plans to get married, and his father immediately invited us to live with him in his three-bedroom apartment. Tim was still refusing to be baptized.

We had the wedding plans made before I told my dad. My biggest fear was that he would try to put me away in a reform school just for spite. That was always his favourite threat when he was trying to keep budding teenagers in his complete control. We all believed he was mean enough to put us in one. He told us reform school was a prison for runaways.

My older brothers and sisters had been through similar threats, but Harry was the only one that had not been baptized as a Jehovah's Witness. Dad and Gram did not put the same pressure on Harry to get baptized that they put on the rest of us because of his lame leg and because he didn't seem to listen as well. He was this nice, quiet, stay-to-himself person who preferred letting the Watchtower conversations go in one ear and out the other. He never wanted to speak at strangers' doors with the *Watchtower*, no matter how much he was threatened with dying at Armageddon. In fact, he never paid any attention at the meetings or to anything Gram was saying at the doors. He had become an annoying distraction to our grandmother, and she gave up on him.

Since Harry had never been baptized, no one at the Kingdom Hall cared what he did. As a matter of fact, Harry got even more attention and visits after he was married, because they wanted to get him and his new wife into the Witnesses. To their chagrin, his wife wasn't listening either.

When I finally told Dad that I had been to the doctor and was definitely pregnant, my mother was sitting nearby for moral support. Mom never defended herself against my father's abuse because, after all, he was over six feet and she was barely over five feet tall. In spite of that, I knew that Mom would not just sit there and watch him beat a pregnant girl; she was on full alert, sitting on the edge of her seat. I knew in my heart that Mom would have intervened and taken the beating for me before she would let Dad hurt her grandchild.

Dad didn't get violent when I told him I was pregnant and wanted him to sign papers so Tim and I could get married. He was very angry, to say the least. He called me names, cursing at me with hateful words that were literally spitting out of his mouth while he threw knives at me with his dark, hard eyes that were glaring and twice as cold as ice cubes.

Glancing over at Mom every few seconds, my dad was blaming her as well as me. "You have not been a very good Witness example for your children!" I thought he might start beating on Mom the way he had in the past when he was very angry, but he seemed to be more concerned about what Brother Einhart and the committee at the Kingdom Hall would think of this problem. It seemed that he didn't want to do anything they might frown upon.

I thought, "Perhaps the committee knew about my father's abusiveness when he was drinking. It might have been discovered when they were questioning my mother about their marriage during the Ross incident. Mom never claimed to be a Witness, so why is it her fault? She never wanted to go to the meetings, but sometimes my father forced her to attend. Mom always showed us love."

My father showed very little love to anyone. He was much nicer to other people than he was to his family, and he didn't seem to care that Mom had been experiencing physical problems in the past year like shortness of breath when she became upset and dizzy spells that would send her to bed for a few hours of rest. Her family had a strong history of heart disease. The only thing my father was concerned about was that if she would have a heart attack and die, she would leave him alone with four young children.

Dad had always been annoyed that Mom was not enthusiastic about the Kingdom Hall meetings. When he forced her to be there, she did not participate or even sing along with everyone else out of the Jehovah's Witness songbook. Mom was always humming to herself at home, but when she got to the Kingdom Hall, her mouth was sealed.

There were several times over the years that I asked Mom, "What song are you humming?" and she usually would say, "You don't know this song. It is an old one." It annoyed me that Mom hummed and didn't tell me what she was humming. I actually thought, "Mom might be going a little crazy from living with my dad and having nine children. Mom doesn't even know what she is humming." It occurred to me that it might be some kind of a coping mechanism.

Now Dad was blaming Mom for not being responsible enough to watch me more closely than she had, as though it was all her fault that I had gotten pregnant. But then, he blamed Mom for getting pregnant nine times from him also, like he had nothing to do with the whole thing. At the Kingdom Hall he pretended he didn't really intend to have such a big family, but we knew he viewed us as his security blanket if he couldn't work anymore. My father was not a good husband to my mother.

I thought, "My father literally kept my mother pregnant, barefoot, and at home for more than twenty-five years of her life. She never drove a car and hardly ever went more than a few blocks away from home." I knew my dear, sweet mom was wondering, "How long do we have to listen to his ranting and raving? How long will he continue before he calms down and stops his screaming?" I had learned how to read my mother through the years because although Mom never said much, I could feel what she was thinking. She was also thinking, "I don't care what Brother Einhart or the Kingdom Hall committee says." She was there for me no matter what happened. All of her glances at me were supportive and loving ones. On the other hand, my father was more concerned with what other people wanted.

Dad went with Mr. Einhart to see the committee and supposedly spoke on my behalf, but when he dropped the bombshell that I had just found out I was pregnant, they were not very sympathetic. They said they had been lied to, and this changed everything. My dad pleaded, "We had no way of knowing she had gotten pregnant when you held the first committee meeting." The men did not care what he said.

The committee pretended they had been tricked into putting me on a secret probation in an attempt to escape being disfellowshipped, and now they said, "We are angry that we were not fully informed of the facts at our first meeting. The only recourse we have is to publicly disfellowship her on grounds of immorality." I knew in my heart that the reason for this action was only because everyone would eventually know that I was pregnant. If I had not been pregnant, everything would have been kept quiet. Everyone knew the public image of the organization must be protected at all costs from public reproach.

At the next committee meeting about me, a letter was prepared telling everyone that I was disfellowshipped on grounds of immorality. The speaker read it publicly to everyone in the Kingdom Hall at the next meeting. It said something like this, in part: "No one is allowed to speak to or associate with Arlene until she has fully repented and written a letter of apology for her sinful conduct and asks to be allowed back into the organization." The Witnesses knew that an undetermined amount of time, about a year, was always the time it took for someone to be allowed back into the fold. If someone immediately wrote a letter, it would have been laughed at and thrown away. They wanted to publicly shun and embarrass people who did not obey the rules. It was a warning to other people that they should not break any of the rules.

After the letter was read to the whole congregation, Tim and I continued going to the meetings even though we had serious doubts about the teachings and practices of the Watchtower. It didn't bother me too much that the Witnesses were shunning me. I owed it to my older baptized brother and sisters to be back in good standing with the Kingdom Hall. My brother and sisters were the ones that mattered. I wanted them to treat me like part of the family again.

The entire thing with my family was really quite bizarre when I look back at those days. I didn't really want to be a Witness anymore, but it was what I was raised with, and I didn't know how to be anything else. I felt condemned to this life I was raised with and therefore accepted the responsibility and punishment.

Chapter 27

Tim and I were married one cold Saturday morning without family or fanfare. It was as gloomy a day as my baptism had been. Tim had his best friend and I had a co-worker friend from the sewing machine factory as witnesses to the marriage in the home of a Justice of the Peace. Both of our friends said, "We are shocked to know how the Jehovah's Witnesses have treated you. You are better off without them." I had boxed up all of my belongings, and we stopped to see my mother and pick up the boxes. I told Mom we were just going to the justice by ourselves.

We had been tempted to invite some old, worldly school friends and have a party, but that would have been wrong according to the Witness teachings, so the four of us just went out to a nice restaurant for dinner. Tim had a sister named Louise in New Jersey. She would have come to spend the day with us, but was busy giving birth to her first child. Now it was time for me to make my own decisions.

I decided that I wanted to attend the Kingdom Hall and get reinstated in order that my Witness family would talk to me again. My younger brothers were not being pressured to be baptized, and they were very kind and understanding toward me. They were still living with Dad and had to be quiet when he was around. They strengthened their resolve to "never get baptized by Jehovah's Witnesses and be owned by the Watchtower Society," so my getting disfellowshipped resulted in some good. Mom said, "You are welcome to visit me anytime you want to visit. Call me whenever you want to and I will call you too." Mom would never ignore any of her children.

It wasn't easy to go to the meetings and be ignored as though I wasn't even there. There were more than one hundred fifty Witnesses that I had seen and known all my childhood and teen years. We all knew each other by name and knew who was part of what family and who was married to what other family. It is a close-knit society at the Kingdom Hall—as long as you obey the rules. The few other teens looked through me as though I wasn't even there, and if anyone at the Kingdom Hall did accidentally look into my face, they usually became upset with themselves or managed a little sneer as they turned away from me in disgust.

Ironically, they could still be friendly to my husband, the one who constantly put pressure on me to have sex before marriage. Tim had not been baptized as a Jehovah's Witness, and they made no judgment against him. They were still trying to get Tim baptized, so they were love-bombing him while ignoring me. They acted as though they cared nothing about me.

After giving birth to a son, Ronald, I told Tim, "I will not let you hold him at the Kingdom Hall. People are going to have to go through me if they want to see my baby. I don't want any of them to touch him. It was hard enough to get married and have people ignore me, but it was worse having a child and not receiving so much as a congratulations card from people who are supposed to be my sisters and brothers in Jehovah. They just want to shame me for having this beautiful baby." Ronald had blond hair and blue eyes like my mother's eyes. Tim wanted to show him off, but I insisted he would not hold the baby at the Kingdom Hall. He belonged to me. They could wait until I was ready to share him.

After a year of being ignored and shunned, the Witnesses were probably as relieved as I was when a letter was read to everyone at the meeting. It said something like, "Arlene has fulfilled the terms of her punishment by writing a letter to the committee of the Kingdom Hall asking for forgiveness for her sin and acknowledging her failure to put the organization and Jehovah first in her life."

After the meeting some people came to me smiling and said, "We are happy that you remained faithful to Jehovah all year. Can we expect to see you Saturday or Sunday to go door-to-door with the new magazines?" Actually, it felt so good not going door-to-door with the magazines that I wasn't sure I could handle that again. Going back to that would be more difficult than being shunned for a year. I felt like I was going to be sick. Actually, I did get sick. I was pregnant again.

Being pregnant was a good excuse to stay home every morning. Eventually though, the pressure on me increased, and I could not escape going door-to-door on the weekend. My second son, James, inherited the dark hair and eyes of my father's family. By the time he was born, I knew that I was living both a lie and a life that wasn't working. My two sons kept me very busy, but the pressure never stopped to be at every meeting and go door-to-door with the Watchtower literature. I studied harder because I still missed school, but no matter how hard I studied the Watchtower publications, so many teachings did not ring true with other verses from the Bible.

Knowing that my standing before Jehovah was on slippery ground, I probably would never make it through Armageddon because of my unbelief. I began reevaluating my life, saying, "I can never be a good enough Jehovah's Witness to make it through Armageddon. Why try?" I slowly began to withdraw from the Kingdom Hall. It felt like I had been beating my head against a brick wall to be good enough. I didn't feel good enough. I knew, "This is not the life I want for myself and not the life I want for my children." It was now 1960 and there was an empty hole inside of me that was never satisfied. Something was missing! I wanted to feel normal and have a normal life.

Chapter 28

Even though the Witnesses are not allowed to vote in elections, I devoured the newspaper every day and became more aware of politics in America. I was especially interested in the upcoming American presidential campaign. I had a small tabletop radio and had it turned on all day, listening to the news programs. I wanted to learn more about the larger world around me.

At the same time that I was taking a new look at the world, Gram was diagnosed with cancer and came back to Pennsylvania for surgery. I tried talking to her about the upcoming presidential election. She said, "A Catholic will never be the president of the United States because there are too many people that would never allow the Pope to run America. A Catholic in the White House would be nothing but a puppet for Rome." There were Protestant ministers who were concerned about a Catholic in the White House too. John F. Kennedy addressed those concerns in September of 1960. The transcript of his speech is on the Internet. My grandmother didn't believe anything he said.

Gram passed away before the November 1960 election. Surprise, surprise! John F. Kennedy won the election and became the first Catholic president of the United States. Poor Gram was wrong again! With my grandmother gone, I decided, "No one will tell me what I can or cannot read or tell me how to think anymore." Still wanting to keep my family, I did most of this reading in secret where I could be attic alone. Current events were important to me.

Another event in 1960 caught everyone's eyes and ears. Madalyn Murray O'Hair began fighting against reading the Bible and saying the Lord's Prayer in public schools. She was an atheist and did not want her son to be exposed to or influenced by Christianity. Her innocent son was told to leave the classroom and wait in the hall while the rest of the children heard the Bible and said the prayer, but that did not pacify Madalyn. She wanted to have the Bible and prayers removed from public schools. For some reason I thought, "She is just as bad as Jehovah's Witnesses. She is trying to dictate what people may and may not do."

I was twenty-one now and felt more enslaved than ever before in my life. There was no true sense of any adult freedom. Jehovah's Witnesses could have alcohol, but we were not allowed to vote. I began working three evenings a week in a sewing factory for the extra money and to get away from my husband and the two boys for a few hours so I could feel like a normal person. I wanted to interact with normal adult people. It also gave me a good excuse to miss more meetings. I was more interested in the newspaper than I was in the meetings.

A few years later, on June 17, 1963, the Supreme Court of the United States under Chief Justice Earl Warren, delivered its 8–1 verdict ruling in favor of Madalyn Murray O'Hair. The decision by the Supreme Court made me very sad. I felt sorry for all the children that would not be allowed to learn the Lord's Prayer or hear daily Bible readings in school. It had been very important to my development in my school and personal life. My father said, "The prayer has no business being in the schools." Jehovah's Witnesses supported the decision.

Life magazine called O'Hair "the most hated woman in America." The Catholic Church strongly opposed the court ruling. Protestant evangelist Billy Graham commented, "The Supreme Court is wrong. Eighty percent of the American people want Bible reading and prayer in the schools. Why should a majority be so severely penalized?"

I agreed with the churches, but felt very helpless to say or do anything politically. I could not even express my opinion or vote for fear of someone hearing me or seeing me. The Witnesses have a policy of telling on each other if they are heard talking about something they should not talk about, or if they are seen some place they shouldn't be seen, like entering a voting location. It was okay to enter a bar, but it was not okay to enter a voting booth. Any suspicious activity is reported to the elders.

One of my sisters had been verbally chastised because someone reported her for walking down a street with a boy, the boy's arm wrapped around her shoulder. People were called before the committee at the Kingdom Hall for anything that was reported against them. To make the matter worse for my sister, the boy was not a Jehovah's Witness. Secret probation!

I began to realize that the elders are ordinary men, most of them uneducated beyond high school. Yet they are given power over the lives of other people to make judgments and execute punishments.

More and more I withdrew to my own little mental space to feel like I was in the attic alone. The old attic had taught me that I could be happy being alone by myself no matter where I was. I practiced being alone even while in the same room with my husband. He was beginning to show signs of mental illness. Tim didn't mind staying away from the Kingdom Hall; he hated going by this time because of all the pressure he was under to be a baptized Witness. He was still being pressured to go door-to-door with the Watchtower every week, and he could not handle pressure very well.

In 1961, I had called his sister, Louise, in New Jersey and spoken to her about Tim. She was a dark-haired, friendly nurse with a cute pug nose and had previously been in therapy with a psychiatrist. She discussed her problems from losing her mother as a teenager. Louise told me, "Tim's problems, no doubt, are tied to the fact that our father and Aunt Henrietta both accused him of killing our mother when he was twelve years old." This was something I had not known about before.

Louise said, "Our mother was forty years old and almost one hundred pounds overweight with diabetes and a heart condition when she died. She had climbed three flights of steps to our apartment after working an eight-hour shift in the summer heat. Our father and aunt didn't take those things into consideration though. Before our mother died, she told them, 'Tim sassed me back when I told him to come upstairs to clean up for supper.' Then our mother lay down on her bed to rest while our angry father went down the steps. He dragged Tim up the steps, yelling at him to have more respect for his mother. Tim was told to apologize to Mom, but it was too late. She had died of a massive heart attack. Dad and Aunt Henrietta screamed at Tim that he killed his mother." Louise was sobbing and could not say anymore, except that she hated reliving that memory of her mother dying and how her brother had been treated.

As a man, Tim refused to talk to anyone about his problems. As far as he was concerned, he was okay, and the rest of the world was screwed up. Now, in 1962, his father was dying of cancer, and I thought that this was the reason for his hot temper and his increasingly violent mood swings. Louise spoke to him on the phone and told him, "You need to forgive your father, as well as yourself. You need to heal from those accusations that were made against you when you were just a child of twelve." Tim said, "Mind your own business. You don't know what you are talking about just because you went to a shrink, so butt out of my life."

It was hard for her, but Louise forgave her father for many things when he was ill. She had a good healthy attitude toward her father and his problems. About Tim she said, "They never forgave each other for what happened when he was twelve, even though on the surface they appear to have a somewhat normal father and son relationship." I thought to myself, "They are great pretenders too. Are we really just actors on a great stage?" William Shakespeare wrote, "All the world's a stage, and all the men and women merely players."

After his father died, Tim acted more and more like his father. He began to gamble on horses, which was a secret vice that his father had and very few people knew about. Louise told me, "Tim and me resented our father for wasting all his money on the horses." Everyone but Tim and his new racetrack friends knew that when you gamble you would probably spend more money than you would ever win. However, he was so sure he was going to be a big winner that he began skipping days from work to go to the racetracks with a friend of his, Jack the gambler. To me, Jack looked like a typical movie gangster who hung out at the racetracks. He was muscular, with a hard and unsmiling face; he looked like a thug. Jack appeared to know the horses very well, so Tim was hoping he could win enough to quit his job and become a professional gambler. He and his new friend began doing many strange things, like disappearing for a few days at a time. They were traveling from one racetrack to another.

When I spoke to Louise about this, she said, "He is trying to live our father's life. Our dad died with little money because he gambled it all away. Tim resents that our dad lost all his money and maybe he wants to show that he is better than our dad by letting everyone know he is gambling. Maybe he wants to prove that he can win lots of money." I didn't know what to think about her opinion, but she was better educated than me and had been under the care of a psychiatrist for her own problems. After speaking with Louise, Tim and I completely stopped going to the Kingdom Hall.

In the Watchtower Society, independent thinking is prohibited and leads to punishment that is usually in the form of some kind of isolation like shunning. Controlling groups are like a person's parent that you must obey; you must do what you are told to do. When people begin to break free of the isolation of the group and begin thinking outside of the box, as Tim and I were doing, they usually leave the organization. The problem was that Tim and I were thinking in two totally different directions. I was seeking normalcy for the first time in my life, while he was seeking a life as a professional gambler.

Chapter 29

One night in 1962, Tim and I were fighting about everything, from his attitude toward me to my attitude toward him. Suddenly he made a fist and slammed me in the face. It felt like the right side of my jaw had been pushed up past my ear. I saw stars! Spinning around in great pain, I put some distance between us as I felt a great fury rising up inside. Turning back to face him again, I screamed with rage, "*Don't you tread on me!*"

The words shocked both of us back to our senses momentarily. I realized that I must have looked wild-eyed and crazy, because that is exactly the way I felt. I instantly knew my mind had snapped back to a day long ago in sixth grade when I had studied about the American colonial flags and what they all meant. We were told to pick one of the flags we liked and write a report about the origin and the reason why we'd chosen that flag. I wrote a report on the *Don't tread on me* flag. It showed a coiled rattlesnake that was ready to strike.

The rattlesnake was a symbol of the American colonies. The flag is called the Gadsden flag after Colonel Christopher Gadsden. It appeared at the first fighting mission of the Continental Navy. I chose that flag because at the age of eleven, I had already decided that when I grew up and was over twenty-one, no one would ever hit me, beat me, or walk on me. No one was going to tread on me like my father treaded on my mother. I had resolved to fight back with deadly force if anyone ever put me in that same situation—and now, someone just did. No one was going to use me for a punching bag. There was a coiled rattlesnake in me that would strike back.

Realizing why those words had come out of my mouth, I was ready to strike and began to scream at Tim like a wild banshee. "No one is going to abuse me!" He was so surprised that he backed farther away across the room from me, half tripping over a discarded toy. He did not know what to expect next. My words were cold, hard, loud, and furious as they flew out of my mouth.

"If you ever hit me again, you're a dead man!" I screamed. "I'll wait for you to go to sleep, and then I'll take a sharp butcher knife, and I will slit your throat from one ear to the next!" I roared like a lion. That coiled rattlesnake inside of me was ready for action. Surprised, Tim tried to joke by saying that if I did that, I would go to jail. I screamed again at him while taking slow and deliberate steps toward him. "If you think I'm kidding, try me! Right now! Hit me again right now! I dare you! I double dare you!" My angry eyes were throwing hateful knives at him. Tim turned and left the house without saying another word.

Without any kind of counseling, Tim continued to get worse, and the marriage was truly finished the night he physically, sexually assaulted me. I woke up to find him tying my wrists together. Not knowing what was going on, I began to struggle. As I began to pull myself free, he forced me down and began speaking vulgar, unprintable things to me that made my stomach churn. I fought him off and managed to turn away from him, but he was like a crazy man and pinned me down again. He smelled like my Dad. It turned my stomach.

He forced himself on me, and I was bruised from trying to fight him off. I was hurt, stunned, and yet numb at the same time. I wanted him dead, but I felt paralyzed and couldn't move. I didn't know what to do next. I was somewhat rigid with the fear and shame of what had just happened; it was brutal.

I seriously considered getting a knife and killing him that night as he slept, but I couldn't seem to move, and so I didn't. One thought stopping me was my love for my two wonderful sons. Early the next morning, I packed up my two little boys and drove to see his sister Louise in New Jersey. After discussing everything with Louise, I asked Louise to come home with me again and get him to a psychiatrist.

Louise came home with me and spent a few days trying to talk Tim into seeing a doctor. Tim insisted there wasn't anything wrong with him, and the only reason he had forced himself on me so brutally was because he had been drinking. He said, "I was drinking and feeling sorry for myself because Arlene wasn't being affectionate enough toward me." In others words, it was my fault! I screamed at him, "Don't you dare blame it on me!"

This reasoning was so typical of Jehovah's Witness thinking. Everything was always the woman's fault. The men rule! According to the Watchtower book, *Let God Be True*, published in 1946, women are merely a lower creature whom God created for man as man's helper. After his sister talked to him, he apologized to me for what he had done. Back then in the early 1960s, it was unheard of for any wife to bring rape charges against a husband.

The general attitude was that a wife couldn't be raped by her husband because she was, after all, his wife, like his property. I didn't tell anyone in my family or anyone from the Kingdom Hall what was going on in our marriage. Louise was the only person I could talk it over with. I didn't want my mother or father involved because I knew that Mom would feel my pain, and Dad would tell me divorce was out of the question. There had never been a divorce on either side of the family.

The old saying was, "When you make your bed, you must lie in it." In other words, when you make your own decisions, you must be prepared to suffer the consequences. That meant that no matter what he did to me, I was expected to take it and be quiet. Back in 1962, it was commonly thought that the woman was responsible for being raped. She would be asked questions like, "What were you wearing? What were you doing? Why were you there?"

Women were thought to be "asking for it." Many victims would not report being sexually assaulted because of the attitude toward women who were raped. A Watchtower magazine in January of 1964 had an article that asked, "Is Rape Fornication If the Woman Does

Not Scream?" The magazine went on to say that if she submitted to the man's passion without screaming, she would not only be consenting to fornication or adultery but should be plagued by the shame. This article dealt with the rape of single and divorced women.

In 1966, the National Organization of Women was founded. The leaders wanted women's liberation, and they wanted women to be treated respectfully at work and at home. Spousal rape and domestic violence are two of the things they fought against.

An article of the *Watchtower* in June of 1968 said that if a Jehovah's Witness woman doesn't scream while being raped, she has committed fornication or adultery, and she could be disfellowshipped. To give a brief idea of the Watchtower view on rape, it took more than another twenty-five years for their leaders to recognize that a rape victim should not be punished.

In the late 1960s, around 1968 or 1969, a woman in America filed charges of rape against her husband. It made the national news, as though no woman had ever charged her husband with rape before this. It became a big debate on television. Even the general population of the 1960s (and earlier) thought a married woman could not be raped by her husband because they were married, and sex was his due. Rape, including spousal rape, became a big women's issue in the early 1970s because of a growing number of women who were saying, "We will not take this anymore!"

An *Awake* magazine published in 1974 by the Watchtower Society said that if a Jehovah's Witness woman did not scream while being raped, she would ruin her relationship with Jehovah God and be disfellowshipped by the Witnesses. An October 1980 *Watchtower* said a Christian woman is under obligation to resist, because the issue of obedience to God's law to flee from fornication is involved.

In June 1984, the victims of rape were cut a break when some new light was shed on the Watchtower leaders. In their *Awake* magazine, they wrote that for the victim to be considered guilty of fornication, there would need to be proof of willing consent.

In 1986, the Watchtower decided that if a woman was raped, she would not be sacrificing her cleanliness before God. Finally, in March of 1993, they simply stated that a rape victim is not guilty of fornication. It had taken Jehovah over one hundred years to reveal that new truth to the leaders of the organization. In the meantime, Witness women were disfellowshipped and shunned for being raped.

Chapter 30

Louise, being a woman and a nurse, understood the entire issue. She often thought ahead of her time. I was fortunate to have her to talk with. She helped to keep my spirits up when things were bad. She gave me good advice and was good company for me. I was really hoping she could help her brother.

Louise went home after spending three days and nights talking to Tim and trying to help. Within a week after Louise left, I knew there wasn't any hope for this marriage. I felt uneasy about being alone with Tim because he had made promises to Louise that he would not keep. Nothing had really improved or changed. We needed things to change.

I found an evening job and started working five nights a week so I could stay away from him. I hated going home after work, but that is where my sons were. Tim agreed that he would leave me alone. I told him, "If you ever attack me again, I will kill you. I promise you that!" This threat was becoming old, but he knew he could not trust me with sharp knives in the house. He did get the message that I would not allow him to abuse me. Tim lost his job before discovering that I was pregnant with child number three.

I continued to work thirty hours a week because we really needed the money more than ever with a third child on the way. Tim said, "I'm willing to accept the responsibility for what I did. I am sorry. I love you and do not want to lose you." Tim even gave up his never-do-good gambling friends and worked steadily for a while.

Somewhere, he came up with enough money put a down payment on a small house. I was very skeptical about getting a house with him, but maybe he really had grown up, so I gave him another chance. It was so frustrating that he could earn good money when he was willing to work steady, but he liked hanging out with his racetrack friends. They were not family oriented.

When the baby was born, she was an eight-pound three-ounce bundle of sweetness. She was the best little baby girl in the world, with a tiny beauty spot right in the center of her throat. She looked like a mini-me. I named her Lisa because the month before she was born in February of 1963, the famous Mona Lisa masterpiece was on a train exhibit traveling from New York to Washington, DC, where it was shown in the National Gallery of Art. As it turned out, the name Lisa was the number one baby girl name in 1963.

The pressure and responsibility of a house and another child began to build, and Tim began cracking again. Within a short time, he was running around with his friend Jack the gambler. The bills did not get paid, everything was overdue, and finally, he was fired from his job. He didn't tell me he was fired; he left the house every day as though he were going to work.

My thirty-hour-a-week night job was not enough to pay the utilities and mortgage. When I confronted him with the unpaid electric and telephone bills, which, by the way, said that our service was being cut off, he admitted that he didn't have a job anymore and was going around with Jack every day trying to figure out how to make some money.

He had a string of jobs that he quit within days because he didn't want anyone telling him what to do or how to do his job. He thought he knew everything and tried to start a business with another friend who knew a little bit about carpentry and plumbing, but the first job they contracted to remodel a bathroom turned out poorly. The irate homeowner refused to pay them in full. Tim drove a cross-country truck, but he thought that was too hard. Our savings were gone, and he had begun to borrow money from friends.

Tim announced that he and Jack the gambler were going to California for a few weeks to see Jack's cousin who owned a boat and should be able to help them find work. I asked, "What does owning a boat have to do with finding a job?" He didn't have an answer. He said, "I will send you some money as soon as we find a job and get paid." Months went by without a word from him, and no money was ever sent to me. I was, in fact, totally abandoned with three children, because he gave me no money before he left and did not call or send any money from California.

I could not continue to survive on a thirty-hour paycheck and needed to work longer hours, even if it meant working two jobs. My children needed me to support them because Tim was not trustworthy anymore. He was giving me nothing but aggravation and grief. I felt a new freedom and decided that we did not need him in our life.

Chapter 31

After three months of juggling a new full-time job and several babysitters, I asked Mom and Dad if we could use an empty bedroom on the third floor for a few months. I needed to work my full-time job plus overtime to support the children and get back on my feet financially. There were bills that needed to be paid before I could afford my own house expenses. Mom said, "Yes!" immediately, but my father said, "Okay, as long you pay for your own expenses, like the extra electric and any of our food you might eat." I said that was fine.

Dad reluctantly agreed and I put the house, fully furnished, for rent on a six-month lease. The renting family had their furniture in storage. They needed to move to this area, but they had contractor problems with the house they were building.

Dad was unfriendly to me, but Mom was very happy to have the children and watch them when I was at work. Dad accusingly asked me, "What did you do to make Tim leave?" This was so typical of Jehovah's Witness thinking—everything was the woman's fault. He thought that I must have done something terribly wrong or been a terrible wife.

I did not want to tell him about the personal problems we were having and didn't want Mom to know about the abuse. My father was going to think whatever he wanted to think, so there was no point in answering him. I sent him some cold, hard daggers with my eyes. He taught me how to do that, and it was the only time I purposely sent them to him. The children and I brought our clothing. I left everything else at the house for the tenants to use.

Before six months had passed, Tim came back from his travels and wanted to move in with us at Mom's house. He was broke, unemployed, unshaven, smelly, and dirty. I turned him away, saying, "You have aunts and uncles you can turn to, or you can drive to Louise's house in New Jersey. You are not welcome to stay here with me and the children at Mom's house or anywhere else. I am supporting the children by myself, and I have no intention of supporting you too. I will not put up with your nonsense anymore!" He left in a terrible rage.

No one knew where Tim had gone, so he couldn't be served with papers to appear for a child-support hearing. After six months of living with Mom and Dad, the children and I moved back to our house. The whole arrangement had turned out well. Financially, I was back on my feet and able to support the children by myself. I loved my children with all my heart and would never give them up, so I worked a Saturday part-time job to supplement my full-time job.

My full-time job was with Western Electric, a large electronics company. My department earned bonuses once a month for our output. We had a government contract and were making electronic components for the Apollo space program to put the very first man on the moon. President John F. Kennedy set a goal of reaching the moon by the end of the 1960s. It was a good-paying job, but my new babysitter was not working out well. She was a sweet retired woman who needed the job, but she confessed, "It is too hard for me to be here for nine hours every evening during the week. I will look for shorter hours, and you should start looking for another sitter."

A neighbor girl, Joyce, came to see me and explained, "I stayed home with my mother after my graduation from high school last year because she had her leg amputated and needed help during the day." Hearing about my babysitter problem, she asked, "Can I take care of your children while you work your second-shift job? I can come over every day at three o'clock in the afternoon and stay with them until you come home." It made me very happy that she offered to watch them. Joyce was a very pretty, petite girl with bright blue eyes that twinkled and long dark hair. She had a steady boyfriend, and asked, "Can Richie be here after dinner?" That was fine with me.

Joy made the children dinner, cleaned up, bathed them, and put them to bed every night during the week. She was a tremendous help and even did the laundry for me. She knew I didn't get any support for the children and asked for little money. Her boyfriend, Richie, was very nice too and would bring ice cream or other treats for my children. It was so nice to come home to a clean house, clean children, and no dishes in the sink.

On Saturday mornings the children went to a neighbor's house to play with the children who were close in age. Anne Trapp, the mother, told me, "No, I won't take any money from you. It makes me happy that my children have other children to play with on Saturdays. They all get along so well." Anne would often do nice things for us. She was a thin, petite woman and a bundle of energy. Her children inherited her blonde hair and blue eyes. Every Sunday morning I saw the family leaving the house to go to Sunday school and church.

Anne called my two boys over to her house one Sunday morning after they came home from church. The boys came back home and presented me with a Happy Mother's Day cake and card. I was overwhelmed at this kindness shown to me and cried—because this was my first celebration of Mother's Day. I resolved that we would celebrate every holiday and birthday. I telephoned my mother and surprised her with, "Happy Mother's Day, Mom!" We would not be deprived of this kind of happiness ever again. Spring was beautiful that year and life was good.

Luckily, because I had the Western Electric job, there was enough money to support the children and keep the house, but there were times when it was very difficult to make my paycheck stretch enough to cover all our needs. There were times when I felt overwhelmed, hanging onto my own sanity by a spider's thread. I had a frightening dream about falling into a black, bottomless pit where a spider thread was hanging. Grasping the thread broke my fall.

In the dream, as I looked upward from the pit, there was a bright light beckoning to me. There was no spider seeking to devour me, only a warm, inviting white light. Thoughts of the dream kept bothering me, which was unusual. I always forget my dreams shortly after waking up. I didn't want to fall into that scary black pit of death. I wanted to climb the spider's thread to the white light that was my future. That black pit was the past.

A few months after we moved back to the house, Tim showed up at the door one night and said, "I need some gas and food money to get to a new job in New Jersey." His friend Jack was waiting for him in the car. Furious with him that he would even have the nerve to ask me for money after he had abandoned us and paid no support for the children in an entire year, I told him in no uncertain terms to, "Get lost and stay lost!" Enraged, he forced his way into the house as I was shutting the door. He began twisting my arm and threatened me: "If you don't give me all the money in your wallet, I will move back into the house and you will have to support me until I get a job!"

Taking him by surprise, I scratched his neck and then kicked and pushed him to break free from his grasp. The children began screaming, but I ran to the bedroom, locked the door, and called the police. When I told the policeman what was going on, he asked, "Is there a court order for child support or a restraining order?" There wasn't, so he said, "There is nothing we can do to help you because if his name is on the house, he can legally stay there if he wants to."

Tim was shouting and banging on the door, the children were screaming, and the policeman could hear everything, but said, "There is nothing we can do unless someone is injured." Crying, I told the policeman, "If Tim hurts me or the children I will surely kill him while he sleeps." He replied, "Give him all the money in your wallet, if necessary, to get him out of the house. Then go to the courthouse in the morning to swear out a restraining order and an order for child support. Give them my name and tell them I sent you to ask for a bench warrant. Put his address as unknown. That way, if he comes back again, we will arrest him, put him in jail, and enforce an order for child support. If you find out where he goes to live in New Jersey, call the police where he lives and tell them you have a bench warrant to have him arrested. Then call us, and we will make sure it is sent to them. He will be put in jail and forced to pay child support."

Heartbroken that he would take money away from his children, I opened the door and said, "Okay! Okay! I will give you all the money in my wallet if you go away and promise not to come back here again!" He never even looked at the children as he grabbed my wallet from my hand, emptied the wallet, and stormed out of the house with my money. He was angry that it had taken so long.

I found out later that he had stopped at Louise's house in New Jersey and asked her for money also. He told Louise that he and Jack had a job to go to in New York. She fed them, allowed them to sleep in her living room, and gave Tim some money when he left the next morning. She said, "A few days later, an agent from the Department of Revenue showed up at my house looking for him. Tim used my address and telephone number on a job application for his place of residence, and the agent wanted to question him about a robbery of a government shipment of money that was on a truck Tim was driving." Louise and I did not hear anything from him or about him for the next five years.

Chapter 32

We didn't know where Tim had been for five years of his life, but then discovered he was living in Atlantic City. A friend of my younger brother Lenny saw him there. Lenny called me, and I called the Atlantic City Court House to talk to them about arresting him. "He is probably living somewhere in or near Atlantic City and might be hanging out at the racetrack. There is a bench warrant for him in Pennsylvania. Can you find his address? I will have the police send you the papers." The local police arrested him with the bench warrant they received from Pennsylvania. He began paying child support for the first time, but it didn't last very long. In a few weeks he left for parts unknown again. It wasn't easy for me to love or trust anyone after what I had been through with Tim and the Witnesses, but I needed to make a decent life for my children. I wanted a normal life too, one that didn't include Tim or the Watchtower Society.

In the five years that Tim was missing, I spent the first year working two jobs. We were making it one day at a time and were able to be happy. Life as a Witness had been hectic and scheduled. Meetings rolled around so fast that it was sometimes impossible to study the material before rushing off to the meetings. Now, life was going along on an even keel, and I was trying to stay away from anyone that might tell me to get back to the Kingdom Hall. This was a new life with my children. It felt good to be a strong and independent woman.

I had changed departments at work, and on my first day I noticed a man. He was a handsome, fit, and trim Irish-looking young man with dark, thick wavy hair and warm blue eyes. When I first met Jim, I was sitting at a workstation assembling small transistors for the first Apollo moon landing program. He was the assistant supervisor of the area and would stop to talk to Diane, a woman who sat near me. She was the same age and size as me. We looked similar, except her hair was a milk chocolate brown. My hair had changed from dark blonde to a light brown color. Diane was happily married, and if she could have, she would have zapped every married couple with the same happiness she knew. She introduced me to Jim, who was in the process of getting divorced from his wife.

Diane liked and respected Jim a great deal. She said, "It makes me angry that some of the promiscuous gals in this department are always trying to seduce him. They know his wife is seeing other men, and they want to date him just so they talk about him. I hope he doesn't go out with any of them." Diane remarked, "Jim is the right man for you." I just laughed at her.

His father, Patrick, had come directly from Ireland and married Veronica, a typical Pennsylvania Dutch farm girl. The marriage was volatile, and Jim was the only child. He had been baptized as an infant and raised Catholic for a few years, but stopped going to church when his parents separated. He was eight or nine years old at the time. His family, aunts, uncles, and cousins had stopped going to church because of alcohol and abuse problems. His mother was angry with the Catholic Church because she didn't agree with its position on divorce. When Jim graduated from high school, he joined the Air Force and was stationed in Washington, DC, where he worked at the Pentagon as a personnel specialist.

After the Air Force, he took a job at Western Electric and began going to night school at Muhlenberg College. He met Judy, and they married the next year. Jim, who did not drink, expected and hoped to have a more peaceful marriage than his parents had, but after only three years, his wife Judy was very discontented and wanted to be single again. She began frequenting bars and dating other men. She would have preferred that Jim remain in the house and be her financial support, but he did not want that kind of a marriage. They separated, and Judy filed for a divorce. Immediately after the divorce, she married an older man who could give her more financial security, and they moved to Boston.

One Friday night after work, Diane said, "Some of the people in our department are going out for sandwiches and drinks to celebrate our big bonus for the month. Go along with us, we will make sure you get a ride home." Diane was secretly acting as Cupid; she arranged for me to be seated between Jim and his friend George from the next department. I didn't quite realize what she was doing, and neither did Jim, but it turned out well, and Diane was pleased. She asked Jim if he could drive me home, and later he asked me to go out to dinner Saturday night.

Our first date was at Volpe's Lounge on Tilghman Street. It was a nice romantic little restaurant and bar in those days. I had no intention of getting serious with Jim, but the following week he met my children when we went to the company picnic. We had a great day. They liked him immediately, and he liked them.

Jim was very easy to get along with because of his kind, generous nature. The next time Jim came to our house to take all of us to a drive-in movie, my daughter Lisa asked him to marry us. We thought that was cute, but we needed more time to know and trust each other. Everything we did that summer was centered around the children and providing for their needs. Jim enjoyed swimming, playing tennis, and miniature golf with the children.

He introduced us to his mother, Vicki, and his stepfather, Reds. They spent a great deal of time getting to know my children. Vicki was working part-time and would come by my house at least once a week to see us. She was about five foot three inches tall and heavyset, with short curly hair that was turning gray. She had glasses with gold frames and usually wore dresses with a large print. Reds was the same height as Vicki and was always smiling and happy. His hair, of course, was red. Actually it was more of a strawberry blond color that was turning white. They were very accepting of the children and me. They treated us well and were very happy to see us with Jim.

I divorced Tim on grounds of abandonment. Since no one knew where Tim was at that time, an ad was put in the newspaper for several weeks. It said that legal action was being taken against him. Tim never responded, and the divorce went through uncontested.

There was a work slowdown in electronics and I was put on unemployment. My check was not meeting our needs, so I took a job in a silkscreen shirt company. I enjoyed the work and the people I worked with. Silk screening is such a pleasant and happy art medium. It is partway between handmade and mass production.

Silk screening requires a different screen for every color on the shirt. The screen is placed on the shirt, and a squeegee is used to apply one color of ink. The screen is removed, and the second screen is placed on the shirt, and then a second color of ink is applied with another squeegee. We often had five colors for one shirt. I enjoyed working there even though it was less money than at the electronics company.

In the colder weather, Jim liked to watch football games with my boys and always provided the snacks and sodas. He bought the children sleds for Christmas, but gave them on Christmas Eve because it was snowing. He took them sledding that Christmas Eve on the dead-end road off of my driveway while I stayed in the house and kept warm. Things had escalated quickly from my daughter's proposal of marriage, and we began planning a future together. Jim was very easy to love.

We were married the day before Mother's Day in a wedding chapel by a justice of the peace and had a small family reception at the lovely country home of Jim's cousin Fran. We had a daughter, Kerin, in March 1967. I wanted to name her Patricia. Jim wanted to name her Erin, so we compromised on Karen, only Jim wanted to spell it Kerin and pronounce it as care-in. He still managed to get "erin" in her name. He is proud to be half Irish, and Kerin was the sweetest little baby. She has dark brown eyes and resembles me, just as Lisa does. When we were out to lunch one time, the waitress remarked, "Wow! The apples did not fall far from the tree," meaning we looked so much alike.

Two of the Jehovah's Witness brothers came by our house one Saturday to see me. They started asking questions about the divorce from Tim and my new marriage to Jim, to determine if I had broken any of the Witness rules regarding these matters. I knew I had broken many of the Witness rules, and I was furious with them for even asking me any questions. They were investigating me years after I left them.

Where were they when I had been abandoned and was struggling to put food on the table for my children? Did they care about the years when I was living alone and supporting three children by myself? How dare they question me about my life when I had not been attending meetings in several years and had no intention of ever going inside a Kingdom Hall again? I didn't want to be a Jehovah's Witness anymore!

I broke many of their rules and didn't care anything about those rules. I told them that my life was none of their business, and they should not bother me again. That was the last time those so-called brothers showed up at my door. I had just willingly disfellowshipped myself.

Jim and I enjoyed celebrating all of the holidays with the children, and I registered to vote in political elections. I had discussed the dynamics of my Jehovah's Witness family with Jim, and he understood the need for some secrecy. I had a new and happier life, but didn't want to totally alienate my Witness family from us, especially my three sisters, so we didn't tell them anything that we did.

My sisters barely tolerated being in the same room with me after I had disfellowshipped myself. Mom always accepted me with open arms; she was a warm and loving mother. When we went to visit her, my father would ignore me and start preaching to Jim so he could count time on his service report. The other Witnesses in the family were cold like Dad and only spoke to me if they absolutely needed to, because that is what they were taught to do.

They believed that giving me the cold shoulder was showing me love, and it would get me back to the Kingdom Hall so I could be in the family again. It was simply intimidation. They told me to come back to the Kingdom Hall before it was too late. The new Armageddon prediction was for 1975. They said, "You are killing your children because they will die with you at Armageddon." I was upset with them and didn't want to be around that kind of talk.

Jim transferred to a new job location in the next county. It was a big step for us to take, but I knew that I could trust him to do what was best for us. When Jim and I were preparing to move, we were surprised to find that housing was so much more expensive in Montgomery County. We decided to rent for a year until we found a house that we wanted and could afford to purchase.

Chapter 33

Moving an hour away and a county away from my family changed my entire life. I felt a new freedom that I had never known before. It was like getting out of bondage—like invisible chains had been broken from my body. This began a completely new chapter of my life.

Jim and I watched with amazement when the Apollo 11 landed on the moon in 1969, and the first man walked on the moon. We were actually watching Commander Neil Armstrong stepping onto the surface of the moon. It is estimated that one-half billion people around the world watched this important event on television. Armstrong planted the American flag on the moon. The watching world heard Commander Armstrong say those now-famous words, *"That's one small step for man; one giant leap for mankind."*

We felt proud of the little effort we had contributed to working on the space program. To our surprise, the electronics company mailed Jim a thin plastic record with the recording of the astronauts speaking with the space center. It was historical. It seemed that life was speeding by.

Changing counties changed our lives in many ways. It always surprised us when we received small kindnesses from others. A gift of a cake or some cookies was usually accompanied by a church bulletin. We had good neighbors and they made us feel very welcomed to the area. Our life was happy.

When Jim and I compared our lives and our backgrounds, we were amazed at the differences in the way we were raised religiously. Neither one of us wanted to be what we were raised to be by our families. We agreed that we both believed in God, but after that we didn't really know how to define what we believed and what we didn't believe.

Now we were openly and joyfully celebrating the birthdays of the children instead of doing it secretly and quietly. We had big parties and cakes; we bought many presents and sang with their new friends. Before the Christmas season I boldly and happily decorated the entire house. My Witness family never came to visit us, so they would not know about our celebrating Christmas. Jim bought a large evergreen tree at the local nursery. It was a big thrill to buy new tree ornaments. We purchased and wrapped many gifts, sang Christmas carols, sent cards to friends, and played holiday music.

I found the address for my childhood neighbors and friends, the Herb family, and sent them a Christmas card with a letter expressing my appreciation for all they had done for me. I told them, "I left Jehovah's Witnesses and moved an hour away." Responding immediately, Catherine and Mary sent me a card, with a letter from Catherine telling me, "We are so happy you left the Witnesses. Mary and I never married, and we are still living with our parents. I work and Mary stays home to take care of our mother and father. They are not in good health." It felt so good to establish contact with this wonderful family again. She wrote, "We still love you, and you are welcome to visit us anytime." We continued sending cards and writing letters. They lived quite a distance away, so it was hard to visit. We exchanged phone numbers and eventually I did visit them several times. I didn't have any Witness friends anymore.

I felt that it didn't matter what Watchtower rules I broke because we were all going to die at Armageddon before or else in the year 1975 anyway. If we only had a few years left, then we would enjoy life and live normally and happily until the world ended. There was one problem though—I could not enjoy my own birthday, and I would get very depressed.

After trying and failing to give me a happy birthday, Jim concluded that there was something deeply wrong with me when it came to that day. He asked, "Why can't you just relax and enjoy your own birthday the same way you enjoy others?" I began telling him how awful it was to think of my childhood and how terrible it was that my mother was beaten for trying to bake a secret birthday cake for me. "I don't deserve a happy birthday," I said. The floodgate finally burst open. All the guilt that I was holding within myself broke free in a torrent of tears.

Sobbing, I told him about that day so long ago in my mother's kitchen. I had never talked about it with anyone before. Jim held me in his arms and comforted me; he said that my mother would have been beaten that day even if it had not been my birthday. He helped me to understand that Mom had not been beaten because of my cake but because my father was drunk and wanted to find an excuse to beat my mother.

Jim's father was an alcoholic too, so he understood what it was like for me. He told me about the time he saw his father chasing his mother around the house with a large butcher knife, trying to kill her for no reason. Fortunately, he was so drunk he couldn't catch her. His father's drinking is why they left him, and then she left the church when the priest told her she should not get divorced. She wanted to get on with her life and find someone to spend it with.

Knowing that the beating my mother took that day really wasn't my fault meant so much to me. I experienced a feeling of deep healing in my life. I finally stopped blaming myself and put the blame where it belonged: on my father and his alcoholism. After that, I really learned to enjoy my own birthdays, as well as other things that I had not been allowed to do or enjoy.

While living in our rental house, a Vacation Bible School was starting at a nearby Mennonite church, and the boys asked if they could attend. At first I said, "No, you might need to be a member of the church to join the Bible School." My sons brought a few neighborhood boys home who said they went every year even though they weren't members. Since, in my mind, we were all going to die at

Armageddon anyway when it finally came, I signed the registration permission forms for them to take back to the church.

My sons went every day for a week with their neighbor friends and brought many papers and crafts home with them. I glanced over the papers and saw that they were all about Jesus. I wondered, "What is wrong with this church? Why aren't they teaching the children anything about Jehovah God?"

The summer seemed to speed by, and we enjoyed a Labor Day picnic with neighbors. In September, shortly after the boys started school, they came home asking if they could join Cub Scouts. I remembered what it was like for me when the girls in elementary school asked me to join the Brownie troop of Girl Scouts. It sounded exciting and like so much fun, but my mother told me that my father would not allow me to do that because the Brownies met in a church. He hated the churches because of the three-headed God, so I could not join Brownies. Now, I remembered how sad I was each time I saw the other girls in Brownie dresses going to the church after school.

Looking into the happy faces of my two sons who were so excited about Cub Scouts, I told them they could join. "Why not," I thought, "we are all going to die at Armageddon anyway, so it makes no difference what they enjoy." A few days later the leader of the den mothers, Mrs. Haines, called me. She told me where I could buy scout uniforms for the boys and said, "We don't have enough den mothers for all the boys; would you help by having a den at your house? Your younger son would be one of your Cub Scouts, and your older son would be with the older group. You would need to collect materials for crafts, supply refreshments, have a flag for them to salute, follow the leader's book of instructions, and maybe take them on an occasional field trip."

This excited me! Wow! I would be part of a scout group! It would make up for not being allowed to be a Brownie twenty-five years ago! I was very happy to say, "Yes!" to Mrs. Haines and thought to myself, "Why not teach a Cub Scout den? I always wanted to be a teacher." She was thrilled that I accepted her offer and came by the house with all kinds of information, supplies, and suggestions for me to use each week. She was a very motherly, friendly person. When she told me, "Occasionally, you need to attend an evening meeting at the church with all the other scout dens," my heart started racing because I had not thought about going to a church. I thought, *The roof might fall in on me, or Armageddon will start.*

The old fears from long ago began to creep up on me, and I asked, "Why do we need to go to a church meeting? There is a scout cabin nearby and I have seen the scouts meet there." Mrs. Haines explained, "It isn't really a church meeting we are attending. It is a scout meeting for all of the dens to get together at one time. Everyone goes in the side door of the church and down the steps to meet in the large social room. The scoutmaster, Sam Danryple, conducts the meeting, which includes a short discussion or film, games, and refreshments. We also have the awards ceremony there when the boys earn their patches and pins." It sounded quite harmless, so I agreed to be at the meetings.

My desire to be with the scouts was stronger than the old fears. It is so strange that after leaving cults, some bondage is still present for many years, and the old fears that were instilled in a child could still cause fear in the heart of an adult. I didn't want to fear normal things anymore. I wanted and tried to leave all that baggage behind, but I was having a problem even thinking about entering any churches.

Chapter 34

The scoutmaster, Sam Danryple, was very good with the boys. He was a little pudgy, with brown eyes and thinning brown hair. He had a healthy appetite for camping and cooking, two good things for a scoutmaster to enjoy. Mrs. Haines introduced us, and he asked me, "Have you found a church home yet?" I replied, "No, we're not really looking for one." Sam came by the house one evening with a businessman friend of his named Frank Roberts.

Frank was like a carbon copy of Sam, and he asked, "Aren't you attending any church with the children?" Jim and I told him, "We don't attend any church, but we do believe in God." He asked, "Do you know God?" That question dumbfounded us. "Know him?" we asked. "What do you mean?" He said, "Do you know, the Father, the Son, and the Holy Spirit?" We just stared at him, so he asked, "Do you have a personal relationship with Jesus?" We didn't know what he was talking about. He read some scriptures from his Bible and told us that we "needed to be saved." Frank could have been an evangelist.

He said, "Jesus loves you and died for you. Would you like to pray and ask Jesus to enter into your hearts?" Frank wanted us to pray with him to Jesus and accept him into our hearts right there and then, but this kind of talk was scary to me. It was totally contrary to everything I had learned as a Jehovah's Witness. As a matter of fact, the Witnesses might think these people were demonized, and I had been taught very well to be afraid of Satan and his demons.

I thought, "Only Jehovah is God. Jesus isn't God. Jesus is Michael the Archangel, and the Holy Spirit does not even exist except as God's invisible power, so how can I possibly pray to Jesus? We should only pray to God." I still had the impression that some churches might have a three-headed image of God, and I couldn't get into a god like that. Besides, "If Jesus is Michael the Archangel, I can't pray to an angel, can I?" Frank kept talking.

"Where do you expect to spend eternity?" Frank asked. "In the grave," I answered, "dead as a doornail, sleeping forever." Frank said, "You will either be in heaven or in hell. It is your choice." I looked at Jim and could see he was uncomfortable with this talk because he had been baptized into the Catholic Church and confirmed a long, long time ago. He wasn't sure where he was going.

I told Frank, "I don't believe in hell as a place of fire and suffering, and I don't believe in going to heaven. I will just sleep forever." Frank said, "If you are right, then I don't have anything to worry about, do I? But what if all the Christian churches that teach and believe in heaven and hell are right? What if my beliefs about heaven and hell are right and yours are wrong? Then where will you spend eternity?" I was stunned. I never gave that possibility a thought before. "What if I was wrong and the churches were right? Where would I spend eternity?"

I couldn't bring myself to answer him, so I used an old Jehovah's Witness smokescreen tactic of changing the subject. I began talking about the end of the world. Frank said, "Please don't change the subject!" I smiled. He wasn't going to let me take him off his track of thought. He said, "If you don't mind my asking, what exactly is your religious background?"

I told him, "I was raised a Jehovah's Witness," and his eyes became round as saucers and seemed to bulge out of his head. He almost fell off the chair he was sitting on. He said, "No!" and I replied, "Yes!" Then Frank said, "Jehovah's Witnesses don't let their children join Cub Scouts!" Then I laughed and explained that I did not consider myself to be a Witness anymore.

Frank asked if he could pray for us and we said, "Sure you can." We didn't know he meant right then and there, but he did. We were a bit uncomfortable when Frank wanted us to stand and join hands with him and Sam in a circle. We were so uncomfortable; we did not even remember what Frank was praying, but he was talking to Jesus about us. Frank made me more than a bit nervous because I had never heard anyone pray to Jesus before or ask for things like this. Frank and Sam both told us "We are going to be praying for you and your family," and then they said, "Good night," and left our house.

A few months later, Jim and I bought a house and moved a few miles away. The children needed to change schools and make new friends. Our oldest son, Ron, needed surgery, and I admitted him to North Penn Hospital at Eighth and Broad streets in Lansdale. I felt so helpless because there was nothing I could do to help Ron or make him feel better.

He was having tests done most of the morning. I left for lunch, and upon returning to his hospital room that afternoon, Mr. Danryple was there. He was on his knees next to Ron's bed, holding his hand and fervently praying, "Jesus, protect Ronald from all harm during surgery and the recovery. Heal him completely in body and soul."

Backing away from the doorway, I slowly walked to the window at the end of the short hallway and looked out at the large, gray, stone church across the street. "Mr. Danryple is doing something for Ron that I don't know how to do," I thought. Gazing at the church across the street, I longed in my heart so badly to go over there and ask someone, "Help me to pray," but I didn't think anyone would be there in the middle of the week in the middle of the afternoon. Suppressing the urge to go over to the church, I went back to the room and thanked Sam for praying for Ron.

Realizing what a void I had in my life without a religious faith, I questioned, "Where can I turn when bad things happen? Who can I confide in or talk things over with? My son will come through the surgery just fine, but what about the next time something happens? Who can I depend on for advice? Call Mr. Danryple? Would that be the right thing to do? What do other people do? Do they call a minister or a priest when bad things happen? What can they do about anything?"

I began thinking about prayer. I wasn't sure I knew how to pray outside of the Watchtower rules. I had been ignoring God for so many years—it was almost ten years since my last prayers—but those prayers by the Watchtower rules meant nothing to me. Feeling guilty about my lack of prayer, I remembered how much I had loved the Lord's Prayer in my childhood and began praying it almost every day.

Chapter 35

Our lives settled down after two years of moving, meeting new people, making friends, and joining groups. I took a part-time job when the three older children were in school. My employer sat me near Edna, a small, thin woman who was singing quietly under her breath while she was working. It was almost like humming, but not quite. It was more like talking to oneself. It wasn't anything I could actually hear or understand, and it was getting on my nerves, so I finally asked Edna what she was saying. Edna had large brown eyes on her small, thin face. She was only about five feet tall, and her long hair was pulled back into a French twist. She reminded me of a Mennonite woman for some reason.

"Don't you go to church?" Edna asked. She seemed surprised that I did not know what she was singing. "I sing in the church choir, and I'm trying to memorize all the verses so I don't need to depend on my music sheet. This is a very old and well-known hymn." I told her, "I don't go to church, so I don't know any hymns." A few weeks later Edna invited me to visit her Baptist church. I didn't go, but Edna and I became friends. Other Baptists crossed my path.

At the supermarket one day, I saw a very short, thin, elderly woman with white hair pulled back into a bun and very thick glasses. She was trying to stretch up on her tiptoes and reach something on the top shelf. I stopped and asked the woman if I could help her get the item; she said, "Yes. Thank you." I reached up to the top shelf, and when I was putting the glass jar in her shopping cart, the woman reached into her cable-knitted sweater pocket and said, "Here, let me give you something." "Oh! No!" I replied, backing away from her. "I don't want anything." I thought the dear old woman was pulling a dollar out of her pocket, but it was a small paper pamphlet, called a tract, that said, "Jesus Loves You!"

I accepted the tract and thanked the woman for it; I needed someone to tell me again that Jesus loves me. After I drove back home, I did read the tract, but still could not believe that Jesus died for me. There was a small prayer to ask for salvation on the tract, but it seemed that it was a selfish prayer, the kind that Frank prayed, and the kind that the Witnesses would never think of praying. I wasn't sure what to think.

Then one day, Jim and I met the secretary in the elementary school office. She asked, "Have you found a church home yet?" We said, "No," and she began telling us, "You should visit my Baptist church. We have so many programs for the children to enjoy. It is a wonderful church." It seemed that every time I turned around there was another Baptist or church-going person.

I began to think that everyone in the community had a church except us. Our next-door neighbor invited us to an independent Baptist Church where they belonged, and when I declined, they offered to take the children. My oldest son, Ron, was standing right there, and he said he wanted to go to church with them. He went regularly.

After a few weeks, I felt the need to call his schoolteacher one Monday morning to say that Ron might be talking a little strange at school. I explained, "Ronald came home from the Baptist Church yesterday all happy and very excited. He said he was saved and wanted to be baptized." His teacher just about shouted, "Praise the Lord! That's the best thing in the world that could happen to him!" and I thought, "Oh no! Not another one! These Baptists are everywhere."

Ron told us he was going to be baptized, and he gave us a paper with the date and time. I thought to myself, "It will not hurt to let him go through with this because after all, we will all die at

Armageddon anyway with the rest of the world. What harm could it possibly do if it made him happy?" It was a Sunday evening service, so Jim and I went to see Ron and other people get baptized and watch what was going on. We were not very impressed and decided early in the hour that we didn't think very much of the minister. He would read the Bible and then pound his fist on the podium, and he actually jumped up and down a few times trying to get his point across on what living for Jesus was about. We couldn't wait to get out of there when Ron was finished.

Ron continued to attend this church, but Jim and I wanted nothing to do with going there again. He came home one Sunday and told me the minister said, "If parents love their children they will beat them when they are bad. 'Spare the rod and spoil the child,' is in the Bible." "Fine," I said, "the next time you are bad, go get me a rod, and I'll beat you with it. Okay?" Ron just smiled at me. I smiled back at him.

This was something I could relate to because my father and grandmother practiced the same thing. Ron stopped going to the church regularly after two years, but I knew it had made a big difference in his life. He seemed kinder to others than before.

Chapter 36

About this same time, my dad was going back strongly with Jehovah's Witnesses. Mrs. Ross had died of cancer, and no one could accuse him of anything anymore, so he went back to all the meetings at the Kingdom Hall. Mr. Ross had moved, and my father probably felt like he was free to start preaching to everyone again.

Dad wrote and mailed my children a two-page letter telling them that he cared about them and said, "If your mother has a Bible in the house, you should read the Bible stories about Noah and the Flood, Moses and the Ten Commandments, and Daniel in the Lion's Den." He gave them a brief version of the stories in his letter.

He told them, "You can write to me if you have any questions after reading the stories." The children thought the letter was nice, and they called him on the telephone to thank him for it. The next week he wrote a five-page letter to the children telling them about Noah's Ark, the flood, and how Jehovah God had spared their lives and killed everyone else on the earth.

He told them, "Jehovah's Witnesses are God's modern-day chosen family, and they will be the only ones spared at Armageddon, just like Noah and his family were spared." He wrote, "Everyone else living on the earth will die." He quoted scriptures to them out of context and told them that in the next letter he would explain more about the Bible.

The children brought the letter to me and said, "What kind of a story is this, Mom?" "That's a Jehovah's Witness story," I said, while studying their faces to see what kind of an impact it had on them. They said, "If he sends us another letter like this, we don't want to read it." It was obvious what he was doing, and the children did not like what he wrote.

It probably took him about two hours to write the letter, and he could count that as service time on his report that he turned in at the Kingdom Hall. When the next letter came, the children opened it, saw it was seven pages of the same kind of death and destruction preaching, and threw it away. After a few more weeks of thick letters that were thrown away unopened, I called him and said, "Stop sending letters to my children because they are just throwing them away without opening them. They don't like what you are writing."

Dad was very annoyed to say the least. I said, "You are just using my children to put time on your Jehovah's Witness service record, and I resent that you are using them." He raised his voice, saying, "You better get back to the Kingdom Hall before it is too late because Armageddon will come by 1975, and you will be destroyed with your children. It will be one generation of sixty years after Christ returned in 1914, and he said this generation would not pass away before the end comes." His scolding me meant that he could count the telephone call as service time because he had preached to me. Getting hours on their service record at the Kingdom Hall is of upmost importance to Jehovah's Witnesses.

My father's preaching went in one ear and out the other. I had been told all of my life, "Armageddon is coming at any moment, any day," and I was tired of living in fear of that day of death and destruction for all those that were not pushing the Watchtower magazine. I was tired of being afraid, wanted to wait out the few years left, and then sleep forever. Being normal for a short time was better than spending forever with the Witnesses in the new world. Then I began thinking of what Frank said. I thought, "What if the churches are right? Will my children go to heaven or hell?" I need to pray more.

The Lord's Prayer was something that I could hang on to. It was in the Bible, and it was what Jesus told his followers to pray. At times like this, I was very thankful that Mrs. Fisher had taught me to say the prayer many, many years ago. It felt good to tell my father that my children were not interested in what he said in the letters he wrote. It felt good to tell him that they were thrown in the trash unopened. I did not want him to instill fear in them or to mess with their heads. They had happy and active lives. The Watchtower had no place in our lives.

In Watchtower-land, Mr. Knorr and his fellow leaders encouraged the Witnesses to earn only what they needed to survive until 1975 and the end of the world. Many Witnesses sold their homes and lived off of that money as they went full-time, knocking on doors, trying to convert people to the Watchtower doctrines.

Those people were praised at local weekend assemblies for what they did, but ended up very broke and disillusioned. Some of those people close to retirement had little money left and needed to depend on the goodness of the government to feed and house them. When the end of the world did not happen, some Witnesses were left destitute. Some were suicidal. The Watchtower claimed they were guilt-free because they never asked anyone to sell their houses or use their retirement savings.

Other Witnesses ran up large credit-card balances because they thought they would never need to pay them. They actually charged necessities instead of working forty hours a week. They were knocking on doors full-time, trying to convert people. The false prophecy destroyed some families, both financially and emotionally. Most of them still clung to the organization.

After 1975, many Witnesses who worked for the Watchtower publishing company in Brooklyn for room, board, and a small allowance began to study the Bible together without the Watchtower magazines and books. They were still trying to figure out why Armageddon did not come by the end of 1975. As a result, many of them were ordered to leave Bethel. Others left by their own decision.

They left the Watchtower's Bethel home. They left the Witnesses, and they went back to their hometowns where they told people what they had learned. Their independent study revealed to them that there had been other false promises, and all the end-time dates had proven to be false. Hundreds of thousands of Jehovah's Witnesses began to question the Watchtower. I prayed then and still pray that all Jehovah's Witnesses will be illuminated and set free from this wealthy, controlling publishing company.

Chapter 37

My two sons joined a local baseball team, and believe it or not, Frank Roberts, the scout leader's evangelical friend, was the manager. He came home with the boys after the first practice and said he was happy to find us again. He knew we had moved, but he didn't know where. As it turns out, we now lived only four blocks away from Frank and his family.

He came by our house to see us one evening when we had new friends visiting us; we were playing cards, having some drinks, and smoking. I assumed he might be offended at the scene since he was so religious, but he said he could stay a little while.

I introduced him to our friends, and he began preaching to them about the need to be saved and have a personal relationship with Jesus. They were not interested in what he was saying and began looking at me like, "Who is this guy?" Frank opened his Bible and began to read verses to them. They were obviously uncomfortable with Frank, so I told him, "Frank, I think you should leave because our friends have their own religion, and besides, you interrupted our card game."

Frank put his hands up and said, "Nice to have met you. Sorry I interrupted your card game. I'm leaving." I walked him to the door, and he turned around, waving a finger in my face. He said, "I'm going to ask the Lord to forgive you for what you just did. You stopped me from preaching Jesus to these people."

I was so surprised that, first of all, he would shake his finger in my face like that, and second of all, because he was going to pray for me to be forgiven. I didn't know if I wanted his prayers anymore, but we saw a great deal of Frank over the next two years. He stopped at our house whenever he was in our neighborhood. He kept inviting us to his church and encouraging us to attend any church. He told us, "Make sure you read the book of John in your Bible," but we didn't get around to reading it before he visited us again.

One day Frank asked, "Can I take you on a trip down the Roman's Road in the Bible?" We had never heard of this before and asked, "What do you mean by a trip down Roman's Road?" Frank opened his American Standard Version of the Bible and said there were four important things for us to see, namely:

1. Man is a sinner. Romans 3:10 and Romans 3:23:
   As it is written, There is none righteous, no, not one. and
   For all have sinned, and fall short of the glory of God.
2. Death is the price for sin. Romans 5:12 and Romans 6:23:
   Through one man sin entered into the world and death by sin;
   so death passed upon all men, for all have sinned. and
   For the wages of sin is death.
3. Jesus paid the price for sin on the cross. Romans 5:8:
   God commended his own love toward us, in that, while we were yet
   sinners, Christ died for us.
4. We can be saved by faith in Jesus. Romans 10:13:
   For whosoever shall call upon the name of the Lord shall be saved.

I realized that I was living in some kind of a spiritual void since separating from the Witnesses. Some of these verses were new to my ears. I had never heard of that scripture before that says, "For whosoever calls upon the name of the Lord shall be saved." I wanted to believe that Jesus loved me and died for me like Frank said he did, but it was so hard to shake the teachings of the Watchtower Bible and Tract Society out of my brain.

Each time I read the Bible, it was with the interpretation of the Watchtower in my head. Frank said, "Accept the Bible at face value.

Read it chapter by chapter. Start with the gospel of John and pray." He was about to give up on Jim and I and our family.

In desperation for our souls, he told me, "I have been telling you for at least two years that Jesus loves you and wants to be part of your life. I don't know why you don't want him in your life, but that is your decision. If you ever need someone to talk to, just talk to Jesus about everything. Talk out loud to him as though he is in the same room with you. Jesus said he would hear our prayers and answer them. Is there anything in your life that you would like to change? Ask Jesus to help you with anything you want to change in your life. He is waiting to hear from you."

Chapter 38

Frank made us think about things. We really admired his zeal for Jesus and his intentions to help other people find a place for Jesus in their lives. We liked everything Frank told us about him. I composed a poem of reflection upon my life to that point. I still longed for my attic at times when wanting to be alone or needing to think.

Attic Alone

Attic alone in my childhood state
Attic alone seems to be my fate
Escaping from the people who bring me down
In my heart I would rather be a clown

Attic alone at the Kingdom Hall
Attic alone I answer the call
Working with others who do the same thing
I'm one of many who follow the ring

Attic alone I don't feel great
Attic alone as I graduate
The long promised new world did not appear
The world keeps going on year after year

Attic alone I set a new course
Attic alone I fight the force
Leaving the grip of all those that I know
I sail away now and go with the flow

Attic alone as a young adult
Attic alone with many a doubt
When living becomes a most painful choice
I'm full of despair and my eyes are moist

Attic alone with my children around
Attic alone and I feel so bound
Straining to break the old chains that still bind
I cannot bear to leave my young ones behind

Attic alone with seas of faces
Attic alone in newer places
Transcend to a place where love abounds
The world is my friend and no one frowns

Attic alone with God on my mind
Attic alone I am not quick to find
Answers to life that will give me some peace
I yearn for a love that will never cease

At this point in time, my life was a happy one, but I thought, "Something is missing. What more could I want? Is it personal prayer? It does not come natural to me. What is acceptable prayer and what is not acceptable prayer? The Lord's Prayer is acceptable, but old fears creep up on me from time to time. I am thankful that my children do not have the same fears that I have."

Chapter 39

In November of 1973, I had a chest cold that made me feel miserable. I thought, "Wake up! You know these cigarettes are not doing your health any good, and you have four children who need you." Feeling unable to give them up, what Frank Roberts said came to my mind. He said I could, "talk to Jesus and ask him to change things, ask him for anything." The children were in school all day, so I began to talk to Jesus as though he were in the room with me.

"Jesus, I don't know if you can hear me or not, but our friend Frank told me that you would listen if I talked to you. I'm putting my cigarettes away in a bag where I won't see them anymore. I don't ever want to smoke another cigarette as long as I live, but I'm putting them where I can find them if this doesn't work. I want to believe everything that Frank says about you, and I want to believe that you do love me and care about me, but it is so hard for me to believe because this is totally different from everything I was taught as a child. I want to believe everything Frank read from the Bible about you. If you know and care about everything I do, like Frank says you do, then please, please hear me, and help me to stop smoking. I really do want to believe in you. Are you there, Jesus? Do you care about us? Do you even hear me talking, Jesus?"

It was a new experience for me, and since I thought we were all going to die at Armageddon anyway, it didn't matter what I said or did. This was definitely worth a try, and I thought it would feel strange, maybe kind of crazy to talk to Jesus out loud. However, it was a very good feeling to think that maybe, just maybe, he was out there somewhere and maybe he did hear me. Maybe Frank was right about Jesus.

He seemed to be far, far away up in space. As that first day wore on, I called on Jesus and talked to him and asked him for help every time the urge to smoke a cigarette got stronger, like every half hour or hour of the day. It was difficult for me not to take one of the cigarettes, so I began pleading, "Can you hear me, Jesus? Are you really God, Jesus? If you are God, help me understand, Jesus! I can't do this by myself! If you don't help me, then everything Frank told me about you is a lie! I want to believe you hear me! I want to believe you care about me!" Then I would feel much better for another hour and start pleading again.

I told Jesus, "The children will be home from school soon, and I need to depend on you to help me through the rest of the day without the children or my husband thinking I am going crazy." Some kind of a peaceful feeling came over me that I had never felt before, and I began to pray to him silently in my head almost constantly, interrupted only by the requests and needs of the family.

I went to bed mentally and physically exhausted, thinking, "I might have psyched myself out all day saying those prayers. Jesus, let me know if you really heard my prayers and if you helped me." Then I fell asleep.

The next morning, I noticed my cigarettes and ashtray were not on the kitchen counter. Looking for them, I remembered the bag and putting them away. Now, about to go for the bag, I wondered, "Did I really psych myself out yesterday, or did Jesus really hear me talking to him?" It was time to talk to Jesus again.

Silently I asked, "Jesus, stay close to me all day. Please don't let me take a cigarette." I could hardly wait for Jim and the children to leave that morning because I needed to speak to Jesus out loud, in no uncertain terms. I was right back at square one! I wanted a cigarette.

Pleading all day for his help and mercy, I told him, "I cannot do this by myself. I am sorry for thinking I had psyched myself out yesterday. Lord, if you help me again like you helped me yesterday, I'll believe everything that Frank told me about you! I'll believe that you love me and died for me, that you shed your blood for my sins, for my stinking cigarette habit, for my lack of prayer, for every sin that I have ever committed! Just please, please, help me through this day without a cigarette!"

By the end of that second day, Jesus was not way out there in space anymore like on day one; I began to feel like Jesus was near to me as I walked around the house talking to him. Again, I went to bed exhausted! I fell asleep praying to him for forgiveness for ever thinking I had psyched myself out, and I admitted to him that he was the only one who helped me through the day.

Chapter 40

On day three, my chest cold was gone. I was feeling good and running around the house with lots of energy to clean and do laundry. About lunchtime, while going down the basement steps, a small voice or thought in my head caught my attention when it said, "Hey! Don't you want a cigarette?" How strange is that? Stopping in my tracks, I said, "What is a cigarette?" I couldn't remember what that was! I needed to take a few seconds to think, like when you are trying to remember the name of an old acquaintance or movie star and can't quite dredge it up from the depths of your mind. "Oh! A cigarette! No, I don't want a cigarette!"

Trembling, I turned around on the steps and wondered what to do next as I returned upstairs. "Is that you, Jesus? It is gone, Jesus! I've been flying around this house all morning feeling on top of the world and never even thought of having a cigarette. The desire is gone! Thank you, Jesus! What now, Jesus?"

I cried as I climbed the next set of stairs to my bedroom, thinking everything Frank told me about Jesus was true. I got down on my knees in prayer, thanking Jesus for being there, for being real, for hearing my pleas, for helping me, for loving me, for dying for me. I asked Jesus to dwell with me, change me, and accept me as one of His own.

A tremendous *peace of God, which passes all understanding* (Philippians 4:7, KJV) came upon me; it felt like warm oil being poured on my head, or a blanket of love, starting in my heart, in my chest, and then folding over me. My entire being was flooded with the warmth of that love. I spent the next three hours on my knees in prayer with Jesus, confessing my sins and rejoicing in His forgiveness, without realizing how much time had passed. Suddenly, I heard the children coming home from school. Getting off my knees and going downstairs, I knew that inside, I was a different person.

According to Jehovah's Witnesses, this kind of thing is not real. It is a trick of Satan to deceive people away from Jehovah God. Anyone who feels like a new person in Jesus Christ is considered to be doomed at Armageddon. It is simply unbelievable to Jehovah's Witnesses. They can be disfellowshipped for talking like this. No wonder Gram got so upset with me when I asked her, "What does Jesus save?" Now I knew. I was living on my own terms, not Watchtower terms. I finally found what I was searching for and what I needed. That emptiness in me had been filled. It is an unconditional love that will never, never cease. That empty hole inside me had finally been filled. It was God's love that filled the hole. That love is Jesus.

Chapter 41

One might think that I would be declaring this newfound relationship with Jesus to my family and friends, but I kept it attic alone. This new love in me was so precious, and I wanted to hold it, cherish it, and learn more about His love.

I couldn't get enough of reading the Bible every day, beginning with the gospel of John, and it was as though scales had fallen off my eyes. For the first time, I could read the Bible without the dark-filtering glasses of the Watchtower mind control and Jehovah's Witnesses doctrines.

From reading the book of John, I could see that Jesus is God! Jesus became everything to me! He was the Lord of my life! I had been set free from fear! Like doubting Thomas in the Bible, I recognized Jesus as my Lord and my God!

He is not Michael the Archangel as the Watchtower taught me. He is not only one of many sons of God or many angels. He is not just *a* son of God, He is *the* Son of God; He is God the Son, the only Begotten One. He is Emmanuel, God with man. He is fully human and fully divine.

This was a very personal relationship that I had with Jesus, and I needed to keep it attic alone and protect it from outside influences while enjoying time with Him. Even when people later commended me for not smoking anymore, I kept it a secret, saying a quiet "Thank you, Jesus," inside.

Almost immediately, I needed to be able to explain to myself how Jesus can be God. "How does this work, Lord? How does it make sense?" I asked. While making a cup of tea, I put a teabag in a cup and thought, "Father," poured the water in and thought, "Son," then added the sweetener and thought "Holy Spirit. You're my cup of tea."

I thought, "It is so easy to make one cup of tea with three ingredients. Is God not so powerful that if He chose to, He could separate the three parts of my tea? Could not the Creator of the universe and all the known and unknown do a simple thing like that? Of course He could! He created the universe! He parted the Red Sea!"

I didn't understand how He did it, but I knew He did. I didn't need to know how God could be three entities in one God, the great I Am, the Father, Son, and Holy Spirit, but I know that He is. God said He is the *I Am,* and He is. The Father is the Alpha and Omega and so is the Son the Alpha and Omega.

According to the gospel of John, He was with the Father in the beginning. He created. He is the bread of life, the manna from heaven, the light of the world, the way, the truth, and the life. He receives the same honor as the Father. If we do not honor Jesus, we do not honor the Father. He claims to know all things. Jesus called Himself the "I Am" and said He was one with the Father. He claims to be equal with the Father. That was blasphemy to the Jews, and they wanted to kill Him.

Every day there was a new thing to learn about God the Son. It made me even more anxious to celebrate Christmas that year. He came that we might live.

Chapter 42

The Christmas and New Year holidays followed shortly after this spiritual experience, and that new year of 1974 was very extra special. I was thirty-six years old and had just found out that I didn't need to be afraid of dying at Armageddon anymore. I was totally free from Jehovah's Witnesses, and I was a child of God the Father, the Son, and the Holy Spirit.

I watched all kinds of Christmas religious services on TV and understood almost all of what they were saying. Jim and I watched midnight mass from the Vatican and Dr. Robert Schuller from California. We tuned in to Pat Robertson and Jack Van Impe. I knew I was still a bit fuzzy on knowing the person of the Holy Spirit.

When January came, the children went back to school, and I began working a new job for an electronics company. They sat me next to Rose, an older woman who chain-smoked at her desk. She was very pleasant to talk to and go to lunch with. Rose asked if the smoke bothered me, and I said, "No, as a matter of fact, I just stopped smoking recently." She said, "Maybe you should ask for another desk; I don't want to make you start smoking again. It's a terrible habit, but I can't quit."

I responded, "That's all right; there is nothing that you could do that would ever make me start smoking again." I smiled, thanking Jesus inside my heart. As I got to know Rose better, Rose began to talk about her Lutheran church, and eventually I shared my cigarette story with Rose and told her how I received Jesus as my Savior.

Rose's regular lunch table in the cafeteria was filled with women over fifty, but Rose invited me to join them. Not knowing anyone else in the company, that was fine with me. One woman was sixty, short, stout, and permed, just like my mother. Her name was Violet; she was a recent widow, very quiet, and soft-spoken. Violet lived a few blocks away from me and asked if we could carpool since her car was not always dependable.

The arrangement worked out well. While leaving work one day, she asked, "Would you like to come to church with me Sunday?" Not knowing what church she went to, I inquired, and she answered, "Do you know the big, gray, stone church right across the street from the hospital?" My heart literally jumped into my throat as I remembered that day when my son was in the hospital and I stood at the hospital window, longing to go over to that big, gray, stone church to have someone help me to pray. "Yes! I'll go to church with you Sunday!" I replied.

Violet said she usually went to Sunday school first, so I offered to go with her. In the Sunday school class, it seemed as though everything the teacher said that morning about the Father, Son, and Holy Spirit was preparing me for what was to follow in church. I had never heard such a glorious live choir before or the voices of hundreds of people in the pews singing hymns during the service. Everyone was smiling and friendly.

The pastor was excellent. The sermon that morning was about baptism which, unbeknown to me at the time, was directed toward the young people in the church who had been preparing for accepting Christ as their Savior and following Him; they would be baptized on Easter morning. How appropriate it was for me, being a new child of God. The church was beautiful to me.

Chapter 43

We sat in the back of the sanctuary because Violet always sat near the back in the center aisle during the service. The pastor had explained the importance of being baptized "in the name of the Father, the Son, and the Holy Spirit." When everyone stood to sing the last hymn, the pastor gave an altar call, saying, "If anyone is here who has accepted Jesus as their Savior and wants to follow Him with water baptism, please come forward; or if you want someone to pray with you to help you accept Jesus as your Lord and Savior, please come forward while we sing." Following along in the hymnal, I quietly began to sing the hymn.

> *Amazing grace—how sweet the sound*
> *That saved a wretch like me.*
> *I once was lost, but now am found,*
> *Was blind, but now I see.*

Looking up from the page because the words were pulling on my heartstrings and making my eyes teary, I saw several young people and adults walking up the aisle to the front of the sanctuary. There was also an elderly gentleman using a cane. The pastor and his assistant were greeting them.

I knew how much of a wretch I was for spending thousands of hours knocking on doors with magazines that had a false message and false doctrines. In spite of all that, Jesus blessed me with His presence. I knew that I had not been properly baptized. "What should I do next?" I silently asked. A thought spoke to my mind from Acts 8:37 (KJV): "What doth hinder me to be baptized?"

These were the words of the Ethiopian man running through my mind. The rich Ethiopian man was reading the writings of Isaiah while traveling on the road. When he asked what the meaning of the words were, the disciple Philip immediately responded and explained the words of the scriptures to him about Christ. The Ethiopian man was the first recorded black man converted to Christ and the first African. He was baptized and took the message of Jesus back to Africa where it flourished.

Without really thinking any further about what I was doing, I put the hymnal down on the pew, stepped out into the aisle, and walked toward the front of the church. Gliding might be a better description of my trip down that aisle because I wasn't aware of my feet even taking me there.

I wanted and needed to be baptized in the name of the Father, the Son, and the Holy Spirit. My baptism into Jehovah's Witnesses was not a valid Christian baptism, because I was baptized into Jehovah and a man-ruled publishing organization.

Violet was so surprised when I walked down the aisle that she turned around and said to her friends in the row behind, "Where is she going?" She had no idea what was going on in my life when she invited me to church. Later, Violet said that she had never invited anyone to church before, so she was stunned.

As a recent widow, she was feeling somewhat lonely going to church by herself and had been praying in her heart that someone would go with her. Since I lived so close and we were already carpooling for work, Violet felt a very strong urge to invite me to church. She followed that urge with the invitation that I accepted.

At the altar, the pastor asked me if I wanted to pray and accept the Lord into my life. I told him that I had already accepted Jesus in the privacy of my home after several years and many people witnessing to me about Jesus. "This is the first Sunday morning church service I have ever attended, but I believe the Lord wants me to be baptized, and I think this is where the Lord wants me to be," I said.

I agreed to attend a few classes with the other candidates and the pastor before the baptism on Easter morning. When the congregation was dismissed, Violet came up to me with a look of total disbelief on her face. She asked me what was going on. I told her about accepting Jesus as my Savior a few months before in my home and that I had a special reason for accepting her invitation to this church.

Violet gave me a hug and was so happy that she had brought a new Christian to church that tears of joy were running down her cheeks. On the drive home, I told her about that day with my son Ron in the hospital. I had looked out the window at the big, gray, stone church with a longing in my heart to go over there and find someone to help me pray.

We both were rejoicing about the way God works as Violet dropped me off at my home. I was surprised to see what looked like my father's car parked in the front of the house. "Oh no!" I said to her, "Here I am feeling higher than a kite because of my joy in confessing Jesus as my Lord and Savior, and my Jehovah's Witness father shows up to bring me down!"

Violet offered to come in the house with me, but I turned down the offer because I did not want to expose this sweet lady to my father's violent temper and verbal outbursts. Little did I know that Dad was not able to bring me down because *Greater is He that is in me, than he that is in the world*, (1 John 4:4, KJV) or, in this case, than he that is in the Watchtower Society.

209

Chapter 44

Happy and smiling as I entered the house, Dad smiled back at me and said, "We have only been here a few moments; where have you been, all dressed up?" Still smiling, I replied, "At church!" A feather could have knocked my father over! His head jerked back, and his face changed from a smile to shock, to disgust, to red with anger within the minute. Glaring at me with his fists clenching, he didn't say a word.

I distanced myself from him and walked across the room to Mom. I gave her a kiss and an extra big hug because Mom was smiling at me with so much love and acceptance. Dad excused himself to Jim and left the house.

"Where did he go?" Mom asked when she heard the door slam. Jim replied, "He didn't say where he was going, but he muttered that he'll be back later to pick you up, Mom." Dad was gone several hours, and we all spent that time with Mom. We made dinner, ate together, and the girls had my mother read stories to them. That was a good time for me to get the dishes done and clean up the kitchen before we had some cake and coffee.

When my father came back for Mom, he didn't even look at me. He reeked of alcohol; when they left, I prayed that Jesus would not let any harm come to Mom on the highway because of Dad drinking. I began to wonder why my father would show up at my house on a Sunday morning. He had never done that before. He should have been out knocking on doors with the *Watchtower* magazines. Then I thought of the logical answer.

It was 1974, and the Watchtower prediction for 1975 was getting closer. I realized that Dad probably wanted to warn us how close we were getting to the end of the world, and he was going to hound me to get back to the Kingdom Hall. He was going to go after my husband and children too with his end of the world rhetoric. I knew that if he did that, he could count the whole morning as time on his service report. Instead of getting some service time for his report, he had been foiled by two words: "At church!" I had turned him off course without even trying.

That evening, Jim told me, "Your face was absolutely radiant and glowing when you came home from church. What happened there?" I told him the entire story, starting when I prayed to stop smoking and ending with my trip down the aisle to be baptized. He was somewhat shocked and wasn't sure what to make of all this. He thought maybe I had gone over the edge with everything Frank said. I didn't tell anyone outside of my own family what had happened to me, not even my mother.

The Baptist pastor called me about the prebaptism classes on Saturday mornings then asked if he and his wife could come to the house to meet the family. We welcomed them to our home and had a very nice visit, which ended in prayer and the information for the classes. When I went to church the following Sunday, we had a beautiful sermon on the subject of communion for the benefit of all the people getting baptized. The Last Supper was explained in detail.

The classes took a few weeks and were very interesting. The water of baptism is related to the waters of Creation, of the Flood, and of the Exodus from Egypt. It connects us to the goodness of God's creation and to the grace of God's covenants with Noah and Israel. Jesus offered the gift of living water. Baptism is the sign and seal of God's grace. It washes away sin and gives us a rebirth and the Holy Spirit. The Holy Spirit binds us to the body of Christ.

I longed to receive communion, but I knew I must wait until after I was baptized. It was different from the once-a-year communion served at the memorial service at the Kingdom Hall, where Jehovah's Witnesses passed matzoh crackers and wine to people who are not allowed to take any. Heaven had been closed to me when I was taught that people had to be born before 1935 to take communion. Now, heaven was open to me.

Chapter 45

When I spoke with Mom on the telephone, I did not tell her what was going on at church. If she had asked me any questions, I would have been happy to talk about everything. She seemed only interested in the children and what they were doing in school.

As I was preparing for baptism in the Baptist church, I was so happy to be free from the Watchtower mind control and free from their false doctrines. The classes I took to prepare for baptism were like drinking from the waters of the fountain of life. It was so satisfying to learn true Christian doctrines that normal people believed.

Good Friday arrived, and that service was a memorable one for me. I learned that Passover was a dangerous celebration in Jerusalem. The Romans doubled their guards to keep order, and they could be brutal. They didn't like all that singing of *Hosanna!* when Jesus rode into Jerusalem on a donkey. Jesus made a ruckus when He turned over the money changers' tables. The temple was off limits now. His enemies were there. There was probably fear among Jesus's followers. Jesus had warned them that He would be handed over, betrayed, and put to death, but it didn't seem real to the disciples because they knew He was the Messiah. They saw Him cure the ill, give sight to the blind, and raise the dead, but now He seemed deeply distressed.

Luke 22 (KJV) was used in the meditation. At their Passover meal, Jesus spoke about giving His body for them and His blood being poured out. They drank wine and were tired, but followed Jesus into the garden. He asked His closest friends to stay awake with Him for one hour when He prayed in the garden—and instead, they all fell asleep. Sadly, He asked them, *Could you not stay awake with me for one hour?* Imagine beads of blood on His brow falling to the ground. In verses 42 to 44, He called, *Father, if You are willing, take this cup from me; yet not my will, but Yours be done. An angel from heaven appeared to Him and strengthened Him. And being in anguish, He prayed more earnestly, and His sweat was like drops of blood falling to the ground.* Two more times He called to His apostles and they were sleeping. The third time, He told them to "get up" because the betrayer was coming. He knew what to expect. Judas came to betray Him with a kiss.

He would be betrayed, accused, arrested, abandoned, beaten, and bloodied. He was tried and sentenced to death. He was stripped, mocked, and crowned with thorns before He was nailed to a cross with large nails through His hands and feet. He suffered unspeakably as He bore all the sins of man on the cross. Even for those who crucified Him, He said, "Father, forgive them, for they do not know what they do." And to the criminal who turned toward Jesus, He said, "Today you will be with me in Paradise." Never before had I heard such a heartfelt meditation.

My entire being was shaken with the gratitude that I felt for His sacrifice. He was the Lamb of God who shed His blood for my sins. He cried, "Father! Why hast thou forsaken Me?" I came to understand for the first time that Jesus was bearing all the sins of all mankind on His own body, and I wept. With all that sin on Him, He felt separated from His Father. Our sins caused Him to suffer like this.

I was baptized at the Easter sunrise service. Jim and the children were ready early to go to church to see my baptism and then later, breakfast would be served in the social hall. It was a gorgeous morning as the sun peeked over the buildings and rays of bright streaming sunlight shone through the stained glass windows on the east side of the church. A woman deaconess that recently met me was asked to stay with me outside the dressing room behind the baptismal pool until it was my turn to be baptized. We sat together, smiling, listening to the story and hymns of the glorious bodily resurrection of Christ.

No one at the church knew me very well except Violet, but everyone was so friendly and kind toward me. They accepted me immediately as a child of God. When I entered the baptismal pool wearing a long white robe, the pastor held my hands and asked if I knew Jesus Christ as my personal Savior and did I want to follow Him in baptism.

"Yes, I do," was my answer to both of these questions. As he said, "I baptize you in the name of the Father, of the Son, and of the Holy Spirit," he immersed me in the water. The pastor put me backward into the water, gently passing my head under the water and lifting me back up.

He gave me a white handkerchief to wipe my eyes and face before escorting me to the exit stairs of the baptismal pool. He said, "God bless you always." What a difference from my first experience of being hastily dunked into Jehovah and his organization. What a glorious resurrection morning!

After the communion plate full of bread squares was passed, a short prayer was said and the words of Jesus were read from the scriptures. *"Take, eat; this is My body."* We ate the bread. This was my first communion. How precious it was. Next, everyone held the tiny cups of grape juice that had been passed through the pews on a polished brass tray. How precious that cup was! I stared into the cup and saw a shining cross looking back at me, as though the contents had caught a light above and it was reflecting crosswise in my little cup.

I thought, "Thank you, Jesus, for the cross," and then, thinking that this would be a great spot to sit in every communion Sunday, I looked up at the high ceiling to see where the light was in relation to my seat, but there wasn't a light fixture that could possibly be reflecting in the tiny cup. I looked back to the cross in the glass, stared in amazement, and didn't take my eyes off of it until I heard the words of Jesus, *"Drink from it, all of you, for this is My blood of the new covenant, which is shed for the remission of sins."*

I tried to repeat the experience again on following communion Sundays by sitting in the same spot, but I was not able to see the cross in the cup again. I took seeing the cross that one time as a gift from God, and I cherish the memory of that day. Everyone welcomed Jim and the children as we enjoyed breakfast in the social hall. They continued to attend church with me.

Jehovah's Witnesses deny that Jesus died on a cross and they deny the bodily resurrection of Christ. Sad to say, they are told that Jehovah probably disintegrated his body into gas and just made it disappear. Some think His body was stolen. Both of these theories have been studied and debunked by leading Bible theologians.

Chapter 46

When Mom called on the afternoon of Easter, one of my children told Mom that they saw me get baptized at the Baptist church. She didn't say anything to me. Mom knew I had been baptized, but still invited me and my family to the cookouts she enjoyed giving in her large flowering yard in the summertime.

Dad was not being friendly. At the last cookout for the summer, he was drinking rather heavily. He began to talk about a news magazine article that showed a long-haired teenager being baptized in a river and the words "Jesus Freaks" emblazoned across the cover.

He began berating the Jesus Freaks, with their love slogans and gospel music. He said, "They are disgusting in Jehovah God's eyes, and they'll find out at Armageddon that their Jesus can't save them and never did. The Devil is in them, not Jesus. We don't have much time left before the end of everything."

Appalled because my father believed that Jesus does not have the power to indwell man, but the Devil does, I said, "Dad, you should be careful what you say about these people. You don't even know them! You don't know what they believe about Jesus."

Not appreciating my comment at all, he bellowed, "I know the Bible, and I know Jehovah God doesn't want us to think that Jesus is God. There is only one God, Jehovah, and He is a jealous God. He said, 'Thou shall have no other gods before me.' You'll find out too when Armageddon starts. It will be too late for you then."

I sighed and tried to keep quiet, but I couldn't sit there and let him say that Jesus is not God. "If you haven't studied what they believe, you don't know what could happen to you. All you need to do is ask Jesus into your heart." Dad almost choked on the beer he was drinking.

With the help of the Holy Spirit, I began to witness to him for Jesus. I thought of the ABCs of salvation.

Admit you are a sinner and ask God's forgiveness.
Believe in Jesus and become a child of God by receiving Christ.
Confess with your mouth that Jesus is Lord.

If thou shalt confess with thy mouth the Lord Jesus, and shalt believe in thine heart that God hath raised Him from the dead, thou shalt be saved. (Romans 10:9, KJV)

At the name of Jesus every knee should bow, of things in heaven, and things in earth, and things under the earth; and that every tongue should confess that Jesus Christ is Lord. (Philippians 2:10–11, KJV)

When they saw Him, they worshipped Him: but some doubted. And Jesus came and spake unto them, saying, All power is given unto Me in heaven and in earth. (Matthew 28:17–18, KJV)

I asked, "How much power is *all* power? Jesus has it all!" I never could have done this without the Holy Spirit giving me the scriptures. I never experienced anything like this before because my memorization skills are not that good. My father sat there absolutely rigid as I spoke. He turned about a dozen shades of red and purple before I finished all the verses flooding my mind and flowing from my mouth. Then suddenly he bolted off his chaise longue and stalked toward me with his eyes glaring and both his large fists clenched. I gasped a huge intake of air.

Jim was sitting in the chair next to me, and he stood up. I cringed and held my breath in anticipation of a physical confrontation. Dad was more than halfway to me, still glaring and with balled fists, when he suddenly stopped! He made a forty-five degree turn and walked toward the house. We didn't see Dad the rest of the day. I had been spared.

No one said a word! Everyone sat there staring at me. They were stunned that first of all, I had the nerve to argue with Dad like that, especially when he was drinking heavily, and second of all, that I had quoted scriptures to him to refute his argument.

Everyone in the yard was in shock from the encounter that had taken place. It was so quiet. No one said anything for what seemed like a full minute. My three Jehovah's Witness sisters began looking at each other, and their faces were all in agreement. I was disowned. My younger non-Jehovah's Witness brothers and my brother Harry and sister-in-law Gerri were staring at me with their mouths hanging open. They were speechless! They could not believe what had just happened. Neither could I—but I knew the Holy Spirit had just helped me recall those verses from the Bible.

Finally, my mother, God bless her, broke the silence. I looked at Mom. She was standing at the charcoal grill and smiling at me from ear to ear, asking, "Would anyone like another hamburger?" My brother Harry stood up. "I'll have one!" he said and walked over to the grill, followed by Jim and some of the children. One of my younger brothers put music on the radio, and some began talking to others, but no one came near me for a while except my husband and children.

I was silently thanking Jesus for the Holy Spirit and the way He had just helped me, thinking, "I cannot believe what just happened. Those scriptures just tumbled out of my mouth. Thank you, Holy Spirit! I am thankful that somehow, my face is still in one piece. My father and his wrath were turned away from me."

The family members who are Jehovah's Witnesses didn't speak to me again. I went from being barely tolerated as a fallen-away Witness to being totally shunned for being an apostate. I was dead to them. My brothers who had never been baptized as Jehovah's Witnesses recovered from the initial shock. They began talking to me and to my family as though nothing had happened.

When we left Mom's house that day, I knew that my sisters Jean, Millie, Judy, and their families would not want to see or speak to me again. I knew they would get home and immediately contact our older Jehovah's Witness brother and his wife to inform them of what I had done. My other non-Witness brothers and sister-in-law were kind, friendly, and loving to me as they hugged me good-bye and invited me to come visit them soon. Harry whispered in my ear, "I am so proud of you," as he gave me a big hug and kiss. I hugged him tightly and kissed him, saying, "I love you, Harry." Harry said, "I love you too." I think at that moment any leftover rivalry from our childhood vanished. Mom observed this between us and smiled with tears in her eyes. She gave me a big, long hug and rocked me in her arms. She asked, "Are you okay?" and I replied, "I'm fine, Mom." I looked into her eyes and could see that she was very proud of me.

Later that month, I was telling some friends at church about the encounter with my father and how Jim stood up when Dad came at me with his fists clenched. Jim took no credit for turning away Dad's wrath. He claims, "I was not paying attention to what you and your father were talking about. I was watching the girls and then was still hungry, so I stood up to see if there were any more hot dogs and hamburgers on the grill." No matter what his reason was for standing up at that moment, I felt sure that he had been prompted by the Holy Spirit to stand and save me from being pummeled by my Dad.

Then 1975 arrived, the year of Armageddon. Nothing happened. I never heard another word about it from anyone in my family. Nathan Knorr died in 1977, and the next president, Fred Franz, ran the organization until 1992 when he died at age ninety-nine. He was a very thin man with a birdlike face. He had many problems keeping control of the Witnesses. Fred Franz himself had predicted that 1975 was the cutoff date for this old world. His own nephew, Raymond Franz, resigned in disbelief from the organization headquarters in New York. He wrote an expose of the Watchtower called *Crisis of Conscience,* in which he describes the meetings and workings of the leaders who claim to be prophets of God. He had been one of the governing body members. Many people were leaving the Witnesses after the predicted end of the world didn't occur in 1975.

After Ray Franz was disfellowshipped for being an apostate, he wrote a second book called *In Search of Christian Freedom.* No Jehovah's Witnesses are allowed to read his books because they would be disfellowshipped and shunned for reading them. By 1978, most of the remaining Witnesses had accepted the reasoning that the "last generation" would continue for a short time.

Chapter 47

My mother had a heart attack during the winter of 1978 that put her in the hospital for two weeks. There was quite a lot of damage done to her heart, and I prayed fervently, "Lord, don't let her die without knowing you." We only saw her two times while she was in the hospital because of the blizzard of 1978. We lived more than an hour away. People were snowed in for days and large cities were paralyzed. Some people froze to death in their cars before the freeways could be opened.

Mom recovered, but we all knew she was on borrowed time. Her full strength did not come back, and she needed more rest than ever before. She was told not to get too excited about anything. She did well for two years before she suffered another attack. She recovered, but was weaker. In early April that year, she asked my father to drive her up to the coal regions to visit some of the places from her childhood.

She took a camera with her, and the next time we went to see her, Mom sat at the kitchen table with me to show me three of the pictures she had taken. There were (1) the remains of the little wooden Methodist church that she attended as a child, (2) the small stream where she was baptized, and (3) the cemetery where both her mother and father were buried next to each other, with big crosses on their graves.

The pictures brought tears to my eyes, and Mom had tears in her eyes, but I could not bring myself to discuss her salvation with her because my father was in the next room, right around the corner. Not wanting to take the chance that Mom might get very emotional if the floodgates of her soul ever opened up, I just gave Mom the biggest, longest hug that I had ever given her. We hugged and rocked each other, a mother and daughter comforting and loving each other without a word. I was not welcome in the house except for visiting my mother. My father was afraid to get her upset by denying me entrance.

Mom's health became very fragile after another heart attack within the year. That attack put her in the hospital for a longer stay. She told me that an old neighbor couple had come to visit her in the hospital, and Dad got angry because the neighbor man asked if he could pray for Mom. My father made the couple leave and told them not to come back. Then he told the nurses at the nurse's station that Mom could have no visits from neighbors anymore.

I told my pastor that I thought Mom had a personal relationship with Jesus, but needed confirmation from someone else to be sure. He offered to drive to the hospital, an hour north on a busy highway, and visit her. I warned him, "Don't go in the room if my father is there. He will be very nasty to you." Luckily, or as my pastor said, "Providentially, your father never knew I was there to visit your mother and pray with her." He had called me when he returned to the church and said, "Your mother does know Jesus in her heart. He has been with her since she was twelve years old." "Thank you, Pastor!" I cried. "Thank you, Jesus."

Chapter 48

Mom passed away on the seventh day of April 1981, a few days after Jim and I and the children visited her. Dad had her buried as a Jehovah's Witness. It was just awful for me to sit through the funeral service because, true to form, the Witnesses saw this funeral as an opportunity to preach their doctrine for one full hour to those who were not Witnesses and might not listen to them at the doors. The speakers always take advantage of a captive audience. At least fifty of our old neighbors came to her funeral.

I tuned out after a few minutes, but when the Witness brother began to loudly proclaim that, "Her hope is in the promise of a resurrection in the new world after Armageddon," I heard those words clearly and knew what a lie it was. Looking at my four children, they looked back at me and shook their heads, knowing what I was thinking. The children took Mom's passing almost as hard as I did because she was so loving and gentle. We all would miss her very much. My children share the same heavenly hope that my mother had. The same one I have.

A few weeks after the funeral, Jim and I bought some new clearance-priced long-playing record albums at a flea market. While ironing some clothes a few days later, I decided to put some music on the stereo. Among the unopened albums was one with a picture of a small, wooden church, set in a wood, not unlike my mother's church might have looked when it was new. It was called *Church in the Wildwood*. I played it while I was ironing and suddenly realized that I was humming. "Oh, no," I moaned, "I am not a hummer!

"Why am I humming? I never hum! This is not like me! Why is it so familiar? Have I heard this song before?" I was surprised and listened intently to the words and melody as I went back to ironing. *"When the roll is called up yonder, when the roll is called up yonder, oh, when the roll is called up yonder, when the roll is called up yonder, I'll be there!"*

I was humming again and realized that it was one of the songs my mother hummed! Crying and humming at the same time while ironing was too much for me, so I pulled the plug on the iron.

I stopped ironing and just sat down while crying, rejoicing, and humming along with the old gospel songs that I now knew my mother kept in her heart all those years of being abused. There was "The Church in the Wildwood," "Old Rugged Cross," "Abide with Me," and "In the Sweet By and By," all known to my mother and hummed to my siblings and me when we were young children.

I began to play the album every day until I knew all the words. Jim and the children appreciated the album too. It helped them to grow in their faith. I thanked God for that album. I believe the Lord wanted to give me peace and reassurance for the third time that Mom was His. First, it was the photographs Mom took and shared with me. Second, it was the confirmation from my pastor. Third, it was the album. Mom had passed on before all of my four children were baptized, but baptized they were.

Years later I shared this story about Mom with the entire audience at an ex-Jehovah's Witnesses weekend conference at the Blue Mountain Christian Retreat Center. I was pleasantly surprised the next morning by the musically gifted family of five that played piano, guitars, and directed the singing for the attendees. Everyone at the conference enjoyed breakfast in the cafeteria. When we gathered together to begin the first session, the music and singing began. After some peppy music to make sure everyone was awake, they slowed the tempo down and then finished with *Old Rugged Cross*.

When they began playing and singing this old gospel hymn, all in the performing family looked at me. I immediately choked up and had tears of joy and appreciation running down my cheeks. Most of the other people gathered there turned to look at me as they sang, and I was the only person that wasn't singing. I tearfully listened and dabbed at my nose as this impromptu choir of about three hundred ex-Jehovah's Witnesses paid honor to my dear mother with this hymn:

On a hill far away, stood an old rugged cross,
The emblem of suffering and shame;
And I love that old cross where the dearest and best
For a world of lost sinners was slain.

So I'll cherish the old rugged cross,
Till my trophies at last I lay down;
I will cling to that old rugged cross,
And exchange it someday for a crown.

O that old rugged cross, so despised by the world,
Has a wondrous attraction for me;
For the dear Lamb of God left His glory above,
To bear it to dark Calvary.

So I'll cherish the old rugged cross,
Till my trophies at last I lay down;
I will cling to that old rugged cross,
And exchange it someday for a crown.

In that old rugged cross, stained with blood so divine,
A wondrous beauty I see,
For 'twas on that old cross Jesus suffered and died,
To pardon and sanctify me.

So I'll cherish the old rugged cross,
Till my trophies at last I lay down;
I will cling to that old rugged cross,
And exchange it someday for a crown.

> *To the old rugged cross I will ever be true;*
> *Its shame and reproach gladly bear;*
> *Then He'll call me some day to my home far away,*
> *Where His glory forever I'll share.*
>
> *So I'll cherish the old rugged cross,*
> *Till my trophies at last I lay down;*
> *I will cling to that old rugged cross,*
> *And exchange it someday for a crown.*

The death of my mother was a big blow to me, but I knew that she believed in a God of love who would take her to heaven. We were separated, but not forever. I am eternally thankful that my pastor and the Baptist church were there for me and taught me things about life after death that Jehovah's Witnesses refuse to accept from the Bible.

Chapter 49

Contrary to what the Jehovah's Witnesses taught me, the Baptist church explained the immortality of the soul. Death in the Bible means separation, not annihilation or destruction of our soul. When the Bible says, "The soul that sins, it shall die," it is misunderstood by Jehovah's Witnesses, and they deceive many others into thinking their way. They believe the soul is the body, and it ceases to exist when the body dies. Many people in the secular world believe there is nothing after life, and they are easy prey when the Witnesses come knocking on their door.

With this new insight, I could better understand many scriptures that puzzled me about the soul and death. My walk with the Lord was nourished and strengthened through studying the Bible and attending church and group Bible studies every week. I began speaking to Sunday school classes in my church and other churches about how to witness to the Witnesses. Eventually, I began doing seminar work with Honor the Son Ministries of Pottstown. The ministry was founded by a schoolteacher who is married to a Witness. I learned a great deal from this teacher about defending the deity of Christ.

He told me that many Christians have a life verse, a Bible verse that they try to live by. His life verse is John 5:23 (ASV), *That all men should honor the Son, even as they honor the Father. He that honors not the Son, honors not the Father who sent him.*

I prayed about this and asked God to give me a verse, because there were so many that I wanted to pick in the book of John that I could not make a decision. I prayed for God's will in this matter. After praying for His will, He gave me three verses. They were not in the book of John; they were words written by the apostle Paul.

I opened my Bible and my eyes immediately fell upon 1 Thessalonians 5:16–18 (NKJV), *Rejoice always, pray without ceasing, in everything give thanks, for this is the will of God in Christ Jesus for you.* I was thrilled to have these three verses that actually said it was God's will for me in Jesus. Living by those words are difficult. People don't always feel like rejoicing or praying or being thankful. It is in the times when I least feel like living by those words that I really need to put forth the effort to rejoice, pray, and be thankful. The Holy Spirit helps.

As a Jehovah's Witness, I thought the Holy Spirit was God's active force or power. He was a nonentity to me. When a weekend retreat was offered by the Baptist church for the purpose of learning more about the Holy Spirit, I signed up. I had experienced His help, but my mind was still a little fuzzy about the work of this entity. I attended the retreat in the Pocono Mountains.

The leader of the retreat identified and taught about fourteen gifts of the Spirit and nine fruits of the Spirit. "There are more gifts than that," he said, "but our workbooks do not include all of them." A search on the Internet revealed eighteen gifts and seventeen fruits of the Spirit.

The gifts of the Spirit presented to us were prophecy, service, teaching, exhortation, giving, leadership, mercy, wisdom, knowledge, faith, healing, miracles, discernment of spirits, and speaking in tongues. The gifts of the Spirit must be used in order to produce the fruits of the Spirit.

The nine fruits presented to us were: love, joy, peace, longsuffering, gentleness, goodness, faith, meekness, and temperance. After hours of discussion, fun, and meetings, we were given a tri-fold evaluation form that had fourteen sections for the fourteen gifts of the spirit. Each individual chose his or her answers for the many, many questions. The choice of answers to all the questions were: (a) yes,

(b) no, (c) sometimes, (d) most of the time. After a break and some music, we went back to our forms and tallied the questions we answered as *yes*.

By reading those questions again and taking note of the section title, we discovered where our strengths were. We then tallied the questions we marked as *most of the time* and could see patterns developing that revealed our most important gifts to the least gifts. My first gift was somewhat of a tie between service, teaching, and exhortation. A few other gifts straggled behind. Everyone was encouraged to use their gifts to the glory of God and told to pray every day for ways to use their gifts and talents.

All the Baptist friends I made spent many hours doing work for the church and having a good time together. The women had monthly mission workshops, and some of the ladies worked on projects every week. The projects included knitting and crocheting baby blankets, sewing small quilts that were used as lap robes in nursing homes, rolling bandages, making Church World Service kits, and making food to deliver to homeless shelters in Philadelphia.

Our ladies made many kits for Church World Service. CWS is supported by many Christian denominations. Some of us sewed school bags for children in Africa, and others filled them with school supplies. We put together hygiene kits and first aid kits to be sent to disaster areas. Everything was done joyfully with love. No work was forced on anyone.

One of the good friends I made, Kate, was known for her cooking and baking. She was my size, five foot one inch, with brown hair. She smiled a great deal, even when there was not a reason. Kate worked for the school district food services and did private catering. Baptists are well known for serving good food at their banquet dinners, as well as their potluck dinners.

Every January, in the dead of winter, our church had a soup dinner either one night during the week or before the Sunday evening service. All the women would prepare a pot of homemade soup and a dessert to bring to the social hall. The church provided the bread. Jim and I always asked, "Which pot belongs to Kate?" We enjoyed tasting so many different soups that we never made at home. One year Kate made cream of squash soup, and I almost did not take some. It was not the most appealing-looking soup, but the aroma tempted me. It was truly delicious. Her specialty dessert was cheesecake, and we were often blessed with one. Baptists are very social-oriented people.

They are also very mission minded; many members give as much to missions as they give to the local church. Locally, they have community outreaches and give aid to those in need. The national ministries help those across our own country, from the cities to poor mountain regions. The international ministries give to the world. There are many missionaries around the world, doing extraordinary work, that receive support from the churches. They nourish people physically as well as spiritually. One of their philosophies is stated, "If you give a man a fish, you feed him for a day. If you teach a man to fish, you feed him for a lifetime." This is true not only for Baptist churches; other Christian denominations have strong mission programs too.

The churches are very accepting of people and help people when they are down. That is what Jesus did—He healed people physically and spiritually. When we reach out to others, we are doing it for Jesus. When asked about her Catholic mission work, Mother Teresa of Calcutta summed it up by pressing each fingertip on her hand, saying the words of Jesus, "You—did—it—to—Me."

This is taken from Matthew 25:40 (NASV): *The King will answer and say to them, "Truly I say to you, to the extent that you did it to one of these brothers of mine, even the least of them, you did it to me."* On one occasion someone said to her, "Mother, I would not do what you do for a million dollars." She smiled and replied, "Neither would I!" Mother Teresa did it all for the love of Jesus. She saw Jesus in the hungry, the thirsty, the strangers, the naked, the sick, and the imprisoned, because Christ made the correlation Himself when speaking of the sheep and the goats. She said, "When we touch a sick person or a needy person, we are touching the suffering body of Jesus." She is one of the most famous modern-day mission workers.

The Baptist church does all their mission work out of love for Jesus too. Working in missions at the Baptist church was very fulfilling for me. It felt as though I had many sisters and could talk with them about everything. I missed my three sisters that were shunning me, but I had friends that became like sisters.

Chapter 50

My family members who are Jehovah's Witnesses still shunned me except for one time after Mom passed on. My sister Millie was chosen to visit me in the summer of 1982 and conveyed a message from the leaders. "The door is wide open for you to come back to Jehovah's Witnesses because our leaders are granting full pardon to all who left no matter what they did or how much they sinned. There will not be a committee meeting at the Kingdom Hall to ask you any personal questions before they take you back into the Watchtower Society." Millie was smiling and said, "It is for a limited time only, so you will need to act quickly."

"Imagine that!" I said. "A limited-time offer to be fully pardoned and redeemed by the Watchtower! I am absolutely amazed!" Millie thought it would be a tempting offer for me. I could tell by the smile on her face that she expected me to be thrilled with the offer so my family would speak to me again after years of shunning.

"Millie, do you really think I could accept everything the Watchtower tells me to accept, believe everything they tell me to believe, do everything they tell me to do? Do you think I would ever knock on doors with their magazines again? The Witnesses believe that anyone who professes a personal relationship with Jesus is misled by Satan and probably demonized. Yet here you are trying to tell me that I would be automatically pardoned by the organization and welcomed back with open arms?"

I explained to my sister in no uncertain terms, "The Watchtower Society is a mind-controlling cult. Following the writings and dictates of old men in Brooklyn does not lead to salvation! There is only salvation in Jesus, and no one needs a one-hundred-year-old publishing company to tell them if they are approved by God or not."

Millie was shocked that I didn't accept the offer. She sat there quite speechless for a while before coldly telling me, "I must leave now. I'm sorry you won't take the offer and sorry you feel that way." I realized that Millie was sorry because she could not accept me or love me as her sister. I was sorry for my sister because she is so deceived.

When Millie was at the door, she turned to me and said, "We all believe that we will be in the new world before the year 2000, and you and your family will be destroyed by Jehovah. In 1994 it will be eighty years since Jesus returned, and a generation should not be any longer than that." I prayed for my sister after she left.

"I wonder if the *Time* magazine article had anything to do with this unusual development," I said to myself. There was a large article in the February 1982 *Time* magazine about the shake-up at the Watchtower headquarters. *Religion: Witness Under Prosecution* told the story of Raymond Franz, nephew of the Watchtower president and a member of the governing body. The magazine told how he was disfellowshipped for apostasy, for not believing in the Watchtower timetable and dates. Franz and his wife left the Bethel home and moved to Gadsden, Alabama.

It is estimated that one million people left the Watchtower ranks within seven years after the 1975 end of the world failed to happen. The Witnesses insisted they were still growing, thanks to nonstop recruiting. I was told, "Actually, they have eased the requirements for who they consider *active* Witnesses, thereby keeping the numbers high." The end of this old system of things must still occur during the lifetime of people who were alive in 1914 when they say Jesus came again invisibly but only their leaders saw Him with their eyes of understanding. With the rapidly shrinking oldsters, the Witnesses will need to come up with another plan to keep this wealthy multibillion-dollar publishing company afloat.

It was and still is difficult for me to understand how my sisters can continue to trust in and believe in Jehovah's Witnesses and the Watchtower. My grandmother's generation expected to see Armageddon, and they didn't. My father's generation expected to live through Armageddon, and now they are gone. My brother and sisters expected to see Armageddon and be in a new world by 1975, and now our generation is dying off. They all expected my family and me to be dead. It seems that they have been waiting half of their lives for me to be destroyed. They have been shunning me for half of my life, for thirty-six years.

Don't they realize that Jesus never shunned anyone? He ate with a hated tax collector and healed a prostitute of demons. Peter denied Him three times, and all of His followers ran away from Him after He was arrested. Jesus never shunned them. Jesus appeared to them after His resurrection. He had already forgiven them all of their sins and shortcomings.

I often pray for my brothers and sisters to know the same God that I know—a God who loves unconditionally and sent His only begotten Son, Jesus, to bear our sins on the cross. I turn to Him when I think of my sisters. I miss them and wonder if they still miss me.

Chapter 51

Nineteen eighty-three was not a good year for me because I had major cancer surgery, and neither my father nor my Witness brother and sisters called me or sent me a get-well card. My other brothers and their families sent cards and came to visit me. I appreciate them very much. They were very loving toward me.

I was already dead to the Witnesses, but still I wrote a letter to my three sisters to tell them that I loved them and they were in a high-risk group for this kind of cancer. They needed to inform their doctors that it occurred in one their sisters. There was no response. It is very possible that they never read the letters. It is possible that the letters went out with the trash, unopened.

When there was no reply from my sisters or even a card, it hurt. However, I knew how to take my pain and suffering to the Lord in my prayers. As I cried to God, He comforted me. I could feel His arms around me—I felt as though I was being held on His lap. He was large, and I was little, like a little girl being loved and comforted by her Father—love and comfort I had never known from my earthly father. I cried, "Abba, Father—thank you. Thank you for holding me." I know I have a heavenly Father who loves me.

It was time for me to forgive my family immediately and completely. They were trapped in a belief system that has little compassion for anyone on the outside. I knew that harboring bad feelings toward them was the wrong thing to do and was not in

God's will for me. I let go of them completely and since then I feel healed.

I read a book in 1985 called *Unconditional Love,* by John Powell. It had a great impact on me. *Conditional love* is not love at all, but a way of controlling another person. Conditional love is love with limits: I will love you if you do this or do that. It can cause great damage to the person being controlled.

Unconditional love is different. Unconditional love wants what is best for the other person and also does what is best for the other person. It has no strings attached. The book helped me to see that unconditional love never asks another person to be a doormat or to be a blind follower who will obey any command. Unconditional love does not shun or hurt the other person. This is the love that Jesus showed.

My mother always showed unconditional love to me; but my father, grandmother, one brother, three sisters, and Jehovah's Witnesses never did. Their love was always conditional and had many strings attached. Even if I sent this book about love to my sisters, they would not be allowed to read it—it was written by a Catholic priest.

Powell, in his eighties, is now retired in Michigan. He worked as a professor of theology at Loyola University from 1965 until his retirement in 1996. During that time, he held spiritual retreats and wrote popular books. After his retirement, he was accused of sexually assaulting five girls in the 1960s and 1970s. He has never been charged with a crime, but acknowledged there was some abuse and agreed to a settlement. It is truly unfortunate that a priest who helped so many people should have injured any young girl. We all sin and need forgiveness.

Mahatma Gandhi said, "If we practice an eye for an eye and a tooth for a tooth, soon the whole world will be blind and toothless." How true. Forgiveness does not come easy for most of us. We don't naturally overflow with mercy, grace, and forgiveness when we've been wronged.

In 1996, Jim's ex-wife was diagnosed with cancer. She had divorced her second husband and was living in Oklahoma near her sister and family. After two years of treatment, she passed away. Shortly after that, I was told that my ex-husband had passed away in the state of Wyoming. Someone in the family had found his obituary on the Internet. He had disappeared again; his sister had no idea where he was for the last ten years of his life.

How thankful I am that my life is on the road I traveled. I had escaped and found great freedom. My children, though touched by some of the negativity of the Witnesses, embraced Christianity.

My oldest son, Ron, was married in the Baptist Church and, within ten years, became the father of three sons named Ronald, Matthew, and Christopher. Unfortunately, his marriage ended in divorce after twelve years, but he fought for joint custody, and we were a continuous presence in the lives of the grandsons. Ron is a trade-school graduate and works in his chosen field as a plumbing technician and field-service technician for the world's largest water purification company. He has worked for the same company since he was eighteen as the company changed hands several times, growing from a regional business to a national company and then to an international corporation.

My son Jim married in the Lutheran church to our sweet daughter-in-law, Nancy. They have been happy for twenty-five years and counting. Even though they were not blessed with a pregnancy, their love for children prompted them to become foster parents, and Nancy became a stay-at-home mom. She is a trained physical therapist technician so they were assigned children needing physical therapy. She and Jim also took special needs and emergency care children into their home, some for a short term until a more permanent foster home was available. Additionally, they were trained for taking care of children with MS and AIDS. Jim and Nancy were among the first foster parents to care for AIDS babies.

One morning they were asked to take a boy, a few weeks old, from the hospital. The child required closely monitored medication for a rare liver ailment, and the mother was not able to properly care for the child. Curtis was a most precious baby, and now that he is a young adult and graduated from high school, he is still precious.

Jim and Nancy fought to adopt Curtis as well as another baby boy that was placed in their home when a week old. They received the abandoned infant at the hospital and came to see me. The baby was wearing a pink blanket and I immediately assumed it was a little girl. I wanted a granddaughter so badly; I was so happy! Then they told me that the hospital ran out of blue blankets—it was a boy! I thought they were teasing me, but they weren't. We welcomed Stephon as our fifth grandson into the family immediately. His legal adoption took three years.

Our son Jim, with a partner, is owner and operator of an auto repair and transmission repair garage in Hatfield. He graduated from trade school also and continues to take classes as new technology develops. They purchased a large building that they renovated, using half of the building for their garage and the other half for a rental office and a small warehouse. The business flourished quickly, and with the additional rental income, it has been a financial success. They transformed a neglected eyesore into an attractive, landscaped business property.

Day after day I am thankful that I left Jehovah's Witnesses. My children escaped the bondage that I was raised with, and they are well-adjusted and successful people.

Back in 1985 when my daughters Lisa and Kerin were in college, I had my first computer and subscribed to the Internet service called Prodigy. I discovered a few Jehovah's Witnesses were also getting on the Internet even though the Watchtower had warned them against doing that. They were discovering the shameful history of the Watchtower, because when they searched the Internet for Jehovah's Witness, they found many ministries that exposed the organization. The Internet has helped many people to leave the Watchtower Society.

On bulletin boards, I met women who had recently left the Watchtower Society, and this helped me to keep up-to-date with what was happening and changing. There were many good Christian ministries that were forming on the Internet; they have a big impact on helping Jehovah's Witnesses to be set free of false doctrines.

A few years later when I switched to another provider, I discovered the chat rooms were a ministry. I could enter a chat room where religion discussions were often hot and heavy between Christians and Jehovah's Witnesses. I spent many hours in discussion with Jehovah's Witnesses even though I told them I had disfellowshipped myself. They were willing to read my comments because no one at the Kingdom Hall could spy on them. They were very brave souls who were seeking answers to questions about the Bible that contradicted the Watchtower teachings. I pray that I planted many seeds along the way.

I offered them my friendship, because no one understands an ex-Jehovah's Witness like another ex-Jehovah's Witness. Many of them live in fear of the future and suffer from post-traumatic stress disorder (PTSD). It is an anxiety disorder that often develops when people are afraid of physical harm or death from terrible events such as natural disasters and wars. They have similar health problems caused by stress and feel limited in their abilities and choices.

Some women that I met on the Internet did not finish high school before 1975 because they were pressured to quit and spend a hundred hours a month knocking on doors and pushing the Watchtower magazines. Many of their problems are related to low self-esteem and a lack of education.

Chapter 52

In 1986, I began working in a Baptist church office. While composing announcements and short articles for the monthly newsletter, I began to think that I should write a book for my children about the Jehovah's Witness experiences that I often shared with Baptist friends. In my spare time I began to record my life, because my sons and daughters often asked questions and wanted to know what it was like to be part of a Jehovah's Witness family. It was difficult for me to dredge up many of the memories and put them into words for my children.

I discovered that it was easier to write about my life than it was to talk about my life and often sat at my computer keyboard, crying as my fingers recorded my experiences. How often I wished that I knew more about my dear mother's life. I was forty when my mother passed on. It was a pity that I had been so busy raising my own family that I neglected to know more about Mom's life. Mom was probably afraid to reveal her Methodist faith to anyone because my father would have opposed her in his typical violent manner. It felt so good to totally release my old hurts and pains. I experienced a great amount of healing in my soul.

My daughters were still in college in 1988, and they began to believe that I really had survived cancer after five years without a recurrence. They asked, "Is there anything that you always wanted to do and never did?" My daughters were thinking I might like to climb a mountain or celebrate my survival by taking a trip to Hawaii, Europe, or the Holy Land.

"Yes," I said, "I always wanted to go to college." They, as students, were somewhat surprised that college was number one on my list, but they said, "Go to community college. Take a few classes and see how you like it."

They encouraged me to visit the college and speak to a counselor, so I did. The counselor was a tall, thin, and attractive woman with a great smile that showed perfect teeth. She made me feel very comfortable after my initial nervousness about the appointment. After looking at the selection of courses, I said, "I want so many of them." She remarked, "Maybe you should be a full-time student. Do you want to take courses just for fun, or do you have a specific goal in mind?" I said, "I am taking this very seriously, because I was not allowed to go to college when I was young." She suggested, "Take the business courses, because you have some computer and office experience."

The thought of being a full-time business student thrilled me. "Yes, why not full-time?" The counselor encouraged me to take the preadmission test. She was very happy that I considered her suggestion and gave me an example of how my courses could be arranged. She also recommended, "Go to the visual aid department of the library and ask for some preadmission aids. Acquaint yourself with the ones that will prepare you for the exam." I took her advice and found that the English essay structure aid was especially helpful.

I didn't know how good a grade I could receive at the age of fifty, but with lots of encouragement from my family, I enrolled. There was little problem with the entrance exam, except algebra. Fortunately, the college has a noncredited Algebra course for students who need help, so I took the classes, and after that, I had no problem with Algebra 101.

Since I was still involved with some Internet websites that had religious interests, it was no surprise that other former Jehovah's Witnesses were being educated. Others who had been denied a higher education in their younger years were enrolling in college and working toward college degrees. I could hear the joy in their email messages.

When I needed to do writing assignments for English 101 and then English 102, I drew upon my life experiences for the assignments. I already had some of them saved on my computer. My professors deeply appreciated reading about my younger years in a Jehovah's Witness family and how it impacted my life. They encouraged me to continue writing.

Writing in college was a healing experience. I looked forward to every class and every writing assignment. The two years went by quickly and I graduated from Montgomery County Community College with a 3.9 average. About the same time, my father-in-law Reds was not feeling well. He said, "I'm just having heartburn from eating too much of mother's good cooking."

Jim's mother, Grammy Vicki, told him, "You need to go to the doctor and get a complete physical exam," but he kept putting it off. Grammy went to the doctor regularly because she was the one that always had health problems, and she was very overweight. Reds had always been very active and just a little on the pudgy side.

One day after putting away groceries, Reds said, "I'm going to lie down and rest a while before dinner." Grammy Vicki said, "I thought he was sleeping too long and wanted to wake him up. I touched him and felt that he was cold. He wouldn't wake up, so I immediately called 911, but it was too late. The EMT could not get any sign of life. He died in his sleep." It was so unexpected for us to get a phone call that he had passed on. We are grateful that he had an easy death, but the shock of it stayed with us for a long time.

Jim and his mother never expected him to be taken so quickly, and she took it very hard. She didn't drive anymore and relied on Reds to do almost everything for her. Jim reassured her that he would spend every weekend with her. His cousin Fran was very close to his mother, like a daughter, and she lived nearby. She said she would help her during the week and buy her groceries. We lived an hour away and were very thankful for Fran.

Our daughters graduated from college and began looking to the future. Lisa graduated with honors and a degree in Computer

Science from Drexel University. While in her senior year, she had a permanent wave put in her long hair that made her hair easier to manage and style. Her graduation pictures were beautiful; one was printed in the *Who's Who Among College Students*. She immediately began working for a consulting firm, and then a large pharmaceutical company hired her.

Kerin, our youngest daughter, graduated with honors from Philadelphia College of Pharmacy and Science with a pharmacy degree. When she was in college her hair became very dark brown like Jim's hair. She always had a natural wave in her long hair and looked beautiful even if she had no time to fuss with having it styled. She could just crunch it up with her hands after washing it, and it would dry extra wavy. She also was hired by a large pharmaceutical company.

Chapter 53

In 1990, I began working as an administrative assistant to the owner of a small specialty company that designed and manufactured test equipment for the glass and plastic industries. Mr. and Mrs. Redner were very nice to me. They were born and lived in Europe before World War II began.

They had escaped from being put into Nazi death camps during the war with Germany. Six million Jews and five million non-Jews died in the Holocaust, for a total of eleven million people. Of the five million non-Jews, three million were mostly Polish Catholics. Two million victims were mostly from other countries including Hungary, Czechoslovakia, Ukraine, Russia, Holland, France, and Germany.

Every European country, even Germany, had those who did not believe in the Nazi ideology. When asked to sign documents of loyalty to the Nazi party, Jehovah Witnesses refused and were forced to wear purple armbands. About ten thousand were imprisoned as "dangerous" traitors. It is estimated that between two thousand and five thousand Witnesses died under the Nazi regime by execution or death camp.

The numbers are small when compared to how many Jews and Christians died, but the Witnesses seek enormous publicity for their members who were faithful to the instructions of the Watchtower. They have a special place in the Holocaust Museum in Washington, DC. What was unique about the Witnesses in the camps is that they were able to get out by signing a paper pledging their support to the Nazi regime. It was a struggle between the Watchtower and the Nazi party.

Lily Redner lost her parents in the Holocaust. She, with her sisters, was hidden by their babysitter's family and then taken to an isolated farm near the border of the country and hidden in a private home. Their life story would make an interesting book all by itself. A Christian minister and his family protected them. Alex Redner and his parents narrowly escaped with their lives and eventually fled to Brazil. After the war, Lily and Alex met while attending college in France. They married and came to America. They are wonderful, well-educated people.

After working in their office during the day, I spent at least two hours every evening having many pleasant conversations on Internet chat rooms and doing emails with women leaving the Watchtower Society. Some of them quickly found their way to churches. One young woman, Jackie, from England, with two young sons, was distraught over the treatment her mother was giving her when she stopped attending the Kingdom Hall meetings regularly. She was twenty-six, the same age I had been when I left the Witnesses.

I could relate to all of her doubts and feelings, so I encouraged Jackie to live her own life for the sake of her children. Her husband wanted the family away from the Witnesses and searched the Internet for the history of the Watchtower. It was difficult for her to believe that she had been so deceived, and she wanted to be free.

I shared my story with Jackie and also shared the good news of Jesus with her. She responded immediately. She prayed and accepted Jesus into her life right there on the Internet. Jackie had a wonderful conversion experience as all the false teachings fled her mind. She immediately went to visit her closest church, which was Anglican, and she enrolled her sons in the preschool. She wanted her sons to be taught about Jesus, not the wrathful Jehovah of the Watchtower.

Jackie grew quickly in her newfound faith and was baptized in the name of the Father, the Son, and the Holy Spirit. She continued to attend church and grow in her faith even though she was being shunned by her Witness family and friends. The next year, she attended a conference of ex-Jehovah's Witnesses in England and spoke about her conversion to hundreds of people. She and her husband have helped many other people leave the Witnesses, right on the Internet.

Most people take a longer time to be free from the Watchtower, and still others cannot be reached, but many seeds are planted. Sometimes those seeds would seem to die or disappear, and then suddenly they would spring to life. Someone else watered and cultivated the seeds.

One young woman named Terri was musically gifted and was looking into New Age types of religion. She became annoyed with others and me for trying to steer her toward Jesus and traditional Christian churches. She said good-bye to us with a bit of an attitude, and then five years later came back on the same Internet group. She was happy that some of us ladies remembered her. She was happy that we were still there.

Terri had experienced a few years of hard times trying to survive in the world of professional musicians, and then, in desperation, she took a job with a professional Christian rock group even though she was not a believer. Her fellow musicians and the music they wrote convicted her heart, and she realized that everything the Internet women had been telling her about Jesus was true. She became a Christian and is now a songwriter. Everyone rejoiced with her.

Another ex-JW woman, Jeri, could not understand for five years how Jesus could be God the Son. She believed He was the Savior that she needed, but she could not grasp the Trinity and thought Jesus was only one of many sons of God. She still believed what the Witnesses taught her, that Jesus was a perfect man who gave His life as a ransom sacrifice in place of Adam, who had sinned against God; a fair exchange, you might say.

It took many hours of prayer and conversing with her before the lightbulb came on over her head, as she described it. She had a wall in her mind that was blocking the evidence, and she could not believe in the Trinity. In spite of that, she wanted to find a church and be a Christian. She didn't know where to go. One day she sat down to prayerfully start reading the Bible from Genesis to Revelation. She read a passage of scripture from the first chapter, Genesis 1:21–25 (KJV):

And God created great whales, and every living creature that moves, which the waters brought forth abundantly, after their kind, and every winged fowl after his kind: and God saw that it was good.

And God blessed them, saying, be fruitful, and multiply, and fill the waters in the seas, and let fowl multiply in the earth.

And the evening and the morning were the fifth day.

And God said, let the earth bring forth the living creature after his kind, cattle, and creeping thing, and beast of the earth after his kind: and it was so.

And God made the beast of the earth after his kind and cattle after their kind and everything that creep upon the earth after his kind: and God saw that it was good.

"Every living thing was created after their kind, after their kind, after their kind," she said to herself. When she understood that each multiplied "after their kind," she paused and thought, "Yes, dogs have dogs, cats have cats, and God has what? Jesus must be God if He is His only begotten Son and there is only one God. God cannot have anything less than Himself." The wall was gone from her mind, and all the evidence my friends and I had been presenting to her over a five-year period began flooding in and became more understandable to her.

After reading the Genesis passage, she immediately believed in God the Son. "The lightbulb over my head went on," she said. She began rejoicing and sharing the good news. The verses that convicted her were ones that my Internet friends and I had never thought of using, but our Lord knew how to convince her. What a happy day! The harvest is His.

Jehovah's Witnesses are discouraged from thinking for themselves because it leads them into other avenues of faith. Many times I have spoken to people who do not know how to cope in the real world when they leave a controlling group. Thanks to the Internet, they can explore and learn new tools for living each day. They can find a large community of believers waiting to help them. When ex-Jehovah's Witnesses find a new faith in Jesus, they might need to be baptized, because the Witness baptism is not a valid Christian baptism.

Chapter 54

In 1992, my father passed away after suffering with cancer for almost a year. I did not attend his Kingdom Hall funeral because he had not spoken to me in almost twenty years. I had forgiven him for being mean and abusive, but I really did not know him anymore. I have no warm or tender memories about him that would draw me to be there. My younger brother and sister-in-law Wanda attended with the Witness family, and when she called me, she said, "There was something very sick about the whole service. It was almost an hour of preaching about the new world. They said very little about your father."

I explained, "That is a typical Witness burial service. They believe that even though his soul died, he is in God's memory because he had faithfully gone knocking on doors with the Watchtower magazines as long as he could walk." Wanda said, "Yes, he was called faithful to Jehovah, and he will be reconstructed and brought back to life on the new earth after Armageddon."

I could not help but wonder if my father had been as disappointed as my grandmother had been that Armageddon had not come before he died. Witnesses wait for it all of their lives and never expect to grow old and die. My one brother and three sisters are doing the same thing. They are the third generation of Witnesses that believed they would never die, and now they are dying.

We lost my dear brother Harry a few years ago. His wife gave him a graveside service before burial. She didn't think the family would come to a church, so she had a Protestant minister officiate—and this time, the Witnesses were the captive audience. Some of the nieces and nephews standing in the back began inching away as though they might get contaminated, but Jean and Millie were sitting on chairs by the grave with our sister-in-law Gerri. Jean uses a walker and could not very well move away. I prayed that the message would reach their hearts. None of them looked at me except Jean. She smiled when she saw me. I know she still loves me and misses me.

Under direction of the Watchtower, they have sacrificed having my family and me in their lives. They are afraid to disobey the organization. Milton Henschel, age seventy-two, bald, with a heavy face, became the fifth Watchtower president in 1992 and was one of the last members of the old Nathan Knorr presidency. He made at least one positive change for the Witnesses. During the early 1990s the difficulty some Jehovah's Witnesses were having in obtaining sufficient employment led to a softening of the anti-education sentiment, though there were still warnings and provisions. After a hundred years of telling people they should not go to college, the Watchtower received new light again and announced that it would be okay for Jehovah's Witnesses to take some college classes.

Working toward a degree was still strongly discouraged, but Witnesses could take some classes for better employment reasons. The November 1, 1992 *Watchtower* had an article titled "Education with a Purpose." The article said it was okay to pursue some higher education with the goal of being able to support oneself part-time and serve Jehovah full-time.

The leadership realized that the computer information age could not be stopped, and the Witnesses needed better job skills to survive. With increased income, they could give more. As a result, Henschel greatly increased the real estate holdings of the Watchtower under his rule. Thousands and then hundreds of thousands of Jehovah's Witness men and women were finally getting some higher education.

When cult members learn to think for themselves, they often begin to leave the controlling groups that hinder independent thinking.

Since the Watchtower still frowns on the Witnesses being full-time students or getting degrees, many Witnesses miss this opportunity to think on their own. Some of them, especially the young ones, do think for themselves and continue in college to earn a degree. I personally know a young Witness who walked away from the Watchtower in his third year of college. I wanted to reach out to help those that were leaving, so I made time for the countercult ministry presentations and seminars. The Internet was and still is bursting with opportunities to talk with people leaving Jehovah's Witnesses.

What an amazing field of ministry it has become. Many fleeing Witnesses are looking for emotional healing and help after suffering different kinds of trauma and abuse. Women-Awake, a Yahoo women's group that is dedicated to helping women leaving the Watchtower organization, is a wonderful group. Friends and relatives of Witnesses also come to Women Awake and other groups to ask how to help free their loved ones from the Witnesses.

There are many more Internet groups helping ex-Witnesses; they can easily be found by searching for support groups. Men who are leaving the Watchtower organization also have a strong presence on the Internet. On the opposite side of the coin, Jehovah's Witnesses are online, looking for people to preach to so they can count service time on their Kingdom Hall report cards without leaving their homes and needing to knock on doors. The Internet has become a spiritual battlefield.

There are yearly conferences and conventions held around the world where former Jehovah's Witnesses gather to tell their stories and discuss ministry to the Witnesses. Every year there are more and more former Jehovah's Witnesses attending these conventions, seeking help from those who have left the Watchtower before them.

These three-day conferences provide the support they need, and they often find a new faith in Jesus before the weekend is over. Many countercult books, videos, tapes, and CDs are available at the conference sites and have been put on the Internet. Some of them can be downloaded on the Internet, while others are made available through many different ministries. Some conferences are nonreligious because many people leaving the Watchtower are afraid to hear another message. I always pray that my Witness family will leave. Most ex-Jehovah's Witnesses have great love and compassion for those they left behind in the organization and try to help others understand what the problems are with the Watchtower doctrines.

Chapter 55

Meanwhile, Lisa planned to marry her college sweetheart in a large Victorian wedding. She did not attend the Baptist church anymore and decided she would have a Methodist wedding, because her fiancé and family were Methodist. She liked the connection it gave her to my mother—and of my four children, she is the one that most resembles my mother.

One day she unexpectedly appeared, wearing her hair differently. It was wavy, pulled back, and kept in place with a one-inch cloth band stretching across the top of her head to hold the hair behind her ears. She took my breath away—I actually gasped. She was the image of my mother as I remembered her in my years of being in the attic alone—it was as though I had been transported back there. Lisa quickly asked, "What's wrong?" and I told her how startling it was to see her wearing my mother's hairstyle and how much she looked like my mother. It brought tears to my eyes.

Lisa had her beautiful wedding in a huge Victorian mansion and moved into a new house. Unfortunately, Lisa's marriage did not last very long because of abuse. Two years later they went through a bitter divorce, and she eventually made a new life for herself in Southern California while pursuing a career as an independent computer science consultant. She landed a contract with the large pharmaceutical company she had worked for, and they sent her to a new research center that opened near Los Angeles.

It made me very sad to see her leave, and Lisa was greatly missed, but she was where she wanted to be. She flew home six times the first year, and that made it more bearable. Lisa always comes home for big events and, of course, would never intentionally miss our family's annual Christmas get-together. She is very close to her sister.

Kerin worked after college graduation and met a handsome young man, Bob. Before she began to go steady with Bob, her future husband, he asked to meet with Jim and me. He was concerned that after raising Kerin in the Baptist church, we would be opposed to our daughter dating a Catholic. Jim and I assured him that we would not oppose him for being a Catholic and that we trusted all of Kerin's decisions.

Kerin and Bob were married in 1992 in a Catholic Church, even though she did not become a Catholic at that time. It was a beautiful wedding followed by a big reception at a country club. They rented a small house until they were ready to build the house of their dreams on a large lot next to where Bob's sister and her family were building a house. Bob has a big Catholic family, so they need lots of room when they all get together.

Jim and I were very happy to see Kerin in this loving family that lived their faith. Kerin and Bob always invite us to their family birthdays, cookouts, and holiday celebrations. We accept when we can, and we enjoy going on vacation with them some years. We did not visit their church after the wedding for a few years.

Kerin always went to church with her husband. When their daughter, Christiane Elizabeth, was born in 1994, I finally had a granddaughter. Jim and I were privileged to be there at the hospital when she was born, and we were also privileged to attend her baptism. Christiane is our one and only precious granddaughter. Kerin and Bob hosted a big party in an Italian restaurant after the baptism, where everyone celebrated the day. It was the first time I had actually seen a baby get baptized in a Catholic church. It was quite a happy experience for everyone. Bob's older sister and her husband are the godparents. Bob is a wonderful man, husband, and father—what one would describe as "a good Catholic."

One thing puzzled me about the Catholics. I did not understand how Kerin could go to church every week, year after year, and not receive communion. It must have been difficult for her. At the time, communion was a sticky point with me because I didn't think it was right that the Catholic rules did not allow non-Catholics to have communion, but I didn't really look into the reasons.

Chapter 56

In 1999, we attended the infant baptism of our new grandson, Anthony James. He is our sixth grandson. Kerin and Bob hosted a party for him afterward, and we enjoyed being there. Bob's family really knows how to celebrate a new life and the bringing of a new child into the family of God through baptism.

The Bible tells us that a Christian convert had his entire household baptized. Acts 10–11 tells the story of Cornelius. As a Roman centurion, he would have had a family and house servants. He and his household were the first-known Gentile converts. Their conversion and baptism helped to resolve the question of whether a Gentile must become a Jew by circumcision to become a Christian. They did not need to be circumcised; they only needed to be baptized.

The story of Cornelius helped me to understand that there was nothing wrong with infant baptism. Infant baptism has been practiced since the early church and is practiced by seventy-five percent of Christians. It is done by the Roman Catholics, Eastern Orthodox, Oriental Orthodox, Armenian Apostolic, Assyrian Church of the East, Anglican Communion, Lutherans, Presbyterians, some Methodists, some Church of the Nazarene, the Reformed Churches in America, the United Church of Christ, and the Continental Reformed. However, infant baptism is not done by the Witnesses or by Baptist Churches.

That same year, I was asked to tell my life story at a "Jehovah's Witnesses Now for Jesus" convention. It was an honor to be part of the program. My story was recorded on a forty-five-minute tape and then translated into several languages. Many copies were sold; it went around the world on tapes and also on the Internet. The audio can be heard at www.towertotruth.org on the Internet.

As I wrote down more experiences and tried to finish writing the book for my grown children, I did not have an ending. A few Baptist friends that knew my story were encouraging me to have my book printed. From time to time I would remember something and write it down, but no conclusion was in sight. I didn't know why I could not write an end to my story, except that I didn't think my story was finished.

I found myself with so-called writer's block in God's waiting room. In my experience, God always answers my prayers. The answers are usually *yes*, *no*, or *wait*. Waiting was a hard thing for me as I put my manuscript away until I could find an ending that would be appropriate. I thought maybe it would just end when I went home to the Lord. This went on for months and years.

I also thought that maybe it was just meant to be a little book for my children so they would have the information for their children as a reminder to be careful, to guard against getting mixed up with any cults that deny the Trinity. I often shared my unfinished story with others who had abusive fathers or childhoods and were searching to rebuild their lives after leaving the Watchtower Society. Sharing it privately was much easier than the thought of actually offering my story to the public in a paperback book. There were so many women and men emailing me that I often felt overwhelmed. I still had my own issues to resolve.

One of the issues I had not fully dealt with in the Baptist church was abortion. When I became aware that my denomination had a pro-choice position, I was very disappointed. Being pro-life, I tried to raise awareness within my local church. I discovered that there were a few others that were strongly pro-life. In the United States, abortion is a civil liberty issue that helps express who we are as a people. We are a very complex and diverse society with strong views about what is right and what is wrong. Religion plays a large role in our opinions and beliefs.

I was serving on the Missions Board of my church and at the annual missions fair, we made a display for the American Baptist Friends of Life, a small group of pro-life American Baptists. In the social hall of our church, where many six-foot-long tables held displays of our missions, we set up a table with pro-life literature. I contacted William Devlin, a pro-life activist in southeastern Pennsylvania, and he agreed to help with our presentation.

Devlin, as he prefers to be called, offered to bring a monitor with a pro-life repeating video for my display, and I gladly accepted the offer. Devlin stayed at the table for the opening of the three-day event while I was busy helping with other displays. Unfortunately, most people attending the fair ignored the video and literature. One of the ignored pamphlets featured this psalm:

You formed my inward parts. You wove me in my mother's womb. I will give thanks to You, for I am fearfully and wonderfully made; Wonderful are Your works, And my soul knows it very well. My frame was not hidden from You, When I was made in secret, And skillfully wrought in the depths of the earth; Your eyes have seen my unformed substance; And in Your book were all written the days that were ordained for me, When as yet there was not one of them." (Psalms 139:13–16, NASV)

It should be said here that Jehovah's Witnesses are against abortion, and I give them credit for that position. However, since abortion became legal, some young, single Witness women who became pregnant had abortions secretly because they thought it was easier than facing a Kingdom Hall committee interrogation, being publicly embarrassed, disfellowshipped, and shunned. Even though the Watchtower and the Witnesses are officially against abortion, it is difficult for me to think of them as being pro-life. They strongly discourage their followers from bringing new life into the world.

Many Baptists are pro-life. I thought we should try another approach to get some support against abortion in my local church. I called some of my friends, and we tried to start a local chapter of

American Baptist Friends of Life in our church. This pro-life group that began within my denomination was struggling to survive.

We submitted a proposal and did a presentation at the annual business meeting of our church, but we were not successful. After our presentation, there were several women that stood and asked to speak because they were strongly pro-choice. Our request to have the church sponsor a pro-life group or use the church facilities for promoting pro-life meetings was voted down. It was a very big disappointment; some of my friends even left the Baptist Church.

Another friend who was strongly pro-life thought it was wrong to leave the church because it was giving up on educating people to the issue. She was a retired schoolteacher and felt that her obligation was to stay in this church and keep the issue alive. She said, "This is my own mission to fight abortion, and this is my battleground." Soon after that defeat, this dear lady fell and broke her hip. She was inactive for a few weeks, but fortunately, she continued being active from her home and soon returned to her battlefield.

Jim and I struggled with continuing to attend the church. We loved the music and the preaching at the Baptist Church. It was traditional, with a great organ and choir. The congregation sang with voices that swelled the rafters of the sanctuary with joyful noise to the Lord. Our pastor helped many people accept Christ. The church was growing so quickly that we were often squeezed into the pews on Sunday morning, before the ministers considered adding another service.

Sitting in tight pews during the church service became too uncomfortable. I was earnestly seeking God's will and wished I could get a clear message about where I should be serving Him. I believed God had led me to this church to be educated as a follower of Christ. I asked Him, "Where should I go, Lord? Where would you have me be? Should we leave this church?"

Eventually, because we were disappointed with the denomination's pro-choice stand and we were tired of being squeezed into the pews on Sunday mornings, we began visiting other churches. We also rationalized that it was best to make some pew room for more new converts that were coming into our Baptist church. Jim and

I began attending a Community Church that had room for the overflow from other denominations. The church had an actively pro-life pastor and a large music ministry that made a very different kind of joyful noise to the Lord.

A band and vocal group, with a guitar-playing lead singer, belted out gospel music that had the attendees clapping and swaying their arms to the beat. It was great music and sometimes felt like a mini rock concert. The loud music made me think of something that happened a long time ago.

One summer evening, Gram and I were walking by a small Holy Spirit church with its streetside windows open. I heard loud music and voices coming from within. My grandmother said they were demonized and we needed to walk on the other side of the street so we would not get hit with the books when they began throwing them out of the windows at us. She said they were spirit-filled with the wrong spirits. Thinking about that made me smile. My grandmother was wrong about all the churches.

This evangelical Community Church was growing quickly, and they were building a new and larger worship center to hold twice as many people. They knew that if they did not expand the seating, people would feel squeezed out and leave the church. The music, understandably, attracted many young people coming from many other churches.

The Community Church prefers to be called interdenominational, as opposed to nondenominational, meaning that people from all different denominations are invited and attend the services. It is a very loving and accepting church; everyone is welcomed. When the new worship center opened, it was quite a surprise to me. It was like walking into a large theater. There was a huge stage with large monitors on both sides. The seats were comfortable chairs with seats that popped up whenever we stood. The church was becoming much more theatrical in content. It was not unusual to have a minidrama during the worship service. Jim and I didn't feel like we were sitting in a church anymore.

On Sundays we enjoyed the pastor's preaching very much, but communion was not served very often. Responding to the desire for more frequent communion services, the Saturday evening meeting began having communion monthly, but we worried about the way it was offered.

During the evening service, they served communion by presenting a big round loaf of freshly baked bread. A cup of grape juice was set on the same table. As the minister said the words of Jesus, "This is My body," the round loaf was torn in half. After saying a prayer for the bread and grape juice, attendees were invited to walk up the aisle and tear or pinch a piece of bread off the loaf and dip it into the grape juice. I saw fingertips and fingernails getting wet in the juice and juice dripping onto the table cover.

I wanted communion, but I didn't like this. "This is no way to treat the Lord's body," I thought sadly, but I didn't want to become a church-hopper, hopping from one church to another, looking for a church that had no problems. It seems that all churches have problems. I knew there was not a perfect church because there are no perfect people. So why did I feel the need to journey onward? Was this the Holy Spirit prodding me?

It seemed that many new people were attending churches as the year 1999 was speeding away. Many were truly concerned that the Y2K disaster would cause untold economic hardships and problems. Many feared that everything operating on computers would come to a standstill. Government warfare systems could malfunction and launch nuclear weapons at other countries. Emergency plans were initiated at record speed. The early programmers set had 0 to 99 for the year turnovers. There was not a 00 turnover for the year 2000. What would happen? Would the whole world as we knew it be turned upside down? Computer experts were working feverishly to protect computer systems from failing. Despite all the fears, the year turned over into 2000 without any major catastrophes, and church attendance began to decline again to a more typical level.

Chapter 57

Great anticipation arose among the Witnesses as the year 2000 slipped away. If Jesus returned invisibly in 1914 as the Witnesses teach, surely this long, long generation would be over. After Jesus gave "the signs of the times" for His second coming, He said that, "This generation shall not pass, till all these things be fulfilled." (Matthew 24:34, KJV). The newest "light" on the generation is that it is an undisclosed amount of time.

There is a Watchtower teaching that Jehovah's Sabbath day of seven thousand years was over in 1975, and faithful Witnesses allowed that they could be a few years off in the counting since the creation days. But now some were questioning how far off could they be.

One way the Watchtower held onto the Witnesses who were growing disheartened over the lateness of Armageddon was to lengthen the years of a generation. This generation went from lasting forty years to sixty years, to seventy years, to eighty years. Recently they are admitting they don't know. The Watchtower says the generation is an undeterminable amount of time. Some Witnesses began questioning and thinking that it might be the starting date of 1914 that was wrong. If the Watchtower ever admitted that 1914 is not correct, the entire belief system might collapse.

Most of the Watchtower teachings are based on the 1914 invisible return of Jesus that was only revealed secretly to the leaders of the

Witnesses and not to the rest of the world. If the 1914 date is wrong, then all other Watchtower doctrines would come under critical scrutiny. The Witnesses know that many people who expected to see Armageddon were long dead. In 1920, President Rutherford had proclaimed, "Millions now living will never die," yet they were all dead or dying.

Old and feeble Mr. Henschel, president of the Watchtower for twenty-three years, voluntarily stepped down from his position in October of 2000. That same year, the members of the governing body resigned their executive positions and became advisors. Don Adams, a long-faced, thin man with glasses, became the next president of the Watchtower in 2000. He is in an administrative position and not in complete control as other presidents had been.

It appears that younger men are making the decisions. After the year 2000 passed, many of the old Witnesses grew discouraged and left the Watchtower. Younger men were taking over the everyday management of the publishing company. The older Witnesses never thought they would see the day when members born after 1935 would be their leaders.

Adam's administration controls the multibillion-dollar company. Decisions made by them manage the billions of dollars worth of real estate in New York. To protect the Watchtower assets (probably from the many sexual abuse lawsuits that it has been plagued with in recent years), the organization has been splitting into many different corporations. One Internet website claims there are one hundred and one of them. This has not been confirmed, but some of those reported are:

Watchtower Bible and Tract Society of Pennsylvania
Watchtower Bible and Tract Society of New York, Inc.
Watch Tower Bible and Tract Society of Britain
Watch Tower Bible and Tract Society of Canada
Christian Congregation of Jehovah's Witnesses
Religious Order of Jehovah's Witnesses
Kingdom Support Services, Inc.
Watchtower Export Services & Trading (West) Ltd.

Watchtower Enterprises Ltd.
Watchtower Enterprises, LLC.
Watchtower Associates, Ltd.
Watchtower Foundation, Inc.

As this book goes to print, it is suspected that the organization is going into the business of providing retirement and nursing homes for their elderly members. Jah-Jireh Charity Homes have been built in England and Canada. The homes are managed by Jehovah's Witnesses for the care of Jehovah's Witnesses.

Many prime real estate properties have been sold and many more are for sale as this giant publishing company plans to move out of the city and relocate closer to Patterson, New York. Perhaps they will claim that they "are fleeing to the mountains," as Jesus advised, when you see you are surrounded and the end of the world is in sight. In times past, we were told the organization was the mountains we must all flee to for safety. Then again, perhaps it is only to reap profits and save money. Cost-saving plans have been initiated around the world.

Splitting the organization into many different entities became necessary to protect its assets. A former elder of Jehovah's Witnesses founded a ministry called Silent Lambs to help protect children from pedophiles within the organization. This former Watchtower elder was shunned for calling attention to the problem, and since then many have referred to the Watchtower Society as a pedophile paradise. The Silent Lambs website has a great deal of information about the sexual abuse within the organization.

The Watchtower settles most of these sexual abuse cases out of court to avoid any publicity. They offer no apologies for their secret dealings. In the secret monetary settlements, the pedophiles are often allowed to continue going door-to-door with Watchtower literature, and the victims are not allowed to speak about the abuse. Hopefully, they will get new light from Jehovah and change the policy someday. Abuse has been a problem since the founding days of the organization.

The very founder of Jehovah's Witnesses, Charles Taze Russell, was accused of sexually abusing a young orphaned girl named Rose Ball, who lived in his home. The scandal was part of a divorce Mrs. Russell was seeking because of mistreatment and because she had witnessed her husband fondling and groping the girl. A search of the Internet will turn up thousands of articles about the Rose Ball and Pastor Russell scandal that was printed in newspapers and in court records.

Under Watchtower rules, there must be physical evidence or two witnesses to the sexual abuse in order to disfellowship anyone who does not confess to the wrongdoing. It is unreal to think a pedophile will willingly confess or allow two witnesses watch him molest a child. To make things worse, some victims claim to have been disfellowshipped for telling others or for notifying the authorities. The predators are still knocking on doors.

Unsuspecting householders have no idea who might be at their doors with the Watchtower literature. While denominational churches are publicly apologizing and paying for counseling and damages for the conduct of a small percentage of sinful priests and ministers who have abused children, the Watchtower tries to sweep all of their dirt under a rug. They pretend they don't have a pedophile problem. Churches have shown great compassion for victims and work to heal their deep emotional wounds and scars. The Witnesses, for the most part, have been protected from knowing the real truth.

The Witnesses are afraid to read anything that reveals the truth of their history and leaders. The Society has published a whitewashed history, and that is the only one the Witnesses are permitted to read. Many people who have firsthand knowledge about the organization have written books, but Jehovah's Witnesses are afraid to read the books. They live in fear, in a mental attic, as I once lived in fear.

Chapter 58

Americans were shocked and dismayed on September eleventh of 2001 when the Twin Towers of the World Trade Center in New York City were attacked. Two airplanes reduced the tall and mighty buildings to a gigantic pile of rubble. Among some Jehovah's Witnesses talking on the Internet, though, the chat was happy because, to them, the towers represented the economic system of this evil world that Jehovah will destroy when Armageddon starts.

They were hoping for a worldwide market collapse or an all-out nuclear war to begin. They look forward to seeing the end of all world economies, governments, and religions. However, there were other Witnesses who were truly sad about the loss of life. Many of them live without any feeling of security from disaster or death, because they don't know if they are good enough to be spared by Jehovah.

Responding to the needs of our country, my daughter Lisa accepted a position with a large civilian contracting company working for the government who were providing computer specialists for the newly formed Homeland Security. After having spent several years in Southern California, she moved back east to Virginia and worked in Washington, DC government offices.

Lisa eventually had assignments with Customs and Immigration, the Treasury Department, and the Department of Defense. After spending some time with the Customs and Treasury departments, she received her Top Security Clearance badge. She settled in with the DOD, which gave the opportunity to travel to many foreign countries she was eager to visit. Lisa always loved to travel and even flew to Australia to attend the wedding of her best friend's sister.

While traveling as a civilian employee with a military group in the Middle East, she spent several days of recreation in the small country of Qatar on the northeast coast of Arabia. It is north of Saudi Arabia, surrounded by the Persian Gulf. The country is attempting to grow by building large chains of resort islands off their coast on the shallow ocean floor. On one stretch of an island, Lisa watched young people diving for pearls and collecting them by the bucketful. Most of the stores in Qatar featured pearls, and Lisa enjoyed choosing her own pearls from a large assortment and having them strung to the exact length necklace that she wanted. She gave me a pearl necklace and pearl earrings from Qatar for Christmas that year.

Lisa made a good life for herself with a successful career and a lovely home in Virginia. The happiness she hoped for as a wife and mother has eluded her, but she never gives up. Her faith in God is strong, and she was very active with her local Methodist church before she recently transferred to a DOD office in Florida.

In 2002, ten years after Kerin was married in the Catholic Church, she told us that she had decided to embrace Catholicism and become a member. When she spoke to me about it, Kerin said she hoped it didn't make me feel bad. It didn't; I was happy for her that she was attending church faithfully and had grown in her faith since she was baptized in the Baptist Church at the age of fifteen.

As for her reasons for joining the church, Kerin said, "The Catholic Church is the original church founded by Jesus on St. Peter. Matthew 16:18 (ASV) says, *And I tell you that you are Peter, and on this rock I will build my church, and the gates of Hades will not overcome it.*"

I knew that scripture about the gates of Hades not prevailing against the church that Jesus founded on Peter. It had a big impact on me at this time of my life when I was unhappy with the pro-choice Baptists and with the way communion was served at the Community Church. Something jolted me.

I knew instantly that it was true that the Catholic Church was the one founded on Peter. When I first heard that portion of scripture, I was a Jehovah's Witness, and they have a totally different interpretation for the verse. The Baptist church also has a different slant on understanding the verse. Now, it seemed to me that the meaning was very clear.

Kerin's daughter, Christiane, was going to be confirmed and receive her first Holy Communion in 2003. Kerin attended RCIA (Rite of Christian Initiation of Adults) classes and received her first Holy Communion on Easter the same year as her daughter. Jim and I attended their services at St. Jude Church. We had always admired the consistent pro-life stand of the Catholic Church and began visiting more often.

About the same month that Kerin told us she was converting to Catholicism, I discovered EWTN, the Eternal Word Television Network, on satellite TV. I told Jim about it, and we began watching the channel in all of our spare time. It is on twenty-four hours a day, and the programs are excellent. I always loved learning about history and began to search for more and more history of the church. I wanted to read the good, the bad, and the ugly.

The more I learned about the church's history by reading books, the more impressed I was. Not all of the history is easy to take. There were periods of church history that revealed corruption and abuse at high levels in the church. Corruption was followed by chastisement and repentance.

It reminds me of the ways Israel and some leaders strayed away from God and needed to be brought back to repentance. Like when King David had his affair with Bathsheba then conspired against her husband, had him killed, and was eventually repentant and reconciled with God. The very fact that Israel is again a nation after two thousand years without a homeland is simply amazing. The Jewish people survived approximately two thousand years without having national borders to call their own, and then they were able to return to the land God gave them. God made an everlasting covenant with Abraham. Jesus gave Peter an everlasting promise.

I asked Jim if he ever thought about returning to the Catholic Church, and he immediately said, "Yes!" He enjoyed the preaching and the gospel music at the Community Church as much as I did, but we both had more reverence for the body and blood of Jesus, and we began to long for the Eucharist. We were watching mass on EWTN every week. While the Community Church had wonderful praise music at their services, the Catholic Church had wonderful worship. The entire mass was worship and prayer—and they had the Eucharist.

I finally knew what was missing from the book I was trying to finish for so many years: the tradition and history of the Church. I had more to learn before my journey could end. Other Christian churches sprang off from the Catholic Church. We are all fellow Christians serving the same risen Lord. There are wonderful teachers of the Word of God, and I will always be thankful for them, but I never learned about the "oral tradition" of the Church that Saint Paul spoke about. The oral tradition of the Apostles was established in the early Church, from the time of Jesus to the written Gospels.

Oral tradition continued through apostolic succession to subsequent Church leaders, the bishops, presbyters, and deacons. The beginning of Christianity spread through the faith and the oral teachings of the apostles and by word of mouth before copies of the letters and books were available. Paul wrote:

So then, brethren, stand firm and hold to the traditions which you were taught, whether by word of mouth or by letter from us. 2 Thessalonians 2:15 (NASV)

The Church preserved and practiced the oral instructions and traditions. Many of them have roots in Judaism. In another letter, Paul wrote:

Be imitators of me, as I am of Christ. I commend you because you remember me in everything and maintain the traditions even as I have delivered them to you. 1 Corinthians 11:1–2 (NASV)

Most Protestant churches are *sola scriptura* (by the Bible alone). Unlike the Watchtower teachings that need to be gleaned from the Bible by jumping all over the Bible, Christian churches take scripture in context, chapter by chapter, to support the basic doctrines. They believe the whole Bible, and that is a good thing. However, not all the writings of the early Christians are in the Bible. There were hundreds of manuscripts to choose from when the first Bible, which means "little books," was put together in one volume by the early Church. There were prayers, traditions, and stories that were not included in the books of the Bible.

The stories are still being told. The prayers and traditions are still being practiced. Since the only way a Witness can defend what they practice is by taking verses completely out of context, it is important for people to know that it is not the right way to learn about the Bible. Scripture should always be taken chapter by chapter in order to understand the times, the people, and the background of any verse. Do not allow the Witness to hop from one verse to another in order to tie verses together to support a false teaching. If people would stop and examine the entire chapter of each verse the Witnesses use, they probably will realize that the chapter gives the verse an entirely different meaning.

The Witnesses cling to the Watchtower Society for dear life, because they are taught that they have no hope outside of the organization. It is their ark when Jehovah destroys everyone but them. The May 1, 1957, *Watchtower* told the Witnesses to show their respect for Jehovah's theocratic organization, the Watchtower, because it is their mother and the beloved wife of their heavenly Father, Jehovah God.

Jehovah's Witnesses are not allowed to honor their own adoptive or biological mothers on Mother's Day with cards or gifts because that would be idolatry, but all were told to honor Jehovah's wife, the Watchtower Society, every day of the year. It is their mother, and they are afraid to leave her.

Chapter 59

Jim and I were getting a great deal of religious news and information from watching Raymond Arroya on EWTN. We told Kerin and Bob that we were going to sign up for the next RCIA classes that started in September of 2004. They were very surprised and happy at the same time; their family was cheering our decision. Kerin immediately offered to be a sponsor/helper for me, and she went with us the first week to help us find St. Jude's school library where the classes were held. Since Jim had been away from the church for fifty-nine years, he wanted to attend the classes. He didn't think he had been fully catechized as a child.

We began attending St. Jude Church every Saturday evening at five o'clock. When mass ended, we stayed until the last note was played and sung. We were in no hurry to leave. It is so nice to attend church because we enjoy it and want to be there.

As a potential revert and convert, Jim and I were presented with a study book and the New American Bible and Catechism. A former student of the class visited our second meeting and recommended the book *Catholicism for Dummies.* We became acquainted with the priests and one of the nuns from St. Jude School who took turns leading our classes. We met two church deacons who also did a wonderful job of teaching our class a few times. We had about twenty people and often broke into smaller groups for discussions.

Several church members attended the classes regularly and joined in the group discussions. Some of them shared their personal stories with us. We began learning more about the saints in our spare time, and some would talk about their favorites before the class began. There were so many wonderful saints!

I was very touched by the story of St. Catherine of Laboure in France and decided to choose her for my patron saint. She had three visions of Mary in 1830. Mary sat in a chair, and Catherine had the privilege of kneeling before her like a child. I felt like a child before Mary, someone that was learning about her and needing help.

Not only that, the painting of St. Catherine reminds me of one of my old favorite comedy shows that I watched with my children, so it stirred fond memories. The show starred Sally Fields as the flying nun. Perhaps many of the older readers enjoyed this popular program too.

The Virgin Mary commissioned Catherine to have a medal made. It is estimated that in four years, from 1832 to 1836, over ten million of these medals were minted in France to meet the popular demand for them. There were many documented miracles, healings, and conversions associated with the medal. It continues to be popular, and many people wear them today. It was designed per instructions from Mary in the vision and is called the medal of the Immaculate Conception. It is also known as the Miraculous Medal.

In 1933, St. Catherine's body was exhumed during the investigation of her sainthood. Her body was found to be incorrupt. I read that it was as fresh as the day it was buried. She had lived for seventy years and was in the grave for fifty-seven years, but her skin was as supple as if she were asleep.

This was very hard for me to believe, but her body is encased in glass and is displayed beneath the side altar in her chapel at 140 rue du Bac in Paris. It is one of the spots where Mary appeared to her. There are pictures of it on the Internet; millions have visited her there.

Chapter 60

As a Jehovah's Witness, I was taught that Catholics were guilty of idolatry because they worship Mary and statues of saints. Some Protestant church members think the same thing, but worshipping them would be against God's commandment and against the teaching of the Catholic Church.

Statues are no different than having pictures of loved ones. The Ark of the Covenant was topped with engraved angelic images per God's instructions. God also told Moses to make an image of a snake: *The LORD said to Moses, "Make a snake and put it up on a pole; anyone who is bitten can look at it and live,"* (Numbers 21:8, NIV). There is nothing wrong with a graven image or statue as long as we do not worship them. Misinformation has caused many problems between the churches.

I was asked by a Baptist friend, "Why is Mary called Mother of God and Queen of Heaven?" I explained, "Mary is the mother of Jesus, and if you believe that Jesus is God the Son, then she is rightfully called the Mother of God. King Solomon's mother is the best example to use for calling Mary the Queen of Heaven. King Solomon's mother was the Queen Mother. The people of Israel had the queen as an advocate for their requests of the king.

"The people went to the queen to ask a favor of King Solomon, who was not always available. The requester would bow to the Queen Mother out of respect for her position, not in worship. If Jesus is the

King of Heaven, then Mary is the Queen Mother. People have always bowed to kings and queens to show respect for their position."

Respect is very important in some countries, like in India. A friend of mine from India told me the story of his journey to America. When he and his bride wanted to come here, he got on his knees to his mother and requested that she give him permission to leave India for the United States. His widowed mother gave her approval. I asked, "What if your mother had not given you her approval?" He said, "Then I would still be in India." Bowing to another person does not make it an act of worship. It is an act of respect that is still practiced in many countries.

Taking a prayer request for intercession to the saints in heaven is a common practice for Catholics. They ask saints to pray for them. In James 5:16 (NIV) we are told that the prayers of a holy person are very powerful.

Therefore confess your sins to each other and pray for each other so that you may be healed. The prayer of a righteous man is powerful and effective.

Who is more righteous than those who have gone to heaven? In some places the Bible tells us not to consult or speak to mediums and spiritualists. That is an entirely different communication, yet some people try to twist it around and apply it to the Catholics. I could not find any restrictions in the Bible against speaking to saints who have gone to heaven.

As a Baptist, I often asked friends to pray for my needs. Many asked me to pray for their needs. If friends can pray for each other's needs, why not ask the saints in heaven to pray for us? Why not talk to my mother when I am missing her? I often speak to my mother since she passed on, and I still buy her flowers on some holidays, but I would never worship her. I still have a relationship with my mother. I don't know if my Mom hears me or not when I speak to her, but it always makes me feel better, and it is comforting to think that she might hear me.

Jim and I were praying about his mother, Grammy Vicky. She was not in good health, and during 2004 it was decided that she could no longer live alone. We always called her Grammy because that is what our children called her. She tried assisted living for a year, but after a hospitalization for heart trouble, it became clear that Grammy needed a nursing home. She was crippled with arthritis, diagnosed with bone cancer, and was virtually bed-ridden. After being in a temporary home where she was unhappy, they found a pleasant new home in a small town only fifteen miles from us. She was much happier there, and it was easier for Jim to visit her every week.

Chapter 61

In the early spring of 2005, Jim and I visited the shrine of the Miraculous Medal in Philadelphia at 475 E. Chelten Avenue. The visit gave me a closer connection to Saint Catherine of Laboure when I saw the paintings of her and her vision of Mary. When I think of Catherine as my patron saint, I am reminded of my old friend, Catherine Herb, who passed away before she was sixty-five. Her sister Mary passed away within the same year. She was named after the Virgin Mary.

Jim and I also visited the National Shrine of Our Lady of Czestochowa in Doylestown. We have no Polish ancestry, but deeply appreciate the shrine because it is only a few miles from our home. It is set on a high hill and draws millions of visitors from all over the world, including Pope John Paul II during one of his trips. It offers many educational opportunities and has a large conference center, bookstore, and gift shop. Jim enrolled in an evening Bible class.

I love all history and enjoyed learning that in 1953, Father Michael M. Zembrzuski, a Pauline monk from Poland, purchased the hilltop farmland near Doylestown in the rolling hills of Bucks County, Pennsylvania, and converted a small barn into a chapel. That chapel grew into a magnificent shrine dedicated to Our Lady of Czestochowa. The large framed picture of her at the shrine is a faithful reproduction of the original that reportedly was painted by St. Luke.

Oral tradition tells us that when Mary went to live with the beloved apostle John after the crucifixion of Jesus, she took along a cypress wood table that Jesus had made. Mary had young virgins to assist her and is therefore credited with starting the first order of religious women, or nuns as we call them today. When the apostle Luke, who was reported to have been a good artist, went to visit Mary, the young women asked him to paint Mary's picture. With Mary's permission, he painted it on the wooden tabletop. While he painted, Mary told him many things about the holy family. Luke recorded these things in his gospel.

Through hundreds of years, Mary's picture was moved, hidden, and protected from those who would have destroyed the table and the painting. It was found in Poland in the fourteenth century. Prince Ladislaus, when traveling with it, hid the painting in the chapel of Our Lady of the Assumption in Czestochowa. While trying to depart the next day with the painting to continue his travels, the horses refused to move even one inch. The portrait wanted to stay in Czestochowa, and that is why it is called Our Lady of Czestochowa.

In the fifteenth century, Hussite heretics ransacked the shrine and tried to destroy the painting. A Hussite soldier slashed the cheek of Mary two times with his sword. When he tried the third time, he froze, fell down to the ground in great pain, and died a terrible death. Church artists later tried to cover and repair the marks, but they always reappeared.

Miracles occurred wherever the painting was displayed. The most astounding one I read about was when three dead people were raised. Three dead youths were taken by wagon to her shrine, and people were asked to pray for the three members of this one family. The Benediction of the Blessed Sacrament was just starting, and the people prayed and sang. As the people sang the "Magnificat," the song of Mary from the gospel of Luke, all three bodies came back to life.

The "Magnificat" words from the Gospel of Luke are:

My soul proclaims the greatness of the Lord,
my spirit rejoices in God my Saviour;
he has looked with favour on his lowly servant.
From this day all generations will call me blessed;
the Almighty has done great things for me and holy is his name.
He has mercy on those who fear him,
from generation to generation.
He has shown strength with his arm
and has scattered the proud in their conceit,
Casting down the mighty from their thrones
and lifting up the lowly.
He has filled the hungry with good things
and sent the rich away empty.
He has come to the aid of his servant Israel,
to remember his promise of mercy,
The promise made to our ancestors,
*to Abraham and his children forever. (*Luke 1:46–55, RCL)

As an interesting part of this history, we learned that in 1656 Mary was proclaimed to be queen of Poland. She protected Poland's people through many battles and problems. As recently as 1920 the Russian army was about to attack Warsaw, and the city was saved by the image of Mary that appeared in the clouds over the city. The Russian soldiers were so terrified they refused to enter Warsaw and peacefully retreated.

If one searches for the history of the Watchtower, it begins in the middle of the eighteen hundreds. Eighteen hundred years after the apostles died, they would have us believe that God finally appointed a Pennsylvania man, C. T. Russell, to lead his believers into a utopian new world.

If you search for the history of Jehovah's Witnesses on the Internet, they carry that name for less than one hundred years. Rutherford, the second president, gave them the name. They grasp onto the Watchtower organization as their mother and cling to her. Unfortunately, their devotion and loyalty are misplaced.

Chapter 62

We discussed many issues during our RCIA classes that had bothered me about the Catholic Church. When I was a Baptist for thirty years, my faith in God was strong, but there were some passages in the Bible that I could not understand. I thought that maybe people were not expected to understand everything and just accept some things on faith. In John 6, Jesus said the bread and the wine were His body and His blood, so that kind of did it for me. I had received communion believing it was, somehow, His body and blood. Jesus said it was. If Jesus said it, I believed it, even though I did not understand how it could be. I knew some things needed to be taken by faith.

Now, in the spring of 2005, we learned about transubstantiation, which means the conversion of one substance into another. It is very important to understand what substance means. We cannot see or taste substance, just as we cannot see or taste faith. In several Christian churches, the doctrine of transubstantiation holds that the bread and wine of the Eucharist are transformed into the body and blood of Jesus, although their appearances remain the same.

The Sacrament of Reconciliation was discussed during one class. This was a real eye-opener for me. I could never understand the verses in the Bible that talked about binding and loosing. When Jesus gave Peter the keys of the kingdom, He said,

A. McGinley

I will give you the keys of the kingdom of heaven; and whatever you bind on earth shall have been bound in heaven, and whatever you loose on earth shall have been loosed in heaven." (Matthew 16:19, NASV)

He said it again in Matthew 18:18 (NASV),

Truly I say to you, whatever you bind on earth shall have been bound in heaven; and whatever you loose on earth shall have been loosed in heaven.

I knew that whenever Jesus said *truly,* it is truly important and one must pay special attention to the statement, but I wondered what He was really saying. In RCIA we learned that there are spiritual and moral bonds of sin. Jesus was granting Peter and the apostles the power to actually forgive these bonds of sin, and that sin was also forgiven in heaven.

This almost blew my mind. To confirm what He was saying, it was restated in John 20:21–23 (NASV):

So Jesus said to them again, "Peace be with you; as the Father has sent Me, I also send you." And when He had said this, He breathed on them and said to them, "Receive the Holy Spirit. If you forgive the sins of any, their sins have been forgiven them; if you retain the sins of any, they have been retained."

Jesus said it very plainly to the apostles that they could forgive sins or retain sins, and the same would be done in heaven. He gave them the Holy Spirit before the day of Pentecost, the day the whole church received the Holy Spirit.

A little gem of information from EWTN was learning that when Jesus breathed the Holy Spirit on them, He was initiating the priesthood. That is what apostolic succession is all about. It began with the first apostles, and they ordained others who ordained others, and so on down through the centuries. The Vatican has a huge archive of records and documents to prove apostolic succession.

Finally, I was able to understand why I needed the Sacrament of Reconciliation (Confession) before partaking of the Eucharist—and that is why non-Catholics are not allowed to partake of the Eucharist at mass. Reconciliation, or confession, having our sins forgiven, is important before receiving the body and blood of Jesus. This does not take away from the fact that it was Jesus who died for the forgiveness of our sins.

In addition to attending the classes, I joined an Internet Yahoo group called Catholicxjw. Jeffrey Schwehm, a college professor and former Jehovah's Witness, founded this apostolate. He started the group for the purpose of drawing together Catholics who were Witnesses at one time and who are willing to support those leaving the Watchtower. We also help other Christians who have encounters with the Witnesses.

Jeff has appeared on *The Journey Home* with Marcus Grodi on EWTN. The apostolate welcomes any Jehovah's Witness, ex-Jehovah's Witness, or those with JW neighbors, friends, or family that would like someone to talk with. All Catholics are welcome to come in and ask questions. In August of 2008, the first Catholicxjw weekend conference convened.

Chapter 63

Purgatory was another one of those Catholic doctrines that Jim and I had difficulty digesting at first. Just as the word Trinity doesn't appear in the Bible, the word *Purgatory* doesn't need to appear in the Bible to be true. The word comes from *purge*.

From my Baptist background, I would concede that one does not need to believe in Purgatory to have a personal relationship with Jesus. Our relationship with Him is separate from things that are difficult to understand. I will only say that we will know when and if we get there. It is something taken by faith or not.

Under Part 1 of the Catechism, "The Final Purification, or Purgatory," I read paragraphs no. 1030 to no. 1032. The entire Catechism is on the Internet and can be researched. The Bible verses most commonly associated with Purgatory are 1 Corinthians 3:11–15 (NASV):

For no man can lay a foundation other than the which is laid, which is Jesus Christ. Now if any man builds on the foundation with gold, silver, precious stones, wood, hay, straw, each man's work will become evident, for the day will show it, because it is to be revealed with fire, and the fire itself will test the quality of each man's work. If any man's work which he has built on it remains, he will receive a reward. If any man's work is burned up, he will suffer loss, but he himself will be saved, yet as through fire.

They were verses of the Bible that I had never understood before. That passage of the Bible talks about fire trying or cleansing every man's work. That is Purgatory. Revelation 21:27 tells us this about heaven, *"and there shall in no wise enter into it anything unclean."* We will be cleansed and saved only through fire and be made clean. We will be holy when we enter heaven. The Catechism is a good resource for understanding the Bible and Church doctrine. Many books have been written explaining Purgatory; Jim bought and read several of them.

The saints were not afraid of Purgatory. St. Catherine of Genoa had this to say about the souls there: "I believe no happiness can be found worthy to be compared with that of a soul in Purgatory except that of the saints in Paradise." One great thing about Purgatory is that it is much better than the alternative place, Hell. Another good thing about Purgatory is that those souls who are there already know that when they leave, they will be holy and ready to enter into heaven.

Jesus said that when He left and went to the Father, He would prepare a place for us. That promise is one that all Christians look forward to obtaining.

Chapter 64

Another thing Jim and I learned was that we needed to get married in the church if we wanted to become Catholics. Jim and I had previously been married to other people and then divorced after a few years. Both of those previous spouses had passed on while in their early fifties; both of them were alcoholics. No annulment was needed, but since Jim and I had been married in a civil ceremony many years ago, Father Shaun told us we would need to be married as Christians and have the Sacrament of Marriage. He said it could be as small and as private as we wanted it to be, or we could have a big church wedding if we so desired.

Jim and I thought it would be wonderful to finally have a church wedding after all of these years of marriage. We agreed, "This is an occasion that the children, their spouses, our granddaughter, and all six grandsons would like to attend." We planned a Saturday morning wedding in February at the church with organ music, flowers, and a photographer. Jim and I picked all the scriptures and prayers from the wedding planner from St. Jude's Church.

It felt so good to get all dressed up in Victorian-style long dresses for this special occasion. Kerin was maid of honor, and her husband was the best man since they were both Catholic, and this was their church. The youngest grandson, Anthony James, was a perfect ring bearer; his sister, Christiane, was a perfect flower girl.

After Father Shaun performed the Sacrament of Marriage, we all went to the Victorian Tea Room for high tea. The menu was scones, soup, salad, finger sandwiches, and, of course, a beautiful wedding cake. Tea was the only beverage served.

It was a very happy and memorable occasion for Jim and I. After all, the children had had lovely church weddings—why not their parents? We said, "How many children get the opportunity to attend church to see their grandparents get married?" It was a fun day our family will never forget. We were collecting many good memories.

One memory we cherish is when, before Easter, our class and each person's sponsor went by bus to the basilica of Saints Peter and Paul in Philadelphia. This is where Cardinal Justin Rigali serves the diocese. Kerin was my sponsor, and we enjoyed the day together. During the service each catechumen walked down the aisle to be blessed and then welcomed with a handshake from Cardinal Rigali. Another good memory was of the beautiful Dominican Retreat House in Elkins Park.

We had a one-day retreat there with the Dominican sisters. It is a lovely old mansion with spacious grounds. There were several lectures for us to attend, and the sisters did an excellent job making everyone feel welcomed and comfortable. We had time to socialize, and we ate dinner together in the dining room. It was a relaxing and educational day.

Our Tuesday evening classes flew by quickly. At the last meeting everyone said, "We are so sorry the classes are finished! We've become good friends, and now we won't be seeing each other as often." We had formed friendships and bonds with each other, but we knew in the course of our everyday lives, we probably would not see each other very much. St. Jude Church is quite large and has four masses each weekend. Jim and I are blessed to see several of our RCIA teachers almost every week at the Saturday evening mass.

The new converts, including myself, were confirmed and received the Eucharist on Saturday evening at the Easter Vigil. One member of the class was baptized first. He is a friendly, witty Jewish man who was married to a member of the church for nineteen years. He had been watching Father Corapi on EWTN and gave his heart to Jesus. His wife and children were overjoyed when he converted to Catholicism after they had prayed for him all those years. All converts to Jesus are welcome to inquire about the classes.

Thanks to the Baptist church, I knew and understood the basic doctrines of the Bible. I still had a lot to learn, but I came to the Catholic Church as a strong and dedicated follower of Christ. For me, no day could emotionally take the place of that day I first encountered Jesus on my knees in my bedroom. Nor was it as emotional an Easter as it had been when I was baptized and received my first communion in the Baptist Church at the age of thirty-six.

I thought of the cross that I saw that first time in my communion cup at the Baptist Church, and I knew that the Holy Spirit had been guiding me all the way. When I was given the Eucharist, it was a holy and glorious moment to receive the body of Christ. It was the culmination of my faith in Jesus. Deep in my soul I was joyful. I was finally where I belonged.

By contrast, many Jehovah's Witnesses live in a shadowy attic of fear—they fear that they are not good enough because they are not worthy enough. They fear that they will not make it through Armageddon because they are not loyal enough to their mother, the Watchtower Society. Most Witnesses are very good people. They are like everyone else on the earth that needs a close relationship with God. They are sinners like everyone else. All sinners need forgiveness and mercy. I pray that all Jehovah's Witnesses will come out of their mental attics and open their hearts to Jesus.

Chapter 65

Church membership is in the heart, and if people harden their hearts against the Lord, they need to repent and come back to Him. We believe the Lord is a very loving and forgiving God. He desires that none should be separated from Him or be shunned.

All prodigal sons are welcomed home with open arms. All they need to do is open their hearts and accept His love and forgiveness. If someone gives you a gift, you must reach out and accept it. Jesus does not force Himself on anyone—He *is* the gift.

I am very thankful for the prayers of a stranger when I was a little girl and for that good Christian man that asked me where I would spend eternity. God gave man free will; each person must decide where he or she will spend eternity.

Jim's mother was ill and not long for this world. He had been telling her for more than a year about our classes and about the homily we heard during mass. He shared the gospel readings with her while faithfully visiting her in the nursing home every weekend. She enjoyed listening to him talk about the Bible portions that were read and the homily that explained those passages of the Bible.

She often seemed to be impressed with his enthusiasm for St. Jude Church. Jim told her that receiving his first Reconciliation and Eucharist in sixty years was very cleansing and uplifting to his soul. He told her he was very happy to be back in the Church. Month by month her hostility toward the Church seemed to decrease. She always wanted to know what was going on at our parish.

Jim's mother, at age ninety, began to wonder what it would be like if she had the Sacrament of Reconciliation and the Eucharist after so many years. She somehow knew that she would never walk again or leave the nursing home alive. When Easter neared, she told Jim she had a surprise for him. During the past few months, she was getting regular visits and prayers from a very nice priest from the Saint Phillip Neri parish near the nursing home in Pennsburg. She told the priest that she wanted to come back to the Church and she wanted the Sacraments.

The priest was happy to hear her confession, all sixty-one years of it. What a joyful and tearful Easter that was when this ninety-year-old woman received the Eucharist and was completely healed in her soul from all that old pain and hostility.

.

Epilog

I suppose I could call this the icing on the cake. Last week Jim and I visited the beautiful Ukrainian cathedral on Franklin Street in Philadelphia to see an exact replica of the Shroud of Turin. I have been reading about the shroud for the past twenty-five years after discovering my first book about the burial cloth. I began writing the story of my life after reading *The Sacred Shroud* by Thomas Humber.

I believe it is the burial cloth of Jesus. Science cannot explain how the image was imprinted upon the cloth. I was speechless as I gazed upon the inch-by-inch replica of the linen cloth that was on loan to the cathedral. The face was mesmerizing. "How appropriate," I thought, "to finish my book by gazing at this exact replica of the shroud." It was a very moving experience.

I deeply appreciate all the love and support of my family, especially my husband, Jim, who encourages me each day and travels with me through life. We know the Catholic Church is not perfect and do not expect it to be. The people in the church are not perfect. A very small percentage of Catholic priests have caused the Church great harm by sexually abusing children over a period of about forty-five years or more, and the Church is paying dearly for the abuse of those priests. The Church is in a period of repentance and reconciliation.

It has great compassion for all the victims and seeks to heal deep emotional wounds and distress. However, some people are unforgiving toward the Church. It might make mistakes in judgment as all other churches make mistakes, but now, with all good intentions, it is attempting to provide treatment not only for the victims but for the offenders as well.

When I told some of my Baptist friends that I joined the Catholic Church, they were not happy about that. They brought up the sex abuse scandal and said, "People are leaving the church over that scandal, not joining it." I asked them, "Is it right for anyone to think poorly of the faithful good servants of God and punish them for the sins of a few unfaithful?" They said, "No, that is not right." Case closed! I know that I have Baptist friends who pray for me. I pray for them too. We love each other in the same Lord Jesus.

Acknowledgments

I thank my husband, children, grandchildren, and friends for being interested in my story. Their love and support mean everything to me. I thank all those brave people leaving the Watchtower for sharing their experiences with me and for being interested in mine. Your prayers have meant so much to me. I thank the Internet for the abundance of cult-awareness ministries and information available.

Jim and I thank the religious leaders and lay leaders who weekly encourage us. We are thankful for all the faith-building classes available. We appreciate them and all of our friends at St. Jude Church in Chalfont, Pennsylvania. Special thanks to Sister Janet Thaddeus who read an earlier version of my manuscript and made so many good suggestions. Thanks to my daughter-in-law, Nancy, for proofreading and helping to find mistakes before this book was published. I thank the publisher and all the gifted contacts I have there, including Ray Leonard and Kathi Wittkamper. Special thanks to my editor, Ellen Peixoto.

General References

http://supreme.justia.com/us/197/11/case.html

http://users.adam.com.au/bstett/JwBloodDoctrineOrigin10.htm

http://www.homeofheroes.com/hallofheroes/1st_floor/flag/1bfc_
pledge.html

http://www.spotlightministries.org.uk/birthdays.htm

http://www.letusreason.org/jw10.htm

http://www.mmoutreachinc.com/jehovahs_witnesses/
jwcommunion.htm

http://www.cfpeople.org/Apologetics/page51a030.html

http://www.randytv.com/secret/wtandwho.htm

http://flu.emedtv.com/spanish-flu/spanish-flu.html

http://www.historycentral.com/TheTwenties/KKK.html

http://www.providence.edu/polisci/students/molly_maguires/

http://www.doctortreatments.com/St-Vitas-Dance-Chorea.html

http://www.carm.org/jehovahs-witnesses-in-a-nutshell

http://www.watchman.org/jw/jwwheat.htm

http://www.jehovahs-witnesses.net/sscc5.html

http://www.bibletopics.com/biblestudy/91.htm

http://www.pfo.org/jwcross.htm

http://www.jehovahswitnesstruth.com/blood.htm

http://members.tripod.com/~Help_for_SDAs/BewarethisCult-
book.html

http://www.freeminds.org/doctrine/bible/translators

http://www.crh.noaa.gov/jkl/?n=appalachianstorm1950

http://www.spotlightministries.org.uk/jwbaptism.htm

http://www.jwfacts.com/Watchtower/-shunning.php

http://www.seanet.com/~raines/mental.html

http://www.coneyislandcyclone.com/about_us.php

http://judaism.about.com/od/deathmourni2/f/mirrors.htm

http://www.links2love.com/love_lyrics_only_eyes_for_you.htm

http://pittsburgh.about.com/cs/pennsylvania/a/death_penalty.htm
http://www.essortment.com/all/selectiveservic_roro.htm
http://www.associatedcontent.com/article/119541/jehovah_witness_suicide
http://www.angelfire.com/mn/coasters/super.html
http://www.mayoclinic.com/health/clinical-depression/an01057
http://www.seanet.com/~raines/phrenology.html
http://www.seanet.com/~raines/mental.html
http://www.npr.org/templates/story/story.php?storyId=16920600
http://pabook.libraries.psu.edu/palitmap/bios/O'Hair__Madalyn_Murray
http://www.artofeurope.com/shakespeare/sha9.htm
http://www.gadsden.info/page/3
http://www.freeminds.org/sociology/women/rape-and-jehovah-s-witnesses
http://www.towerwatch.com/articles/Watchtower_christmas_delimma.htm
http://www.scouting.org/scoutsource/CubScouts.aspx
http://www.whoisjesus.com/whois.html
http://www.aztlan.net/index.html
http://www.jwfacts.com/Watchtower/1975.php
http://contenderministries.org/romanroad.php
http://www.bible.ca/ntx-praying-to-jesus.htm
http://www.allaboutthejourney.org/the-case-for-christ.htm
http://www.allaboutreligion.org/is-jesus-god-aar-afb2.htm
http://www.wholesomewords.org/etexts/ross/jesus.html
http://www.constitution.org/col/amazing_grace.htm
http://www.pclawrenceville.org/baptism.html
http://www.redeemermarin.org/Sermons/GoodFriday2000f.html
http://www.expository.org/eastersermons.htm
http://abcsalvation.org/
http://www.ask.com/wiki/Raymond_Franz?qsrc=3044
http://www.squidoo.com/blizzard-of-78
http://www.bmcr.org/
http://www.hymnsite.com/lyrics/umh504.sht
http://www.godonthe.net/HolySpirit/sgifts.htm

http://www.churchworldservice.org/site/PageServer
http://abclocal.go.com/wls/story?section=news/local&id=3643364
http://www.uoregon.edu/~adoption/topics/fostering.htm
http://www.holocaustforgotten.com/fivmil.htm
http://fcit.usf.edu/HOLOCAUST/PEOPLE/victjeho.htm
http://groups.yahoo.com/group/Women-Awake/
http://www.mtio.com/articles/aissar56.htm
http://www.prolifeamerica.com/right-to-life_pro-life_organizations.
cfm
http://www.intouchmin.net/articles/jehovahswitness/1914.htm
http://news.jah-jireh.org/
http://www.womeninthebible.net/1.11.Bathsheba.htm
http://www.silentlambs.org/
http://www.ewtn.com/
http://www.holyspiritradio.org/
http://www.solagroup.org/
http://www.beginningcatholic.com/catholic-rcia-stages.html
http://www.amm.org/catherine.asp
http://www.catholic.com/library/Mary_Mother_of_God.asp
http://www.czestochowausa.com/
http://www.merriam-webster.com/dictionary/transubstantiation
http://www.ancient-future.net/reconciliation.html
http://www.ewtn.com/journeyhome/index.asp
http://www.usccb.org/catechism/text/
http://www.catholiceducation.org/articles/apologetics/ap0091.html
http://www.americancatholic.org/features/sacraments/
reconciliation.asp
http://www.catholicxjw.com/
http://www.newadvent.org/cathen/12575a.htm

Breinigsville, PA USA
08 October 2010
246924BV00004B/1/P